✔ KU-324-158

EMPIRE
MOVIE
MISCELLANY
HUNDREDS OF AMAZING FILMIC FACTS

INSTANT FILM
BUFF STATUS
GUARANTEED

Virgin BOOKS

Compiled and written by Kim Newman, Ian Freer and Oliver Richards

Additional entries by James Dyer, Nick De Semlyen, Helen O'Hara

Based on an 'idea' by Colin Kennedy

Illustrations by Mick Brownfield

Production Editor: Liz Beardsworth

Copy Editor: Nick De Semlyen

***EMPIRE* Editor: Mark Dinning**

First published in Great Britain in 2007 by
Virgin Books Ltd
Thames Wharf Studios
Rainville Road
London
W6 9HA

A catalogue record for this book is available from the British Library.

ISBN 978 0 7535 1224 1

Typeset by Phoenix Photosetting, Chatham, Kent

Printed and bound in Great Britain by CPI Bookmarque, Croydon. CR0 4TD

1 3 5 7 9 10 8 6 4 2

INTRODUCTION

If you love movies – *really* love movies – then you can't know enough about them. Any old wannabe film buff can tell you that Tom Selleck was originally going to play Indiana Jones or quote the last line from *Some Like It Hot* ('Well, nobody's perfect!') or name the seven dwarfs at the drop of a hat (Sneezy, Sleepy, Grumpy, Happy, Doc, Bashful, Dopey). But if you want to have real cinephile credentials, be the Yoda of movie trivia, you have to go further than that. Much further.

This is where this book comes in. What you hold in your hands is the collected cream of *EMPIRE*'s troika of movie miscellanies with some added extras to bring things right up to date. Yes, we will tell you all the basics that any movie newbie needs to know, but this is not the usual collection of Oscar winners or box-office champions that usually passes for trivia. Instead, this cornucopia of filmic factology is pulled from every corner of the moviegoing globe, from its pioneering first steps to the latest blockbusters; this book tells you who *voices* the seven dwarfs – that's the level of expertise this guide can instantly confer on you.

Handily sized to conquer any pub quiz – those 'liquid prizes' will be yours! – we hope we've created something that is at once completely pointless yet totally indispensable. More importantly we hope it reminds you of the little details and memorable minutiae that make up why you love movies. If you've ever drifted off in a meeting scrabbling to think of all the Goonies or been kept awake at night trying to remember the subtitle of the fifth *Star Trek* movie, fret no more. Help is at hand …

Ian Freer
Editor
EMPIRE Movie Miscellany

RULES FOR KEEPING GREMLINS

Do not get them wet.

Keep them out of bright light.

Never, ever, feed them after midnight.

THE HOOVER CLAN AND THEIR DYSFUNCTION*

Olive	(Abigail Breslin)	Obsessed with winning kiddie beauty pageant
Dwayne	(Paul Dano)	Nietzschean obsessive on a vow of silence
Richard	(Greg Kinnear)	Control freak motivational speaker
Grandpa	(Alan Arkin)	Porn-obsessed drug addict
Toni Collette	(Sheryl)	Frazzled head of a fucked-up family
Steve Carell	(Frank)	Suicidal Proustian scholar

* from Little Miss Sunshine

STARS WITH A MYSPACE PAGE

Social networking website Myspace is awash with celebrity imposters. Below is a selection of the few stars who have genuinely signed up.

Kevin Smith

Edgar Wright

Zach Braff

William Shatner

Eli Roth

Jenna Elfman

Tim Story (director of The Fantastic Four)

Doug Jones (star of Hellboy and Pan's Labyrinth)

CARRY ON FILMS WHERE SID JAMES PLAYS A CHARACTER CALLED SID

Film	'Sid'
Carry On Up The Khyber	Sir Sidney Ruff-Diamond
Carry On Camping	Sid Boggle
Carry On Loving	Sid Bliss
Carry On At Your Convenience	Sid Plummer

Carry On Matron   Sid Carter

Carry On Girls   Sidney Fiddler

CLOSE ENCOUNTERS OF THE THIRD KIND

In his 1972 book, *The UFO Experience: A Scientific Enquiry*, Dr J Allen Hynek divided UFO activity into three categories. Steven Spielberg not only purloined the last of these definitions for the title of his 1977 sci-fi extravaganza, he also cast Hynek as a scientist in the movie – in the film's conclusion, he is the one with the white hair moving through the crowd.

A close encounter of the first kind is a sighting of an unidentified flying object or objects. Reports of fast-moving lights in the night sky or 'flying saucers', unattributable to human technology, can all be considered close encounters of the first kind.

A close encounter of the second kind is an observation of physical evidence of extraterrestrial visitation. Footprints, heat or radiation damage to terrain and crop circles, found in the vicinity of a UFO sighting, could be considered examples of close encounters of the second kind.

A close encounter of the third kind is an observation of one or more aliens associated with one or more crafts.

MOVIE ACRONYMS

BAPS Black American Princesses

CHUD Cannibalistic Humanoid Underground Dwellers, or Contamination Hazard Urban Disposal

DARYL Data Analyzing Robot Youth Lifeform

DOA Dead On Arrival

FUBAR Fucked Up Beyond All Recognition

IPCRESS Induction of Psycho-neuroses by Conditioned REflex with StresS

M*A*S*H Mobile Army Surgical Hospital

MOTHER (from Hillbillys In A Haunted House) Master Organisation To Halt Enemy Resistance

RoGoPaG Roberto Rossellini, Jean-Luc Godard, Pier Paolo Pasolini, Ugo Gregoretti

SFW So Fucking What

S1m0ne Simulation One

SPECTRE Special Executive for Counter intelligence, Terror, Revenge, Extortion

SQUID (Strange Days) Superconducting QUantum Interference Device

SUSIE Syncro Unifying Sinometric Integrating Equitensor (computer in Kronos)

SWALK Sealed With A Loving Kiss

TARDIS Time And Relative Dimensions In Space

THRUSH Technological Hierarchy for the Repression of Undesirables and the Subjugation of Humanity

TIE Twin-Ion Engine (fighters from Star Wars)

UFO You Fuck Off

UNCLE United Network Command for Law Enforcement

ZARDOZ the wiZARD of OZ

ZOWIE (in the Derek Flint films) Zonal Organisation for World Intelligence and Espionage

ZPG Zero Population Growth

THE QATSI TRILOGY

Godfrey Reggio's Qatsi trilogy comprises abstract, visually driven, feature-length documentaries, all scored by Philip Glass, all centred on concepts borrowed from Hopi Indians. To wit:

Koyaanisqatsi (1983) is the Hopi Indian word for life out of balance.

Powaqqatsi (1988) is the Hopi Indian word for life in transformation.

Naqoyqatsi (2002) is the Hopi Indian word for a life of killing each other.

REAL NAMES

Alan Alda	Alphonse d'Abruzzo
Jennifer Aniston	Jennifer Anastassakis
Antonio Banderas	José Antonio Domínguez Bandera
John Barry	John Barry Prendergast
Jacqueline Bisset	Winnifred Jacqueline Fraser-Bisset
Dirk Bogarde	Derek Jules Gaspard Ulric Niven van den Bogaerde
Albert Brooks	Albert Einstein

Yul Brynner	Taidje Khan
Kate Capshaw	Kathleen Sue Nail
Jean-Claude Van Damme	Jean-Claude Van Varenberg
Danny DeVito	Daniel Michaeli
Vin Diesel	Mark Vincent
Carmen Electra	Tara Patrick
Jenna Elfman	Jennifer Mary Butala
Andy Garcia	Andrés Arturo García-Menéndez
Goldie Hawn	Goldie Jean Studlendgehawn
Ben Kingsley	Krishna Bhanji
Bruno Kirby	Bruno Giovanni Quidaciolu Jr
Julianne Moore	Julie Anne Smith
Meg Ryan	Margaret Mary Emily Anne Hyra
Susan Sarandon	Susan Abigail Tomalin
Jane Seymour	Joyce Penelope Wilhelmina Frankenberg
Charlie Sheen	Carlos Irwin Estevez
Martin Sheen	Ramon Estevez
Kevin Spacey	Kevin Fowler
Skeet Ulrich	Bryan Ray Ulrich
Christopher Walken	Ronald Walken
Bruce Willis	Walter Bruce Willison

THE TWISTS OF M NIGHT SHYAMALAN

Film	The 'twist'
The Sixth Sense	Bruce Willis is dead all along
Unbreakable	Samuel L Jackson is Superhero nemesis
Signs	Rory Culkin's asthma, Abigail Breslin's aversion to stale water and Joaquin Phoenix baseball swing coalesce to kill the alien
The Village	The 19th-century village is actually in the present day
Lady In The Water	Freddy Rodriguez (muscleman) is actually the guardian

SATURDAY NIGHT LIVE SPIN-OFFS

The Blues Brothers (Dan Aykroyd, John Belushi)*
Wayne's World (Mike Myers, Dana Carvey)*
Stuart Saves His Family (Al Franken)
It's Pat (Julia Sweeney)
Superstar (Molly Shannon)
Coneheads (Dan Aykroyd, Jane Curtin)
A Night At The Roxbury (Will Ferrell, Chris Kattan)
The Ladies' Man (Tim Meadows)
Mr Mike's Mondo Video (Michael O'Donoghue)

* signifies disappointing sequel

NB: This Is Spinal Tap doesn't count; the film came before the band appeared on
SNL. Win arguments by remembering Mr Mike was the first *SNL* spin-off character.

THE TASKS OF PAN'S LABYRINTH

Retrieve a key from the belly of a giant toad
Steal a dagger from the lair of the pale man
Spill her half-brother's blood in the centre of the labyrinth*

* This is a trick – by refusing to do as ordered, Ofelia succeeds in this task

LETHAL WEAPON TAGLINES
Lethal Weapon

Two cops. Glover carries a weapon … Gibson is one
(He's the only LA cop registered as a lethal weapon)

Lethal Weapon 2

The magic is back!

Lethal Weapon 3

The magic is back again!

Lethal Weapon 4
The gang's all here!

BARS, PUBS, CLUBS AND RESTARAUNTS

Bagdad Café (Bagdad Café)

The Blue Parrot (Casablanca)

Café Eighties (Back To The Future Part II)

Café Flesh (Café Flesh)

Café Mozart (The Third Man)

Café Sonata (Eyes Wide Shut)

Cantina (Star Wars Episode IV: A New Hope)

Coyote Ugly (Coyote Ugly)

Club Obi-Wan (Indiana Jones And The Temple Of Doom)

The Green Man (The Wicker Man)

The Kardomah Café (Brief Encounter)

Mel's Drive-In (American Graffiti)

McCool's (One Night At McCool's)

Mildred's (Mildred Pierce)

The Neon Boot (Blood Simple)

Rectum (Irreversible)

Rick's Café Americain (Casablanca)

The Sad Café (Ballad Of The Sad Café)

Silencio (Mulholland Dr.)

The Slow Club (Blue Velvet)

The Tall Man (Rawhead Rex)

The Tides Restaurant (The Birds)

The Titty Twister (From Dusk Till Dawn)

The Whistle Stop Café (Fried Green Tomatoes At The Whistle Stop Café)

The Yellow Door (A Bucket Of Blood)

Yoshiwara (Metropolis)

THE HOLLYWOOD TEN

A band of filmmakers who, in 1947, refused to testify for the House Un-American Activities Committee over allegations of communism and were subsequently imprisoned, then blacklisted (although many worked under assumed names).

The ten were:

Ring Lardner Jr (screenwriter: The Cincinnati Kid, M*A*S*H)

John Howard Lawson (screenwriter: Blockade, Sahara)

Albert Maltz (screenwriter: The Naked City, The Beguiled)

Samuel Ornitz (screenwriter)

Dalton Trumbo (screenwriter: The Brave One, Spartacus, Exodus)

Herbert Biberman (director: Salt Of The Earth)

Edward Dmytryk (director: Murder My Sweet, Crossfire, The Caine Mutiny)

Adrian Scott (producer: Cornered, So Well Remembered)

Alvah Bessie (screenwriter: Objective Burma!)

Lester Cole (screenwriter: Born Free, under pseudonym Gerald LC Copley)

THE NOSTROMO CREW FROM ALIEN

Dallas (Tom Skerritt), Ripley (Sigourney Weaver), Lambert (Veronica Cartwright), Brett (Harry Dean Stanton), Kane (John Hurt), Ash (Ian Holm), Parker (Yaphet Kotto), Jones The Cat

HOW SHARKS ARE KILLED IN JAWS MOVIES
Film: Jaws
Killer: Martin Brody (Roy Scheider)
Method: A bottle of compressed air in mouth, canister is shot, detonating the shark

Film: Jaws 2
Killer: Martin Brody (Roy Scheider)
Method: Brody lures shark to chomp on underwater power cable

Film: Jaws 3-D
Killer: Mike Brody (Dennis Quaid)
Method: Brody Jr pulls pin on grenade in hand sticking out of shark's throat

Film: Jaws IV The Revenge
Killer: Ellen Brody (Lorraine Gary)
Method: After an electric gadget disorientates the great white shark, Mrs Brody skewers it with a broken bowsprit

THE ROAD TO ... MOVIES BY DESTINATION

Singapore, Zanzibar, Morocco, Utopia*, Rio, Bali and Hong Kong

* Utopia is the only destination that's not a real place

SEVEN SEVENS
Seven Samurai

Kambei (Takashi Shimura)
Kikuchiyo (Toshirô Mifune)
Gorobei (Yoshio Inaba)
Kyuzo (Seiji Miyaguchi)
Heihachi (Minoru Chiaki)
Shichiroji (Daisuke Katô)
Katsushiro (Isao Kimura)

Se7en's Murder Methods

Gluttony - fed to death by pasta
Greed - forced to hack off own flesh
Lust - stabbed by customised sex toy
Pride - suicide after good looks are ruined
Sloth - chained to bed and fed drugs
Envy - a severed head
Wrath - shooting the person who severed the head

The Goonies

Mikey (Sean Astin)
Brand (Josh Brolin)
Chunk (Jeff Cohen)
Mouth (Corey Feldman)

Andy (Kerri Green)
Stef (Martha Plimpton)
Data (Quan Ke Huy)

Seven Brides

Milly (Jane Powell)
Liza (Virginia Gibson)
Dorcas Gailen (Julie Newmeyer)
Alice Elcott (Nancy Kilgas)
Sarah Kine (Betty Carr)
Ruth Jackson (Ruta Kilmonis)
Martha (Norma Doggett)

Seven Brothers

Adam Pontipee (Howard Keel)
Ben Pontipee (Jeff Richards)
Gideon Pontipee (Russ Tamblyn)
Frank Pontipee (Tommy Rall)
Daniel Pontipee (Marc Platt)
Caleb Pontipee (Matt Mattox)
Ephraim Pontipee (Jacques d'Amboise)

The Seven Dwarves (Disney)

Sneezy (Billy Gilbert)
Sleepy (Pinto Colvig)
Grumpy (Pinto Colvig)
Happy (Otis Harlan)
Doc (Roy Atwell)
Bashful (Scotty Mattraw)
Dopey (Eddie Collins)

The Magnificent Seven

Chris (Yul Brynner)

Vin (Steve McQueen)
Chico (Horst Bucholtz)
O'Reilly (Charles Bronson)
Lee (Robert Vaughn)
Harry Luck (Brad Dexter)
Britt (James Coburn)

24 FPS

This stands for 24 frames per second, the normal speed for 35mm film to run through a camera and projector. As video runs at 25fps rather than 24fps, this accounts for the fact that video running times are shorter than theatrical running times - you lose a frame for every second. The following table converts seconds into feet and frames, the standard measurements for film in the US and UK.

35mm (24 fps) 1 foot = 16 frames

Seconds of film	Feet & Frames	Frames Only
1	1ft 8fr	24 frames
2	3ft	48 frames
3	4ft 8fr	72 frames
4	6ft	96 frames
5	7ft 8fr	120 frames
10	15ft	240 frames
30	45ft	720 frames

Minutes	Feet	Frames
1	90ft	1,440 frames
5	450ft	7,200 frames
10	900ft	14,400 frames
30	2,700ft	43,200 frames
60	5,400ft	86,400 frames

RIDICULOUSLY LONG (AND RIDICULOUS) FILM TITLES

Night Of The Day Of The Dawn Of The Son Of The Bride Of The Return Of The Revenge Of The Terror Of The Attack Of The Evil, Mutant, Alien, Flesh-eating, Hellbound, Zombified Living Dead Part 2: In Shocking 2-D

The Persecution And Assassination Of Jean-Paul Marat As Performed By The Inmates Of The Asylum Of Charenton Under The Direction Of The Marquis De Sade

The Saga Of The Viking Women And Their Voyage To The Waters Of The Great Sea Serpent

You've Got To Walk It If You Like To Talk It Or You'll Lose That Bear

Lina Braake - Die Interessen Der Bank Können Nicht Die Interessen Sein, Die Lina Braake Hat

The Heart Of A Lady As Pure As A Full Moon Over The Place Of Medical Salvation

Little Songs Of The Chief Officer Of Hunar Louse, or This Unnameable Little Broom

The Adventures Of Buckaroo Banzai Across The 8th Dimension

Can Hieronymous Merkin Forget Mercy Humppe And Find True Happiness?

The Incredibly Strange Creatures Who Stopped Living And Became Mixed-Up Zombies

The Death Of The Flea Circus Director, or Ottocaro Weiss Reforms His Firm

The Effect Of Gamma Rays On Man-In-The-Moon Marigolds

The Englishman Who Went Up A Hill But Came Down A Mountain

Gas-s-s-s-s! or, It Became Necessary To Destroy The World In Order To Save It

Introduction To Arnold Schoenberg's Accompaniment To A Cinematographic Scene

I Could Never Have Sex With A Man Who Had So Little Regard For My Husband

Oh Dad, Poor Dad, Mamma's Hung You In The Closet And I'm Feelin' So Sad

Swept Away ... By An Unusual Destiny In The Blue Sea Of August (In Italian: *Travolti Da Un Insolito Destino Nell' Azzurro Mare D'Agosto*)

Who Is Harry Kellerman And Why Is He Saying Those Terrible Things About Me?

AUTHORS WHO APPEAR IN FILMS OF THEIR OWN WORK

Author	Film
JG Ballard	Empire Of The Sun
Charles Beaumont	The Intruder
Paul Bowles	The Sheltering Sky
Arthur C Clark	2010

Robert Cormier	I Am The Cheese
James Ellroy	Stay Clean
Robert Harling	Steel Magnolias
SE Hinton	The Outsiders, Rumble Fish, Tex
John Irving	The World According To Garp, The Cider House Rules
Tama Janowitz	Slaves Of New York
Stephen King	Pet Sematary (and many others)
Richard Matheson	Somewhere in Time
Pat McCabe	The Butcher Boy
Nicholas Mosley	Accident
Scott Spencer	Waking The Dead
Mickey Spillane	The Girl Hunters (as his series' hero, Mike Hammer)
Jacqueline Susann	Valley Of The Dolls, The Love Machine
Gore Vidal	The Best Man
Irvine Welsh	Trainspotting

THE WOLF MAN (1941) RHYME

Even a man who is pure at heart
And says his prayers by night
May become a wolf
When the wolfbane blooms
And the moon is full and bright …
(old folk rhyme, written by Curt Siodmak)

THE 'FREAKS' OF FREAKS*

Actor	Character
Frances O'Connor and Martha Morris	The Armless Wonders
Jennie Lee	Zip
Elvira Snow	Pip
Prince Randian	The Living Torso
Daisy and Violet Hilton	Themselves
Frances O'Connor	Armless Girl
Angelo Rossito	Angeleno

Peter Robinson	The Living Skeleton
Schlitze	Himself
Harry Earles	Hans
Daisy Earles	Frieda
Minnie Woolsey	Koo Koo The Bird Girl
Elizabeth Green	The Stork Woman
Johnny Eck	The Legless Man
Joseph Josephine	Half-Woman Half-Man
Olga Roderick	The Bearded Woman

* From Tod Browning's 1932 horror film about sideshow performers

MOVIE TARZANS

Elmo Lincoln	Tarzan Of The Apes, 1918*
Gene Pollar	The Revenge Of Tarzan, 1920
P Dempsey Tabler	Son Of Tarzan, 1920
James Pierce	Tarzan And The Golden Lion, 1927
Frank Merrill	Tarzan The Mighty, 1928*
Johnny Weissmuller	Tarzan The Ape Man, 1932*
Buster Crabbe	Tarzan The Fearless, 1933
Herman Brix (Bruce Bennett)	The New Adventures Of Tarzan, 1935
Glenn Morris	Tarzan's Revenge, 1938
Lex Barker	Tarzan's Magic Fountain, 1949*
Tamer Balci	Tarzan In Istanbul, 1952
Gordon Scott	Tarzan's Hidden Jungle, 1955*
Denny Miller	Tarzan, The Ape Man, 1959
Jock Mahoney	Tarzan Goes To India, 1962*
Mike Henry	Tarzan And The Valley Of Gold, 1967*
Ron Ely	Tarzan's Jungle Rebellion, 1967*
Steve Hawkes	Tarzan And The Rainbow, 1972*
David Carpenter	Tarzan In King Solomon's Mines, 1973
Miles O'Keeffe	Tarzan, The Ape Man, 1981
Christopher Lambert	Greystoke: The Legend Of Tarzan, Lord Of The Apes, 1984
Joe Lara	Tarzan In Manhattan, 1989

Caspar Van Dien   Tarzan And The Lost City, 1998·
Michael T Weiss   Tarzan And Jane, 2002·

* played the role more than once

· cartoon voice

SELECT FALSE NAMES USED BY STARS SIGNING IN AT HOTELS

Actor	Pseudonym
Marlon Brando	Lord Greystoke
Kevin Costner	Tom Feral
Melanie Griffith	Miss Hoover
Elizabeth Hurley	Rebecca de Winter (from the Daphne Du Maurier novel *Rebecca*)
Courtney Love	Neely O'Hara (character in Jacqueline Susann's *Valley Of The Dolls*)
Madonna	Sugar Kane (Marilyn Monroe's character in *Some Like It Hot*)
River Phoenix	Earl Grey
OJ Simpson	DH Lawrence
Johnny Depp	Santa Del Vecchio, Oprah Noodlemantra

SCREENWRITING GLOSSARY

BACKSTORY – the story of the characters' lives before they enter the story

BEATS – pregnant pauses in dialogue or dramatic action

CHARACTER ARC – the (usually emotional) growth of a character over the course of a movie

DENOUEMENT – the final clarification/resolution of the story

EXT – abbreviation for exterior

INT – abbreviation for interior

MONTAGE – a series of scenes evoking a collective feel or picture

PITCH – a verbal presentation of a script, with a view to selling it

PLOT – the most interesting, dramatic way of telling the STORY

PLOT POINTS – key moments on which the unravelling of the plot turns

STORY – the series of events that form the screenplay in chronological order

SUBPLOT – additional story linking and involving the main characters
THREE-ACT STRUCTURE – a structure that divides the story into three distinct acts:
Act 1 = set-up; Act II = development; Act III = resolution and DENOUEMENT
TREATMENT – a document (generally 25 to 30 pages) describing the plot in the order
it happens in the screenplay
VOICE-OVER – dialogue that runs over the top of a scene

SELECTED ONE- OR TWO-LETTER TITLES

M (1931/1951), O (2001), Pi (1998), Q (1982), W (1973), X (1963), Z (1968), CQ (2001), Da
(1988), Ed (1996), FM (1978), F/X (1986), Go (1999), i.d. (1995), If (1968), IQ (1994), It
(1927), K2 (1991), P.J. (1968), 10 (1979), -30- (1959), X2 (2003)

THE 300 TRAINING REGIME

The cast of Zach Snyder's historical epic followed this fitness plan to achieve that
sculpted six-pack physique:

1. Switch to a low-fat, low-carb, no-sugar or dairy diet. Essentially, your diet should
consist of vegetables and lean meat or fish.

2. Gather together the following tools: the spare tyre from an articulated lorry or,
for preference, a JCB; a wooden box about one-foot square; ropes with rings on
the bottom, about a foot off the floor; a rowing machine; fifty-pound weights; some
ropes; a trained fitness professional.

3. Try the following exercises:

a. Flip the tyre up and down the road, 25m each way.

b. Jump up onto and down from the box as many times as you can, as fast as you
can.

c. Put your feet on the box, your hands on the rings and do push-ups.

4. If you throw up, or need a lie-down after five minutes, well done! You're working
hard enough. Now get up, you maggot, and get back to it.

5. Need motivation? Partner up. Set your partner to rowing, say, 500m, while you do
lunges up and down the room while holding the 50lb weight high over your head.
The catch is that you can only stop when your partner finishes their row.

6. Repeat for two months, for at least two hours a day. Follow with two hours of
sword and fight training.

7. Still not quite there? Follow 300's example and cheat. Yes, it's OK to use airbrushing to highlight your abs and pecs for that Xerxes look.

THE SCIENTIFIC NAMES FOR WILE E COYOTE AND THE ROAD RUNNER

Coyote

Carnivorous Vulgaris, Eatibus Anythingus, Famishus Famishus, Eatibus Almost Anythingus, Eatius Birdius, Eternali Famishus, Famishus Vulgaris, Hard Headius Ravenus, Everedii Eatibus, Apetitus Gigantis, Hungrii Flea Bagius, Overconfidenti Vulgarus, Road Runner Digestus, Famishus Fantasticus, Famishus Vulgaris Ingeniusi, Eatius Slobius, Hardheadipus Oedipus, Carnivorous Slobius, Canis Nervous Rex, Grotesqus Appetitus, Nemesis Ridiculii, Lupus Persisticus

Road Runner

Accelerati Incredibulis, Hotrodicus Supersonicus, Velocitus Delectibus, Delicius Delicius, Digoutius Tidbitius, Tastius Supersonicus, High Ballius, Burnius Roadius, Birdipus Zippous, Speedipus Rex, Digoutius Hot Dogis, Fastius Tasty-us, Tidbittius Velocitus, Burn Em Upus Asphaltus, Velocitus Incalculus, Batoutahelius, Super-Sonic Tonicus, Velocitus Tremenjus, Disappearius Quickus, Semper Food-elius, Ultra-Sonicus Ad Infinitum, Birdus Fleetus

ACTUAL PUNNING PORN MOVIE TITLES

Intercourse With The Vampyre

The Sperminator

Muffy The Vampire Layer

Sperms Of Endearment

Driving Miss Daisy Crazy

Your Ass In The Park

The Maddams Family

Edward Penishands

Hannibal Lickter

Romancing The Bone

Clockwork Orgy

Juranal Park
Jurassic Poke
Sex Trek: The Next Penetration
Tailiens
Babewatch
Bare Ass In The Park
One Million Years AC/DC
Mad Jack: Beyond Thunderbone
Bi Dream Of Genie
Blonde Ambition
Twin Peeks
Doctor Yes
Father Of The Babe
A Few Good Rears
Sherlock Homie
Full Metal Bikini
Jennifer Ate
The Last Anal Hero
A League Of Their Moan
Little Big Dong
Lust, Ties, And Videotape
Other People's Pussy
Plan 69 From Outer Space
Rears In Windows
Single Tight Female
Sleeping With Seattle
Southern Cumfort
Spermacus
The Lust Weekend
Moonlusting
Mystic Pieces
Outrageous Foreplay
The Porn Birds

The Poonies
Pleasure Island
Satisfaction Jackson
Sleazy Rider
The Slutty Professor
A Star Is Porn
Tailhouse Rock
Terms Of Endowment
Top Buns
The Touchables
Wetness For The Prosecution
Sexcalibur
Splendor In The Ass
Tales From The Backside
Thighs & Dolls
Where The Boys Aren't
Against All Bods
Honey, I Blew Everybody
The Search For Pink October
976-76DD
Anal Analysis
Assent Of A Woman
Beetlejism
The Best Rears Of Our Lives
Binders Keepers
Cape Rear
Defending Your Sex Life
In And Out Of Beverly Hills
Malcolm XXX
Wet Dream On Elm Street
Beaverjuice
Beverly Hills 90269
The Boneheads

Bonfire Of The Panties

Butt's Up, Doc?

The Cockateer

Dances With Foxes

Do The White Thing

Erectnophobia

Field Of Wet Dreams

The Flintbones

French Connexxion

Guess Who Came To Dinner?

The Harder Way

I Cream With Genie

Naked Buns 8

Patriot Dames

Pretty Peach

Sex Lives On Porno Tape

Silence Of The Buns

Tale Of Two Titties

Tracy Dick

Total Reball

White Men Can't Hump

Whore Of The Roses

Backside To The Future

Earth Girls Are Sleazy

BONKERS PRESTON STURGES CHARACTER NAMES

Mayor Wilfred H Tillinghast, Madame Juliette La Jolla (The Great McGinty); Mr Bildocker* (Christmas In July); Ambrose Murgatroyd* (The Lady Eve); The Princess Centimillia, Mr Hinch, Mr Osmond, Dr Kluck, Mr Asweld and McKeewie (The Palm Beach Story); Norval Jones, Trudy Kockenlocker (The Miracle Of Morgan's Creek); Woodrow Lafayette Pershing Truesmith, Sgt Heppelfinger* (Hail The Conquering Hero); Harold Diddlebock, EJ Wagglebury, Formfit Franklin (Mad Wednesday); Hilda Swandumper,

Blackie Jobero, Judge Alfalfa J O'Toole, Julius Hingleman (The Beautiful Blonde From Bashful Bend); Miss Fyfyth (Les Carnets De Major Thompson)

* played by William Demarest

SHIPS AND VESSELS

PBR Streetgang (Apocalypse Now)

The Nostromo (Alien)

The Pequod (Moby Dick)

The Nautilus (20,000 Leagues Under The Sea)

The Seaview (Voyage To The Bottom Of The Sea)

The Nebuchadnezzar (The Matrix)

USS Enterprise (Star Trek)

Memphis Belle (Memphis Belle)

USS Caine (The Caine Mutiny)

HMS Defiant (HMS Defiant)

The Blackbird (X-Men)

Herbie (The Love Bug)

Little Nelly (You Only Live Twice)

HMS Torrin (In Which We Serve)

HMS Compass Rose (The Cruel Sea)

The Dark Star (Dark Star)

The Millennium Falcon (Star Wars)

The Discovery (2001: A Space Odyssey)

The Bounty (Mutiny On The Bounty)

Battlestar Galactica (Battlestar Galactica)

The Disco Volante (yacht, Thunderball)

The Liparus (oil tanker, The Spy Who Loved Me)

The Mary Celeste (Mystery Of The Mary Celeste)

The Titanic (A Night To Remember)

The Maggie (a tugboat, The Maggie)

The Titfield Thunderbolt (a train, The Titfield Thunderbolt)

United Planets Cruiser C-57-D (Forbidden Planet)

The Venture (King Kong)

The Protector (Galaxy Quest)
The Rita (Creature From The Black Lagoon)
U-96 (Das Boot)
The Sawfish (On The Beach)
The Antonia Graza (Ghost Ship)
Lewis & Clark (Event Horizon)
The Icarus II (Sunshine)

THE ASTAIRE–ROGERS* FILMS

Flying Down To Rio (1933), The Gay Divorcee (1934), Roberta (1935), Top Hat (1935),
Follow The Fleet (1936), Swing Time (1936), Shall We Dance (1937), Carefree (1938),
The Barkleys Of Broadway (1949)

*real names Frederick Austerlitz and Virginia McMath

IMAGINARY COUNTRIES

Ambrosia (Billy Liar)
Bacteria (The Great Dictator)
Cascara (Water)
Corto Maltese (Batman)
Estrovia (A King In New York)
Euphrenia (The Slipper And The Rose)
Freedonia (Duck Soup)
Republic of Gabel (Ghost In The Shell)
Genovia (The Princess Diaries)
The Duchy of Grand Fenwick (The Mouse That Roared)
Republic of Hatay (Indiana Jones And The Last Crusade)
Republic of Hidalgo (Doc Savage – The Man Of Bronze)
Isthmus (Licence To Kill)
Javasu (Princess Caraboo)
Krakozia (The Terminal)
The Kingdom of Marshovia (The Merry Widow)
Nibia (Ace Ventura: When Nature Calls)
Parador (Moon Over Parador)

Pottsylvania (The Adventures Of Rocky And Bullwinkle)
Ruritania (The Prisoner Of Zenda)
San Marcos (Bananas)
San Monique (Live And Let Die)
Sylvania (Duck Soup)
Tecala (Proof Of Life)
Tijara (The In-Laws)
Tomania (The Great Dictator)
The Republic of Valverde (Commando and Die Hard II)
The Barony of Vulgaria (Chitty Chitty Bang Bang)
The Kingdom of Zamunda (Coming To America)
The Republic of Zangoro (The Dogs Of War)

TITLE CHANGES

UK	US
Harry Potter And The Philosopher's Stone	Harry Potter And The Sorcerer's Stone
The Quatermass Experiment	The Creeping Unknown
Quatermass II	Enemy From Space
Quatermass And The Pit	Five Million Years To Earth
Dance Of The Vampires	The Fearless Vampire Killers
The Damned	These Are The Damned
Monte Carlo Or Bust	Those Daring Young Men In Their Jaunty Jalopies
The Wisdom Of Crocodiles	Immortality
Carlton-Browne Of The FO	Man In A Cocked Hat
Catch Us If You Can	Having A Wild Weekend
Mad Max 2	The Road Warrior

US	UK
Hallelujah, I'm A Bum	Hallelujah, I'm A Tramp
Off Limits	Military Policemen
Off Limits	Saigon
House On Sorority Row	House Of Evil
Sisters	Blood Sisters

Murder My Sweet	Farewell My Lovely
A Big Hand For The Little Lady	Big Deal At Dodge City
The Hot Rock	How To Steal A Diamond In Four Uneasy Lessons
Shoot To Kill	Deadly Pursuit
Joy Ride	Roadkill
Dracula 2000	Dracula 2001
Saving Silverman	Evil Woman
Cannonball	Carquake
Dennis The Menace	Dennis
Encino Man	California Man

PIXAR SHORTS

The Adventures Of André And Wally B. (1984), Luxo Jr (1986), Red's Dream (1987), Tin Toy (1988), Knick Knack (1989), Geri's Game (1997), It's Tough To Be A Bug (1999), For The Birds (2000), Mike's New Car (2002), Boundin' (2003), Jack-Jack Attack (2005), One Man Band (2005), Lifted (2006)

THE DIRTY DOZEN AND THEIR 'SKILL'

Character	Actor	Skill
Joseph Wladislaw	Charles Bronson	Sticks by the Major, sole survivor
Robert Jefferson	Jim Brown	Runs and drops grenades into the bunker
Tom Busby	Milos Vladek	Gets lost in the pack
Ben Gilpin	Ben Carruthers	Goes in the pen with Sawyer
Victor Franco	John Cassavetes	Mafia bigshot who cuts the phone
Roscoe Lever	Stuart Cooper	Gets killed
Pedro 'Mayonnaise' Jimenez	Trini Lopez	Supposed to cut the cable
Seth K Sawyer	Colin Maitland	Goes in the pen with Gilpin
Tassos Bravos	Al Mancini	Lost in the bunch, but ethnic
Archer Maggot	Telly Savalas	Psycho serial killer, causes trouble

| Vernon Pinkley | Donald Sutherland | Impersonates an officer |
| Samson Posey | Clint Walker | Big lunk, thug |

* Also on the mission, but not dirty, are Major Reisman (Lee Marvin) and Sgt Bowron (Richard Jaeckel), both of whom also survive

SELECTED FILMS WITH ALL-DWARF CASTS

The Terror Of Tiny Town (1938), Even Dwarfs Started Small (1970)

UNCREDITED APPEARANCES

Milton Berle (Pee Wee's Big Adventure)

Cate Blanchett, Peter Jackson (Hot Fuzz)

Kenneth Branagh (Swing Kids)

Yul Brynner (The Magic Christian)

Don Cheadle (Ocean's Eleven)

Seán Connery (Robin Hood: Prince Of Thieves)

Joseph Cotten and Marlene Dietrich (Touch Of Evil)

Matt Damon, Jason Biggs and James Van Der Beek (Jay And Silent Bob Strike Back)

Peter Finch (First Men In The Moon)

Carrie Fisher (Austin Powers: International Man Of Mystery)

Bryan Forbes (as Turk Thrust) (A Shot In The Dark)

Ava Gardner (The Bandwagon)

Elliott Gould (City Of Industry)

Ian Hendry (Damien: Omen II)

Glenda Jackson (The Boy Friend)

Boris Karloff (Bikini Beach)

Shirley MacLaine (Ocean's Eleven)

Madonna (Die Another Day)

Leo McKern (Damien: Omen II)

Groucho Marx (Will Success Spoil Rock Hunter?)

Roger Moore (as Turk Thrust II) (Curse Of The Pink Panther)

Jack Nicholson (Broadcast News)

David Niven, Frank Sinatra, Dean Martin and Peter Sellers (The Road To Hong Kong)

Peter O'Toole (Casino Royale)
Arnold Schwarzenegger (The Long Goodbye)
Henry Winkler and Linda Blair (Scream)

SERIAL KILLER NICKNAMES

Nickname	Character (actor)	Film
M	Franz Becker (Peter Lorre)	M
Son of Sam	David Berkowitz (Michael Badalucco)	Summer Of Sam*
The Hillside Stranglers	Kenneth Bianchi and Angelo Buono (Billy Zane and Dennis Farina)	The Hillside Stranglers*
Citizen X	Andrei Chikatilo (Jeffrey DeMunn)	Citizen X*
Maniac Cop	Officer Matt Cordell (Robert Z'Dar)	Maniac Cop
The Boston Strangler	Albert DeSalvo (Tony Curtis)	The Boston Strangler*
The Tooth Fairy, a.k.a. Red Dragon	Francis Dolarhyde (Tom Noonan/Ralph Fiennes)	Manhunter/ Red Dragon
Cyrus the Virus	Cyrus Grissom (John Malkovich)	Con Air
Buffalo Bill, a.k.a Mr Hide	Jame Gumb (Ted Levine)	The Silence Of The Lambs
Diamond Dog	Nathan Jones (Ving Rhames)	Con Air
Bluebeard	Henri Landru (George Sanders)	Bluebeard's Ten Honeymoons*
The Hawk	Stephen Marsh (George Costigan)	The Hawk
The Driller Killer	Reno Miller (Jimmy Laine a.k.a Abel Ferrara)	The Driller Killer
The Shape	Michael Myers (Nick Castle)	Halloween
The Nightstalker	Richard Ramirez (Bret Roberts)	Nightstalker*
Chucky	Charles Lee Ray (Brad Dourif)	Child's Play
Dr Giggles	Dr Evan Rendell (Larry Drake)	Dr Giggles
The Hitcher	John Ryder (Rutger Hauer)	The Hitcher
Serial Mom	Beverly Sutphin (Kathleen Turner)	Serial Mom
The Phone Book Killer	Arthur 'Buck' Taylor (Judd Nelson)	Relentless
Scorpio	unknown (Andrew Robinson)	Dirty Harry

The Stepfather	unknown, a.k.a. Jerry Blake (Terry O'Quinn)	The Stepfather
The Gemini Killer	unknown (Brad Dourif)	Exorcist III: Legion
John Doe	unknown (Kevin Spacey)	Seven
Zodiac	Arthur Allen Leigh* (John Caroll Lynch)	Zodiac

* denotes real person

FRANCHISE SEQUELS AT A GLANCE
The Children of the Corn Saga

Children Of The Corn (1984) a.k.a. 'the one with Linda Hamilton'

Children Of The Corn II: The Final Sacrifice (1993) a.k.a. 'the one with a monster at the end'

Children Of The Corn III: Urban Harvest (1994) a.k.a. 'the one with a big-city setting and a glimpse of Charlize Theron'

Children Of The Corn IV: The Gathering (1996) a.k.a. 'the one with Naomi Watts and Karen Black'

Children Of The Corn V: Fields Of Terror (1998) a.k.a. 'the one with Alexis Arquette and Eva Mendez, not to mention David Carradine'

Children Of The Corn 666: Isaac's Return (1999) a.k.a. 'the one with the creepy kid from the first film coming back as an adult'

Children Of The Corn: Revelation (2001) a.k.a. 'the one with Michael Ironside'

The Friday the 13th Slayings

Friday The 13th (1980) a.k.a. 'the one where Jason's mom is the killer'

Friday The 13th Part 2 (1981) a.k.a. 'the one where Jason wears a sack on his head'

Friday The 13th Part 3: 3-D (1982) a.k.a. 'the one in 3-D that introduces the hockey mask'

Friday The 13th: The Final Chapter (1984) a.k.a. 'the one with Crispin Glover'

Friday The 13th: A New Beginning (1985) a.k.a. 'the one that pissed you off because they lied last time and because some copycat is the killer'

Friday The 13th Part VI: Jason Lives (1986) a.k.a. 'the one where the numerals came back but went Roman and Jason returned from the grave as a zombie'

Friday The 13th Part VII: The New Blood (1988) a.k.a. 'the one with the telekinetic heroine'

Friday The 13th, Part VIII: Jason Takes Manhattan (1989) a.k.a. 'the one where Jason doesn't get to New York 'til way, way too late in the film to make a difference'

Jason Goes To Hell: The Final Friday (1993) a.k.a. 'the one where they ditch the Friday The 13th title and Jason turns out to be possessed by a killer demon slug that hops from body to body racking up more killings, and Freddy's glove pops up at the end'

Jason X (2001) a.k.a. 'the one in space'

Freddy Vs. Jason (2003) a.k.a. 'the one which crosses over with Elm Street'

The Halloween Cycle

Halloween (1978) a.k.a. 'the original'

Halloween II (1981) a.k.a. 'the second one'

Halloween III: Season Of The Witch (1983) a.k.a. 'the one without Michael Myers'

Halloween 4: The Return Of Michael Myers (1988) a.k.a. 'the one where Michael Myers returned and the numbers switched'

Halloween 5 (1989) a.k.a. 'the one called The Revenge Of Michael Myers on the posters but not on the film'

Halloween: The Curse Of Michael Myers (1995) a.k.a. 'the last one with Donald Pleasence'

Halloween H20 (1998) a.k.a. 'the one set twenty years later where Jamie Lee Curtis comes back'

Halloween: Resurrection (2002) a.k.a. 'the one where it turns out she chopped off the wrong guy's head at the end of the last film'

Halloween (2007) a.k.a. 'The Rob Zombie remake'

The Howling Bunch

The Howling (1981) a.k.a. 'the one with E.T.'s mom'

Howling II: Stirba Werewolf Bitch (1985) a.k.a. 'the one with Christopher Lee'

Howling III: The Marsupials (1987) a.k.a. 'the one with Australian pouched werewolves'

Howling IV: The Original Nightmare (1988) a.k.a. 'the one where they adapted the original novel Joe Dante threw away'
Howling V: The Rebirth (1989) a.k.a. 'the one set in an Eastern European castle'
Howling VI: The Freaks (1991) a.k.a. 'the one with Bruce Payne as a vampire and the weird circus setting'
Howling: New Moon Rising (1995) a.k.a. 'the one where all the werewolf footage comes from earlier films in the series and 90 per cent of the running time is taken up by country music'

The Elm Street Nightmares

A Nightmare On Elm Street (1984) a.k.a. 'the one with Johnny Depp'
A Nightmare On Elm Street Part 2: Freddy's Revenge (1985) a.k.a. 'the one with the very gay subtext'
A Nightmare On Elm Street 3: Dream Warriors (1987) a.k.a. 'the one with Patricia Arquette'
A Nightmare On Elm Street 4: The Dream Master (1988) a.k.a. 'the one directed by Renny Harlin'
Freddy's Nightmares (1988) a.k.a. 'the video release that turns out to be episodes of the cable TV series'
A Nightmare On Elm Street: The Dream Child (1989) a.k.a. 'the one without a number'
Freddy's Dead: The Final Nightmare (1991) a.k.a. 'the one with the 3-D climax'
Wes Craven's New Nightmare (1994) a.k.a. 'the one with the postmodernism'
Freddy Vs. Jason (2003) a.k.a. 'the one which wants to be Frankenstein Meets The Wolf Man for the new millennium'

The Police Academy Canon

Police Academy (1984) a.k.a. 'the first one'
Police Academy 2: Their First Assignment (1985) a.k.a. 'the one with Bobcat Goldthwait as the gang leader'
Police Academy 3: Back In Training (1986) a.k.a. 'the one with Bobcat going straight and becoming a cop'
Police Academy 4: Citizens On Patrol (1987) a.k.a. 'the one with Sharon Stone'

Police Academy 5: Assignment Miami Beach (1988) a.k.a. 'the one where Steve Guttenberg got out of the contract and quit the series'

Police Academy (1988) a.k.a. 'the first shot at making a cartoon TV series'

Police Academy 6: City Under Siege (1989) a.k.a. 'the one with a director's credit that gets a cheap laugh - his name is Peter Bonerz'

Police Academy: The Animated Series (1993) a.k.a. 'the second shot at making a cartoon TV series'

Police Academy: Mission To Moscow (1994) a.k.a. 'the one with Christopher Lee'

Police Academy: The Series (1997) a.k.a. 'the TV spin-off you never saw'

The Star Trek Spin-Offs

Star Trek: The Motion Picture (1979) a.k.a. 'the one with V'Ger'

Star Trek: The Wrath Of Khan (1982) a.k.a. 'the one where Spock dies'

Star Trek III: The Search For Spock (1984) a.k.a. 'the one where Spock comes back'

Star Trek IV: The Voyage Home (1986) a.k.a. 'the one with the whales'

Star Trek V: The Final Frontier (1989) a.k.a. 'the one where Shatner complains to God'

Star Trek VI: The Undiscovered Country (1991) a.k.a. 'the one where peace is made with the Klingons'

Star Trek: Generations (1994) a.k.a. 'the one with Kirk and Picard'

Star Trek: First Contact (1996) a.k.a. 'the one with the Borg and time travel'

Star Trek: Insurrection (1998) a.k.a. 'the one with F Murray Abraham'

Star Trek: Nemesis (2002) a.k.a. 'the one with the baldie clone'

MOTHLIGHT

Stan Brakhage's landmark abstract film Mothlight (1963) was made without a camera by pasting moth wings and foliage straight onto film.

WHAT KIND OF ANIMAL WAS?

Andre (a seal)

Asta (a dog - The Thin Man)

Babe (a pig)

Baby (a leopard - Bringing Up Baby)

Balthazar (a donkey - Au Hasard, Balthazar)

Balto (a dog)

Beauty and Beast (dogs - The Hills Have Eyes)

Beethoven (a dog)

Benji (a dog)

The Black (a horse - The Black Stallion)

Bonzo (a chimp - Bedtime For Bonzo)

Buddy (a basketball-playing dog - Air Bud)

Bull's-Eye (a dog - Oliver!)

Catzilla (a cat - Mouse Hunt)

Charlie (a cougar - Charlie The Lonesome Cougar)

Charlotte (a spider - Charlotte's Web)

Cheetah (a chimp - Tarzan The Ape Man)

Church (a zombie cat - Pet Sematary)

Clarence (a cross-eyed lion - Clarence The Cross-Eyed Lion, Daktari)

Clyde (an orang-utan - Every Which Way But Loose)

Cujo (a dog)

Daisy (an alligator - An Alligator Named Daisy)

Danke (a dog - The Ugly Dachshund)

DC (a cat - That Darn Cat!)

Dunston (an orang-utan - Dunston Checks In)

Ella (a capuchin monkey - Monkey Shines)

Elsa (a lion - Born Free)

Flicka (a horse - My Friend Flicka)

Flipper (a dolphin)

Francis (a mule - Francis The Talking Mule)

The General (a cat - Cat's Eye)

Gentle Ben (a bear)

George and Gracie (whales - Star Trek IV: The Voyage Home)

Gertrude (a duck - Journey To The Centre Of The Earth)

Ghost And The Darkness (lions)

Goofy (Mickey's a mouse, Pluto's a dog, Donald's a duck - what the hell is Goofy?)

Greyfriars Bobby (a dog)

Hooch (a dog - Turner and Hooch)

Jack (a hockey-playing chimp, MVP: Most Valuable Primate)

Jake (a cat [from outer space] - The Cat From Outer Space)

Joe Young (a big gorilla - Mighty Joe Young)

John Paul Jones (a cat - Cat People)

Jonathan Livingstone Seagull (yes, a seagull)

Jones (a cat - Alien)

Kes (a kestrel)

Lassie (a dog - Lassie Come Home)

Link and Voodoo (chimps, Link)

Matilda (a boxing kangaroo)

Max (a chimp who cops off with Charlotte Rampling - Max, Mon Amour)

Mij (an otter - Ring Of Bright Water)

Milo and Otis (a cat and a dog - The Adventures Of Milo And Otis)

Moby Dick (a white whale)

Mr Tinkles (a cat - Cats & Dogs)

Napoleon (a pig - Animal Farm)

Old Yeller (a dog)

Orca (a killer whale - Orca Killer Whale)

Paulie (a parrot)

Rin-Tin-Tin (a dog)

Sammy (a way-out seal - Sammy The Way-Out Seal)

Socrates and Ben (rats - Willard)

Sparky (a reanimated dog - Frankenweenie)

Stuart Little (a mouse)

Tao, Budger and Luath (a cat and two dogs - The Incredible Journey)

Tarka (an otter - Tarka The Otter)

Thomasina (a cat - The Three Lives Of Thomasina)

Tonto (a cat - Harry And Tonto)

Toto (a dog - The Wizard Of Oz)

Trigger (a horse, Son Of Paleface)

Velvet (a horse - International Velvet)

White Fang (a dog)

Willy (a whale – Free Willy)

Won-Ton-Ton (a dog – Won-Ton-Ton, The Dog Who Saved Hollywood)

Zoltan (a vampire dog – Zoltan, Hound Of Dracula)

FICTIONAL BOOKS IN MOVIES

All Of Them Witches by JR Hanslett (Rosemary's Baby)

Bare Ruined Choirs by Barton Fink (Barton Fink)

The Bottle by Don Birnam (The Lost Weekend)

Chain Of Command by Youngblood Hawke (Youngblood Hawke)

A Clockwork Orange by F Alexander (Clockwork Orange)

The Garden Of Proserpina by Randolph Henry Ash (Possession)

The Gift by Dr George Waggner (The Howling)

The Hermann Goering Workout Book (Top Secret)

How I Did It by Victor Frankenstein (Young Frankenstein)

I Wake Up Bleeding by Phillip Marlowe (The Lady In The Lake)

The Joy Of Impotence by Dr Max J Eggelhofer (The Front Page)

A Match Made In Space by George McFly (Back To The Future)

Magical Me by Gilderoy Lockhart (Harry Potter And The Chamber Of Secrets)

Misery's Return by Paul Sheldon (Misery)

The Mystery Of The Plantaganet Parakeet by Andrew Wyke (Sleuth)

Pinsky! a.k.a. Women I Would Like To Pork (Throw Momma From The Train)

The Ravagers, The Return Of Angelina and *Romancing The Stone* by Joan Wilder (Romancing The Stone)

The Shape Of Rage by Dr Hal Raglan (The Brood)

Swedish Home-Made Penis Enlarger Pumps And Me by Austin Powers (Austin Powers: International Man of Mystery)

THE COMPLETE ERNEST

Ernest Goes To Camp (1987); Ernest Saves Christmas (1988); Ernest Goes To Splash Mountain (1989); Ernest Goes To Jail (1990); Ernest Scared Stupid (1991); Ernest Rides Again (1993); Ernest Goes To School (1994); Slam Dunk Ernest (1995); Ernest Goes To Africa (1997)

FOREIGN TITLES TRANSLATED

A Bout De Souffle	Breathless (literally, Out of Breath)
L'Age D'Or	The Golden Age
Ai No Corrida	In The Bullrun
Allegro Non Troppo	Fast, But Not Too Fast
À Nous La Liberté	Freedom For Us
Aparajito	The Unvanquished
L'argent	The Money
Au Revoir Les Enfants	Goodbye To The Children
Avanti!	Come!
L'avventura	The Adventure
La Balance	The Informer
La Bamba	The Sting
Il Bidone	The Swindle
Das Boot	The Boat
La Cage Aux Folles	Cage For Fools
Un Chien Andalou	An Andalusian Dog
Les Diaboliques	The Fiends (literally, The Diabolicals)
La Dolce Vita	The Sweet Life
Les Enfants Du Paradis	The Children Of Paradise
Equus	Horse
Festen	The Celebration
La Grande Illusion	The Big Lie
Heimat	Homeland
Hiroshima, Mon Amour	I Love Hiroshima
Kagemusha	Double (as in Lookalike or Impersonator)
Kanal	Sewer
Koyaanisqatsi	Life Out Of Balance
Kwaidan	Ghost Stories
Matador	Killer
Les Miserables	The Unhappy People
Mondo Cande	Dog's World (i.e. 'it's a dog's life')
La Nuit Americaine	Day For Night (literally, The American Night)

Onibaba	The Hole
Padre Padrone	Father Master
Plein Soleil	Broad Daylight
Ran	Chaos
Rashomon	In The Woods
La Regle De Jeu	Rules Of The Game
Rififi	Rumble (literally 'a roughhouse fight')
La Ronde	Rondo, or The Roundelay
Sanjuro	Thirty
Sansho Dayu	Sansho the Bailiff
She's Gotta Have It	She Requires Sex
La Strada	The Street
El Topo	The Mole
Touchez Pas Au Grisbi	Hands Off The Loot
Ugetsu Monogatari	Tales Of The Pale Moon After Rain
I Vitelloni	The Overgrown Calves
Yeleen	Brightness
Yojimbo	Bodyguard
Yol	The Road Of Life
Zero De Conduite	No Marks For Conduct

RAY HARRYHAUSEN'S CREATURES

Movie	Creature
Mighty Joe Young	Joe Young (a big gorilla)
The Beast From 20,000 Fathoms	The rhedosaurus
It Came From Beneath The Sea	The six-tentacled octopus
Earth Vs. The Flying Saucers	The flying saucers and the alien invaders
The Animal World	The brontosaurus, the stegosaurus, the ceratosaurus, the triceratops and the tyrannosaurus
220 Million Miles To Earth	The Ymir (a Venusian reptile)
The Seventh Voyage Of Sinbad	The cyclops, the snake woman, the duelling skeleton, the roc (giant bird) and the dragon
The Three Worlds Of Gulliver	A disappointingly ordinary alligator

The Mysterious Island	The giant crab, the phorocasaurus (prehistoric chicken-thing), the giant bees and the nautilus (tentacled undersea mollusc)
Jason And The Argonauts	The harpies, the hydra (many-headed mythical serpent), Talos (bronze giant), Poseidon (giant fish-tailed sea-god) and the army of sword-fighting skeletons
The First Men In The Moon	The Selenites (insectile inhabitants of the moon) and the Mooncalf (giant caterpillar)
One Million Years BC	The archaelon (giant turtle), allosaurus, brontosaurus, triceratops, ceratosaurus and pterodactyl
The Valley Of Gwangi	Gwangi (an allosaurus) and eohippus (a tiny horse)
The Golden Voyage Of Sinbad	The living ship's figurehead, the homunculus, the living statue of Kali (eight-armed Indian goddess), the centaur (human-horse hybrid) and the griffin (lion-eagle hybrid)
Sinbad And The Eye Of The Tiger	The intelligent baboon, the ghouls, the Minaton (a bronze minotaur), Trog (a giant prehistoric man with a horn) and the giant sabre-toothed tiger
Clash Of The Titans	The Kraken (big sea monster), Dioskilos (two-headed dog), Pegasus (winged horse), Calibos (hulking brute), Bubo (a chirruping mechanical owl) and the Medusa (snake-haired gorgon)

THE DEADLY VIPER ASSASSINATION SQUAD*

Name	Code Name	Actor
Beatrix Kiddo	Black Mamba, a.k.a. The Bride, a.k.a. Mom	Uma Thurman
Elle Driver	California Mountain Snake	Daryl Hannah
Vernita Green	Copperhead	Vivica A Fox
O-Ren Ishii	Cottonmouth	Lucy Liu
Budd	Sidewinder	Michael Madsen
Bill	Snake Charmer	David Carradine

Order of death in films: Vernita Green, O-Ren Ishii, Budd, Elle Driver, Bill
Order of death chronologically: O-Ren Ishii, Vernita Green, Budd, Elle Driver, Bill

*From Quentin Tarantino's Kill Bill Vol. 1 and Vol. 2

FIRST, LONGEST, LARGEST, MOST

The first feature film ever made – The Story Of The Kelly Gang (1906)

The longest film ever made – The Cure For Insomnia (1987), running 85 hours

The best year for US feature film production – 1921 (854 features)

The worst year for US feature film production – 1963 (121 features)

The largest number of fatalities on a film set – 40 on The Sword Of Tipu Sultan (1989)

The first footprints in the Hollywood Walk Of Fame outside Graumann's Chinese Theater – made by Norma Talmadge in May 1927

The first pre-credit sequence – Crime Without Passion (1934)

The most prolific director – William Beaudine, who made 182 pictures between 1922 and 1965

The first film to show the sex act – Extase (1932)

The longest ever interval between original and sequel – 46 years between The Wizard Of Oz and Return To Oz

The largest number of extras – 300,000 in Gandhi (1982)

The most married Hollywood star – Al 'Lash' LaRue, who was married on ten occasions

The first ever remake – The Great Train Robbery (1904) was a remake of The Great Train Robbery (1903)

The most kisses dispatched in one film – 127 by John Barrymore in Don Juan (1926)

The tallest screen artiste – Clifford Thompson, star of Seal Skins (1932), was eight feet six inches

The greatest number of retakes – 342 shot by Charlie Chaplin for City Lights (1931)

The heaviest screen artiste – Ethel Greer, star of Hoopla (1933), who weighed 637lb

The youngest professional film director – Sydney Ling, aged 13, Lex The Wonder Dog (1973)

The first helicopter shot – The Twister Road (1948)

The performer who played the most roles – Tom London, who made 2,000 screen appearances between 1883 and 1963

The first song especially composed for a film – 'Mother I Still Have You' for The Jazz Singer (1927)

The largest assemblage of animals for one movie – 8,552 in Around The World In Eighty Days (1956)

The longest acting career – Curt Bois debuted in Der Fielde Bauer in 1908 and finished in Wings Of Desire in 1987

The most successful documentary at the box office – IMAX space shuttle documentary The Dream Is Alive (1985), which grossed $86 million

The first flashback – The Yiddisher Boy (1908)

The most prolific screen songwriter – Lyricist Vali, who wrote 6,500 songs from 1959

The actor who has played the same role the most often – Hong Kong star Kwan Takhing who played Huang Fei-Hong in 77 out of 104 films

The youngest performer ever to receive star billing – Leroy Overacker, aged six months in A Bedtime Story (1933)

The only soundtrack to outgross the movie – Superfly (1972)

The largest number of cameras for one sequence – 48 for the sea battle in Ben-Hur (1925)

The first director to direct himself – Harold Heath in £1,000 Reward (1913)

The greatest number of retakes for a dialogue scene – 127 shot by Stanley Kubrick for The Shining (1980)

The first film to end with a freeze frame – La Roue (1923)

REASONS FOR DETENTION IN THE BREAKFAST CLUB

Student	Reason
Claire Standish (Molly Ringwald)	Cutting class to go shopping
Andrew Clarke (Emilio Estevez)	Taping a kid's butt-cheeks together
Brian Ralph Johnson (Anthony Michael Hall)	Bringing a flare gun to school
John Bender (Judd Nelson)	Pulling a fire alarm
Allison Reynolds (Ally Sheedy)	Nothing

ACTORS WHO'VE NAMED THEIR PETS AFTER BOOZE

Anne Archer – Bordeaux (dog)

Brigitte Bardot – Gin (dog)

Drew Barrymore - Mocha Bailey (horse)
Linda Blair - Pilsner (dog)
Doris Day - Heineken (dog)
Ronald Reagan - Scotch and Soda (Scottish terriers)

SELECTED ALBUMS MADE BY ACTORS

Album	Artiste
Calypso - Is Like So	Robert Mitchum
How Could It Be	Eddie Murphy
This Is Me	Jim Dale
Saddles 'n' Spurs	Lorne Greene
Albert Finney's Album	Albert Finney
A Tramp Shining	Richard Harris
Heartbreak LP	Don Johnson
Songs Without Words	Dudley Moore
A Transformed Man	William Shatner
Whenever I'm Away From You	John Travolta
The Return Of Bruno	Bruce Willis
When	Vincent Gallo
Private Radio	Billy Bob Thornton
America, Why I Love Her	John Wayne
Ask Me What I Am	Burt Reynolds
A Twist Of Lemmon	Jack Lemmon
Songs I Like	Dick Van Dyke
Little Joe Sure Can Sing	Joe Pesci (as Joe Ritchie)
Jungle Rhythm	James Dean
Who Is There Among Us Who Knows?	Jack Nicholson
They Can't Take That Away From Me	Danny DeVito
Bobby Ogden's Outlaw Blues	Peter Fonda
Do You Wanna Touch Me (Oh Yeah)	Michael Caine

CLAPPERBOARD*

As well as providing the editor with vital data, the idea of a clapperboard placed in front of the shot before the start of each take is to allow the editor to synchronise sound and picture by matching up the image of the closed clapperboard and the sound of the clapperboard snapping.

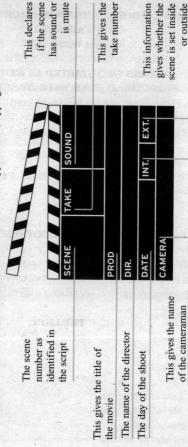

The scene number as identified in the script

This declares if the scene has sound or is mute

This gives the take number

This gives the title of the movie

The name of the director

The day of the shoot

This information gives whether the scene is set inside or outside

This gives the name of the cameraman

*Also the name of a '70s kids' TV film show hosted by Chris Kelly

IN WHICH FILM DOES MARILYN MONROE'S DRESS BLOW UP AN AIR VENT?

The Seven Year Itch (1955)

ACTORS WHO STARTED AS WAITERS

Alec Baldwin, Antonio Banderas, Ellen Barkin, Kathy Bates, Sandra Bullock, David Caruso, Julia Ormond, Ellen DeGeneres, Dana Delany, Robert Downey Jr, Andy Garcia, James Garner, Gene Hackman, Woody Harrelson, Dustin Hoffman, Burt Lancaster, Jessica Lange, Jon Lovitz, Geena Davis, Mary Steenburgen, Meryl Streep, Barbra Streisand, Kathleen Turner, Raquel Welch

ACTORS WHO STARTED AS THE EL POLLO LOCO CHICKEN

Brad Pitt

FILM DIRECTOR BROTHERS

Joel and Ethan Coen; Albert and Allen Hughes; Larry and Andy Wachowski; Paolo and Vittorio Taviani; Joshua and Jonas Pate; John and Roy Boulting; Anthony and Joe Russo; Stephen and Timothy Quay; Mark and Michael Polish; Jean-Pierre and Luke Dardenne; the Mirza Brothers; the Bolex Brothers; the Brutal Brothers

LEO THE LION

There have been four roaring MGM lions over the years. The first Leo was brought to America from the Sudan in 1917, and made his debut in sound only. When Sam Goldwyn merged with Metro Pictures and Louis B Mayer in 1924, the logo was redesigned to show the lion's face. The first Leo was replaced by another from Selig Zoo in LA, who in turn was replaced by Pluto in 1928. It was Pluto who appeared at the front of MGM's first talkie – White Shadows In The South Seas (1928) – and also appeared in a much larger role, mauling Romans in 1936's No Place Like Rome. Pluto was replaced in 1944 when the trademark was updated and the lion head has remained unchanged ever since. Incidentally, the motto 'Ars Gratia Artis' that surrounds the lion means 'Art For Art's Sake'.

TOP GUN CALL SIGNS

Actor	Character Name	Call Sign
Tom Cruise	Lt Pete Mitchell	Maverick
Val Kilmer	Lt Tom Kazanski	Iceman
Anthony Edwards	Lt (JG) Nick Bradshaw	Goose
Tom Skerritt	Cmdr Mike Metcalf	Viper
Michael Ironside	Lt Cmdr Rick Heatherly	Jester
Rick Rossovich	Lt (JG) Ron Kerner	Slider
Tim Robbins	Lt (JG) Sam Wells	Merlin
John Stockwell		Cougar
Barry Tubb		Wolfman
Clarence Gilyard Jr		Sundown
Whip Hubley		Hollywood

WOODY ALLEN'S ON-SCREEN ALTER EGOS†

Victor Shakopopolis (What's New, Pussycat?, Everything You Always Wanted To Know About Sex But Were Afraid To Ask), Jimmy Bond/Dr Noah (Casino Royale), Virgil Starkwell (Take The Money And Run), Fielding Mellish (Bananas), Allan Felix (Play It Again, Sam), Miles Monroe (Sleeper), Boris Grushenko (Love And Death), Alvy Singer (Annie Hall), Isaac Davis (Manhattan), Sandy Bates (Stardust Memories), Andrew Hobbs (A Midsummer Night's Sex Comedy), Leonard Zelig (Zelig), Danny Rose (Broadway Danny Rose), Mickey Sachs (Hannah And Her Sisters), Joe Needleman (Seth Green – Radio Days), Alice Tate (Mia Farrow – Alice), Sheldon Mills (New York Stories), Cliff Stern (Crimes And Misdemeanors), Max Kleinman (Shadows And Fog), Gabe Roth (Husbands And Wives), Larry Lipton (Manhattan Murder Mystery), David Shane (John Cusack – Bullets Over Broadway), Lenny Weinrib (Mighty Aphrodite), Joe Berlin (Everybody Says I Love You), Harry Block (Deconstructing Harry), Lee Simon (Kenneth Branagh – Celebrity), Emmet Ray (Sean Penn – Sweet And Lowdown), Ray Winkler (Small Time Crooks), CW Briggs (Curse Of The Jade Scorpion), Val Waxman (Hollywood Ending)

† all played by Woody Allen unless noted

AMERICANS WHO ARE ACTUALLY CANADIANS

Star	Born in
Dan Aykroyd	Ottawa
James Cameron	Ontario
John Candy	Toronto
Jim Carrey	Ontario
Thomas Chong	Edmonton
Rae Dawn Chong	Vancouver
Lolita Davidovich	Ontario
Michael J Fox	Alberta
Norman Jewison	Toronto
Margot Kidder	Yellow Knife
Rick Moranis	Toronto
Leslie Nielsen	Regina
Mary Pickford	Toronto
William Shatner	Montreal
Martin Short	Hamilton
Donald Sutherland	St John

ABBOTT AND COSTELLO MEET ...

Frankenstein (i.e. Frankenstein's Monster, also Dracula and the Wolf Man)

The Killer, Boris Karloff

The Invisible Man

Captain Kidd

Dr Jekyll And Mr Hyde

The Keystone Kops

The Mummy

FAKE FILMS WITHIN FILMS

Habeas Corpus (The Player)

Mant! (Matinée)

Stab (Scream 2)

The Duelling Cavalier (Singin' In The Rain)

Exorcist IV (Time After Time)
The Spy Who Laughed At Danger (Hooper)
Vampire's Kiss (Body Double)
Codename: Dragonfly (CQ)
The Faraway Mountain (The Bad And The Beautiful)
Holly Does Hollywood (Body Double)
Weeds (ivans xtc.)
Beverly Hills Gun Club (Action)
Groundhog Day (The Monster Squad)
Je Vous Presente Pamela (Day For Night)
Coed Frenzy (Blow Out)
Gump Again (Cecil B DeMented)
Crash Course (The Exorcist)
I Am A Pig (S1m0ne)
Atomic War Brides (Hollywood Boulevard)
Vampire Vomit (Eskimo Nell)
Driving Over Miss Daisy (Stay Tuned)
Hot Pants College II (Love And Death On Long Island)
Jack Slater (series, Last Action Hero)
Teenage Werewolf Meets Teenage Frankenstein (How To Make A Monster)
Asses Of Fire (South Park: Bigger, Longer & Uncut)
TJ Hooker: The Movie (Charlie's Angels)
Helix (Notting Hill)
The Sand Pirates Of The Sahara (The Majestic)
Playback Time (Mr Bean's Holiday)

PA-PAH, PA-PAH, PA-PAH, PA-PAH, PA-PA-PA

The piece of music that accompanies the Pearl & Dean logo is called 'Asteroid' by Peter Moore. For the record, the company was formed by Charles and Ernie Pearl and Robert Dean.

THE GODFATHER'S 'FIVE FAMILIES'

The Corleones, the Barzinis, the Cuneos, the Tattaglias and the Strachis
(NB: the real five families were the Genoveses, the Gambinos, the Bonannos, the
Colombos and the Luccheses)

THE THREE AMIGOS

Dusty Bottoms (Chevy Chase), Lucky Day (Steve Martin), Ned Nederlander
(Martin Short)

FAKE FILM BANDS

Autobahn - three depressing Germans from The Big Lebowski
Barry Jive And The Uptown Five - Jack Black's band in High Fidelity
The Blues Brothers - trivia one-upmanship fact: their original names were Jake
Papageorge and Elwood Delaney
Blueshammer - perform the hilariously ghastly Pickin' Cotton Blues in Ghost World
Breaking Glass - doomed Hazel O'Connor-led New Wavers (featured Jonathan Pryce
on bass)
Buckaroo Banzai And The Hong Kong Cavaliers - Peter Weller's rock group-cum-
super-scientific adventure gang
Camel Lips - all-girl band in Serial Mom (played by less-offensively named band L7)
The Carrie Nations - three-girl combo in Beyond The Valley Of The Dolls
CB4 - Chris Rock's band from the rap parody movie
Cherry Bomb - Lea Thompson's unfortunately named band from Howard The Duck
Citizen Dick - the grunge band teaming Eddie Vedder and Matt Dillon in Singles
The Commitments - Dublin soul
Crucial Taunt - Tia Carrere's band from Wayne's World
Dogs In Space - Michael Hutchence's band from the film of the same name
Deena Jones And The Dreams - Previously The Dreams, then The Dreamettes -
Dreamgirls
Du Jour - the boy band in Josie And The Pussycats
Eddie And The Cruisers - this even had a sequel
Ellen Aim And The Attackers - Diane Lane's band from Streets Of Fire
Fig'rin D'an And The Modal Nodes - the cantina band from Star Wars
Flame - played by Slade in the underrated Flame, a.k.a. Slade In Flame

The Folksmen - A Mighty Wind

The Free World - crap rappers from 8 Mile

Fuck You Yankee Blue Jeans - Silent Bob's Russian cousin's band from Clerks

Future Villain Band - played by Aerosmith in the Bee Gees' Sergeant Pepper's Lonely Hearts Club Band

Hey, That's My Bike - Ethan Hawke's band from Reality Bites

Ivan And The Terribles - longhairs who come to a bad end in Motel Hell

Josie And The Pussycats - long tails and ears for hats, guitars and sharps and flats

Kipper - Robin Askwith's group in Confessions Of A Pop Performer

The Lone Rangers - from Airheads

Marvin Berry And The Starliters - the Enchantment Under The Sea band in Back To The Future

Max Frost And The Troopers - band who take over the USA in Wild In The Streets

No Vacancy - The School Of Rock

N.W.H. - from the 'Spinal Rap' effort Fear Of A Black Hat (the initials stand for Niggaz Wit Hats, and the line-up was Tone Def, Tasty Taste and Ice Cold)

Otis Day And The Knights - the soul band from National Lampoon's Animal House

PoP! - Music And Lyrics

The Quadratics - Welcome To The Dollhouse

The Riptides - Matt Dillon's Beach Boys knock-off from Grace In My Heart

The Rutles - Dirk, Barry, Stig and Nasty, the Prefab Four

The Soggy Bottom Boys - from O! Brother Where Art Thou?

Spinal Tap - This Is Spinal Tap; the grandaddy of all fake bands

Stillwater - Almost Famous

Strange Fruit - a.k.a. the Fruits, Still Crazy

The Stray Cats - supergroup in Stardust, with a line-up including David Essex, Paul Nicholas and Dave Edmunds; Adam Faith was their manager

Sweet Sue And Her Society Syncopators - the all-girl band from Some Like It Hot

Tom, Bill And Mary - trio from Nashville, played by Keith Carradine, Allan F Nicholls and Cristina Raines

The Venus In Furs - from Velvet Goldmine

The Wonders - from That Thing You Do

Wyld Stallyns - Bill and Ted's band

WHAT'S THE FILM WHERE JAMES CAGNEY SQUEEZES A GRAPEFRUIT IN MAE CLARKE'S FACE?

The Public Enemy (1931)

DATES FOR YOUR DIARY

2 February	Groundhog Day#
14 February	The St Valentine's Day Massacre*, My Bloody Valentine*
17 March	St Patrick's Day - cop Andy Kaufman freaks out and guns down a bunch of bystanders, God Told Me To*
1 April	April Fools' Day* (actually, it's all a joke!)
May (second Sunday)	Mother's Day*, Happy Mother's Day Love George*
6 June 1944	The Longest Day§, Saving Private Ryan*§
June (sometime)	Graduation Day*, The Graduate
June (third Sunday)	Father's Day
4 July	Independence Day*, Born On The Fourth Of July§
15 August 1969	Woodstock festival begins
29 August 1997	Terminator 2: Judgment Day
30 September 1955	Death of James Dean
2 October 1988	The timeline fissures in Donnie Darko#
October (first Monday)	Supreme Court convenes, First Monday In October
12 October	Columbus Day - celebrate with a back-to-back videothon of 1492: Conquest Of Paradise, Carry On Columbus and Christopher Columbus: The Discovery
14 October 1947	Proving he has The Right Stuff, Chuck Yeager breaks the sound barrier
31 October	Halloween* (and sequels*)
5 November	Guy Fawkes' bonfires used for handy corpse-disposal in Hangover Square and The Mad Magician
12 November	The Enchantment Under The Sea Dance, 1955 (Back To The Future)*
7 December 1941	Pearl Harbor*§, The Final Conflict*#§
13 December 1886	The plague is unleashed in Twelve Monkeys*#

25 December	You Better Watch Out*, Silent Night, Bloody Night*,
	Don't Open 'Til Christmas*, Home Alone,
	It's A Wonderful Life#, Family Man#
31 December	New Year's Evil*, Last Night*
Moveable feast	Friday The 13th*

*massacre, #timewarp, §America at war

MOVIE ACRONYMS (NON-FICTION)

ACE - American Cinema Editors

AFI/BFI - American/British Film Institute

AIP - American International Pictures

AMPAS - Academy Of Motion Picture Arts And Sciences

ASA - American Standards Association

ASC/BSC - American/British Society Of Cinematographers

BAFTA - British Academy Of Film And Television Arts

BBFC - British Board Of Film Classification

CAA - Creative Artists Agency

CTBF - Cinema And Television Benevolent Fund

DGA - Directors Guild Of America

DVD - Digital Versatile Disc

FACT - Federation Against Copyright Theft

Fps - frames per second

HFPA - Hollywood Foreign Press Association

HBO - Home Box Office

HUAC - House Un-American Activities Committee

ICM - International Creative Management

ILM - Industrial Light & Magic

IMDb - Internet Movie Database

MGM - Metro Goldwyn Mayer

MIFED - Marche Internazionale Del TV, Film E Del Documentario

MPAA - Motion Picture Association Of America

NTSC - National Television Standards Committee

PAL - Programmable Phase Logic/Phase Alternation Line

RKO - Radio Keith Orpheum
SAG - Screen Actors Guild
SMPTE - Society Of Motion Pictures And Television Engineers

THE TOP TEN STUNTS OF JACKASS

Crazy antics undertaken by the Jackass crew during the course of their two big-screen outings:

Alligator Tightrope - Steve-O walks a tightrope across the alligator pool at a zoo, wearing only a jockstrap and helmet and with a chicken hung from his bottom. He falls in and narrowly avoids being bitten. (Jackass: The Movie)

Mousetraps - Ehren McGhehey throws himself into hundreds of set mousetraps, dressed as a mouse. (Jackass: The Movie)

Riot Control Test - Johnny Knoxville is shot by a beanbag projectile from a pump-action shotgun. Two days later, the bruise covers his entire stomach. (Jackass: The Movie)

Rocket Skates - Knoxville comes to England and skates down hills with lit bottle rockets on his shoes. (Jackass: The Movie)

Bungee Wedgie - Does just what it says on the tin. (Jackass: The Movie)

Bull Run - The sequel opens with the gang being chased through an abandoned neighbourhood by a stampede of bulls. (Jackass: Number 2)

Yak Attack - Knoxville, blindfolded, enters the pen of an enraged yak and is rammed. (Jackass: Number 2)

Penis Puppetry - Chris Pontius puts a cotton puppet onto his penis, then dangles it in front of a poisonous snake. (Jackass: Number 2)

Old Lady Flasher - Guest star Spike Jonze cameos, disguised with prosthetics as an old woman whose breasts publicly escape her clothing. (Jackass: Number 2)

Horse Juice - Possibly the grossest moment in Jackass history sees the gang chugging warm stallion semen straight from the source. (Jackass: Number 2)

THE MAN IN THE SUIT

Alien (Boris Balejo), Gort from The Day The Earth Stood Still (Lock Martin), The
Creature From The Black Lagoon (Ricou Browning, Ben Chapman), Godzilla
(mainly Ken Satsuma), Predator (Kevin Peter Hall*), Swamp Thing (Dick Durock),
Moonwatcher, head ape from 2001: A Space Odyssey (Dan Richter)

* Also inside Harry in Harry And The Hendersons

THE CONFESSIONS MOVIES

… Of A Window Cleaner (1974)
… Of A Pop Performer (1975)
… Of A Driving Instructor (1976)
… From A Holiday Camp (1977)

BOLLYWOOD – A GLOSSARY

Bandra - Suburb of Bombay that marks the beginning of Bollywood
Chamcha - The 'yes men' of the stars
Dushum Dushum - A fight sequence; it is onomatopoeic
Holi - The Hindu festival of colour, often a backdrop for Bollywood flicks
Mahurat - The first shot in the can, always celebrated with food and drink
Playback Singers - Professional singers who provide the singing voices for
the actors (often becoming stars in their own right)
Rona Dhona - Scenes of weeping and wailing

MOVIE STAR DEATHS
Car Accidents

James Dean (1955)
Janet Gaynor (1982)
Grace Kelly (1982)
Jayne Mansfield (1967)
Tom Mix (1940)

Plane Crashes

Leslie Howard (1943)

Carole Lombard (1942)
Audie Murphy (1971)
Ricky Nelson (1986)
Aaliyah (2001)

THE CORRECT ORDER OF THE PLANET OF THE APES SEQUELS

Beneath ... (1970)
Escape From ... (1971)
Conquest Of ... (1972)
Battle For ... (1973)

CHARACTERS WE HEAR ABOUT BUT NEVER MEET

Alex Marshall (The Big Chill), Amy (Chasing Amy), Butch Wallace's dad (Pulp Fiction), Cat Dancing (The Man Who Loved Cat Dancing), Ellie Kedward (The Blair Witch Project), Floyd Thursby (The Maltese Falcon), George Kaplan (North By Northwest), Harvey (Harvey), John Connor (The Terminator), the real Pinback (Dark Star), Rebecca De Winter (Rebecca), Rusty Regan (The Big Sleep), Seymour Scagnetti (Reservoir Dogs)

MCGUFFINS*

The crown jewels -The Adventures Of Sherlock Holmes
The valuables of several apartments in a New York brownstone - The Anderson Tapes
An audio recording of an assassination - Blow Out
The intercostal clavicle of a brontosaurus - Bringing Up Baby
Irrevocable letters of transit signed by General de Gaulle - Casablanca
The West diamonds - The Cat And The Canary
An audio recording of an assassination conspiracy - The Conversation
A computerised payment made during a brief Millennium Bug defence procedure - Entrapment
A jewelled snake worn as a brassiere by a supermodel - Femme Fatale
Black-market detonators for nuclear weapons - Frantic
Stolen rubies - Gaslight

A magical youth - The Golden Child

The US gold reserves at Fort Knox - Goldfinger

Breeding sables to be smuggled out of the USSR - Gorky Park

$4 million-worth of heavy gold bullion - The Italian Job

A suitcase full of fissionable material - Kiss Me Deadly

Gold bullion melted down into souvenir models of the Eiffel Tower - The Lavender Hill Mob

A porno movie featuring Hitler - Loose Cannons

A fabulously jewelled bird statuette - The Maltese Falcon

The mask and sword of Genghis Khan - The Mask Of Fu Manchu

A deadly virus - Mission: Impossible 2, The Satan Bug

A stolen jade necklace - Murder My Sweet

Smuggled pre-Columbian artefacts - Night Moves

Variant editions of a book written by the Devil - The Ninth Gate

A Buddha full of microfilm - North By Northwest

Bottles full of plutonium - Notorious

The takings of five Las Vegas casinos - Ocean's Eleven (1960)

The takings of three Las Vegas casinos - Ocean's Eleven (2002)

Microfilm of the 'Lotus X' formula hidden in a dinosaur skeleton - One Of Our Dinosaurs Is Missing

$70,000 ripped off from Mel Gibson - Payback

A submarine disguised as the Loch Ness Monster - The Private Life Of Sherlock Holmes

A suitcase ripped off from Kiss Me Deadly - Pulp Fiction

The contents of the Paris offices of Mappin & Webb jewellers - Rififi

A hijacked New York City subway train - The Taking Of Pelham One Two Three

Stolen money - The Thomas Crown Affair (1968)

A stolen Monet - The Thomas Crown Affair (1999)

* term derived by Alfred Hitchcock that describes the object that drives the plot forward

EIGHT WOMEN

Mamy (Danielle Darrieux), Gaby (Catherine Deneuve), Augustine (Isabelle Huppert), Louise (Emmanuelle Béart), Pierrette (Fanny Ardant), Suzon (Virginie Ledoyen), Catherine (Ludivine Sagnier), Madame Chanel (Firmine Richard)

WEIRD MOVIE JOB TITLES

ADR EDITOR - The editor responsible for recording and placing additional dialogue (ADR stands for Automatic Dialogue Replacement)

BEST BOY - The assistant to the gaffer

BOOM OPERATOR - The sound technician who operates the boom (the telescopic pole with the microphone attached)

CRAFT SERVICES - The team responsible for providing food and drink for cast and crew

DGA TRAINEE - An individual from the Directors Guild Of America's training programme who gets to observe the making of a film production

FOLEY ARTIST - A sound-effects artist who creates sounds that are recorded to match the images on screen (e.g. footsteps on gravel), and named after sound-effects pioneer Jack Foley

GAFFER - The chief electrician on a film set, responsible for supplying, placing, lighting and maintaining the lights

GREENSMEN - The personnel responsible for real and artificial trees/plants on a film set

GRIP - A stagehand responsible for manifold tasks: transporting and setting up equipment, props, setting up and pushing the camera dolly - i.e. must have a firm 'grip' on equipment

KEY GRIP - The individual in charge of the grips

LEADPERSON - The individual who assists the set decorator in obtaining, storing and placing the various set dressings; supervises the swing gang

SWING GANG - The team that sets up and dismantles a set for filming

BILLY WILDER/I.A.L. DIAMOND COLLABORATIONS

Love In The Afternoon (1957); Some Like It Hot (1959)*; The Apartment (1960)*; One, Two, Three (1961); Irma La Douce (1963)*; Kiss Me Stupid (1964); The Private Life Of Sherlock Holmes (1970); Avanti (1972)*; The Front Page (1974)*; The Fortune Cookie (1976)*; Fedora (1978); Buddy, Buddy (1981)*

* denotes starring Jack Lemmon

DIE HARD IN A ...

The original movies and their many imitators:

Die Hard in an office building (Die Hard)

Die Hard up a mountain (Cliffhanger)

Die Hard on a plane (Con Air, Passenger 57, Air Force One, Executive Decision)

Die Hard at a resort hotel (Crackerjack)

Die Hard at a bio-weapons lab (Deadly Outbreak)

Die Hard at a water-purification plant (Lethal Tender)

Die Hard in Alaska (On Deadly Ground)

Die Hard in Beverly Hills (The Taking Of Beverly Hills)

Die Hard in a military school (Toy Soldiers)

Die Hard in an airport (Die Hard 2)

Die Hard in a police station (Assault On Precinct 13)

Die Hard in a traffic jam (Gridlock)

Die Hard in a flood (Hard Rain)

Die Hard in a hockey stadium (Sudden Death)

Die Hard in an embassy (Who Dares Wins, Diplomatic Siege)

Die Hard in New York (Die Hard: With A Vengeance)

Die Hard in prison (Half Past Dead)

Die Hard in a decommissioned prison (The Rock)

Die Hard on a dam (Terminal Rush)

Die Hard on a boat (Under Siege, Speed 2: Cruise Control, Final Voyage, City Hunter)

Die Hard in outer space (Assault On Dome 4)

Die Hard on a bus (Speed)

Die Hard on an oil rig (North Sea Hijack)

Die Hard on a train (Under Siege 2: Dark Territory, Derailed)
Die Hard out West (Rawhide, The Tall T)

PLAN 9 FROM OUTER SPACE*

As described by The Ruler (John 'Bunny' Beckinridge) in Ed Wood's Z-grade classic, Plan 9 'deals with the resurrection of the dead. Long distant electrodes shot into the pineal and pituitary gland of the recent dead'. Plans 1 to 8 remain unspecified.

* Plan 9 From Outer Space was shot in just four to six days

THE SPENCER TRACY–KATHARINE HEPBURN MOVIES

Woman Of The Year (1942)
Keeper Of The Flame (1942)
Without Love (1945)
The Sea Of Grass (1947)
State Of The Union (1948)
Adam's Rib (1949)
Pat And Mike (1952)
Desk Set (1957)
Guess Who's Coming To Dinner (1967)

SELECTED CLOCKWORK ORANGE SLANG

Slang	Meaning
appy polly loggies	apologies
bitva	fight
chai	tea
chelloveck	man
devotchka	girl
doobiedoob	OK
droog	friend
eggyweggs	egg
glazzies	eyes
gloopy	stupid
grazhny	dirty

gulliver	head
guttiwuts	guts
horrorshow	splendid
in-out-in-out	sexual intercourse
lonticks	slices
malchick	boy
malenky	little
milicent	policeman
pee and em	mother and father
prestoopniks	criminal
pretty polly	money
ptitsa	bird
rasoodock	mind
sinny	movies
tashtook	handkerchief
viddy	look
vonny	smelly
yahoodies	jew
yarbles	testicle

CLUELESS SPEAK*

Term	Meaning
Audi	goodbye
Baldwin	attractive guy
Barney	unattractive guy
boinkfest	major league sex session
clueless	uncool
do	have sex
doable	mate potential
dope	smart, cool
hymenally-challenged	virgin
loadie	drug abuser
Monet	attractive only from a distance

smoked out   stoned

surfing the crimson wave   having a period

*As heard in Amy Heckerling's 1995 teen comedy

SHORT HOLLYWOOD MARRIAGES

12 months	George Brent and Ann Sheridan
11 months	Paul Simon and Carrie Fisher
9 months	Joe DiMaggio and Marilyn Monroe
8 months	Richard Burton and Liz Taylor (second time around)
7 months	Artie Shaw and Ava Gardner
5 months	Natasha Henstridge and Damian Chapa
4 months	Henry Fonda and Margaret Sullivan
11 weeks	Porfirio Rubirosa and Barbara Hutton
8 weeks	Drew Barrymore and Jeremy Thomas
38 days	Ernest Borgnine and Ethel Merman
35 days	George Brent and Constance North
21 days	Wallace Beery and Gloria Swanson
13 days	Patty Duke and Michael Tell
8 days	Dennis Hopper and Michelle Phillips
7 days	Robert Walker and Barbara Ford
5 days	Cher and Greg Allman
1 day	Jean Arthur and Julian Anker
6 hours	Rudolph Valentino and Jean Acker

THE RULES OF FIGHT CLUB

1 Do not talk about Fight Club

2 DO NOT talk about Fight Club

3 Someone yells stop, goes limp, taps out, the fight is over

4 Only two guys to a fight

5 One fight at a time

6 No shirt, no shoes

7 Fights will go on as long as they have to

8 If this is your first night at Fight Club, you have to fight

THE VOIGHT KAMPF TEST

In Ridley Scott's Blade Runner (1982), blade runners use Voight Kampf tests to determine whether someone is human or replicant (android). The test involves a series of questions and scenarios designed to prompt an emotional response while an instrument, the size of a music box, measures 'the so-called blush response', fluctuation of the pupil and involuntary dilation of the iris. Voight Kampf scenarios include:

It's your birthday. Somebody gives you a calf-skin wallet …

You've got a little boy. He shows you his butterfly collection plus the killing jar …

You're watching television. Suddenly you realise there's a wasp crawling on your arm …

You're reading a magazine. You come across a full-page nude photo of a girl. You show it to your husband. He likes it. He hangs it on the wall. The girl is lying on a bearskin rug …

You're watching a stage play. A banquet is in progress, the guests are enjoying an appetiser of raw oysters. The entree consists of boiled dog …

NATIONAL LAMPOON VACATIONS

Vacation (1983), European Vacation (1985), Christmas Vacation (1989), Vegas Vacation (1997), American Adventure (TV, 2000)

THE HOLLYWOOD CAREER TRAJECTORY

Who is Ricardo Montalban?

Get me Ricardo Montalban

Get me a Ricardo Montalban type

Get me a young Ricardo Montalban

Who is Ricardo Montalban?

MOVIE STAR INITIALS

F(ahrid) Murray Abraham

Edward G(oldberg) Robinson

W(illiam) C(laude) Fields

James B(arrie) Sikking

P(aul) J(ohn) Hogan

Samuel L(eroy) Jackson

William H(all) Macy

M(anoj) Night Shyamalan

M(ichael) Emmet Walsh

P(amela) J(ayne) Soles (née Hardon)

John C(hristopher) Reilly

D(aniel) B(ernard) Sweeney

Lee J(acoby) Cobb

F(riedrich) W(ilhelm) Murnau

R(onald) Lee Ermey

John G(ilbert) Avildsen

David O(liver) Selznick

E(verett) G(unnar) Marshall

C(hristopher) Thomas Howell

Darryl F(rancis) Zanuck

I(nteractive) A(lgebra) L(eague) Diamond

D(avid) W(ark) Griffith

T(homas) J(efferson) Hooker

Richard E(sterhuysen) Grant

Talent where the initial stands for nothing include Louis B Mayer, Michael J Pollard and Michael J Fox (the J is a tribute to Pollard).

THE DOLLARS TRILOGY

(1) A Fistful Of Dollars (1964)

(2) For A Few Dollars More (1965)

(3) The Good, The Bad And The Ugly (1966)

(1) Joe, (2) Manco and (3) Blondie are the designations of Clint Eastwood's Man With No Name

JAMES CAMERON CREW T-SHIRTS

'Jim's a hands-on director. I have the bruises to prove it.' (Titanic)

'You can't scare me. I work for James Cameron.' (True Lies)

'Waiting on lipstick? I just say tattoo their lips.' (Titanic)

'Life's an abyss … And then you dive.' (The Abyss)

'Terminator 3 - not with me.' (Terminator 2: Judgment Day)

'No animals were hurt during the making of this movie. But the actors were tossed around like Styrofoam cups.' (Titanic)

SELECTED ALAN SMITHEE FILMOGRAPHY

Alan Smithee is the pseudonym, handed out by the Directors Guild Of America, when a filmmaker wishes to remain anonymous after a film has been severely recut or altered.

The Coroner (1999) - unknown

To Light The Darkness (1999) - really Vance Kotrla?

Wadd: The Life And Times Of John C Holmes (1998) (video version) - really Cass Paley

Dilemma (1997) - unknown

Sub Down (1997) - really Gregg Champion

Le Zombi De Cap-Rouge (1997) - unknown

Burn Hollywood Burn (1997) - really Arthur Hiller

Hellraiser: Bloodline (1996) - really Kevin Yagher

Smoke 'N' Lightnin' (1995) - really Michael Kirton

Raging Angels (1995) - unknown

Senior Trip (1995) (segment 'Forrest Humps') - unknown

Bloodsucking Pharaohs In Pittsburgh (1991) - really Dean Tschetter

The Shrimp On The Barbie (1990) - really Michael Gottlieb

Solar Crisis (1990) - really Richard C Sarafian

Catchfire (1989) - really Dennis Hopper

Ganheddo (1989) - really Masato Harada (US version)

I Love N.Y. (1988) - really Gianni Bozzacchi

Putz (1988) - unknown

Appointment With Fear (1987) - really Razmi Thomas

Ghost Fever (1987) - really Lee Madden

Morgan Stewart's Coming Home (1987) - really Paul Aaron and Terry Windsor

Let's Get Harry (1986) - really Stuart Rosenberg

Stitches (1985) - really Rod Holcomb
Gypsy Angels (1980) - unknown
Barking Dog (1978) - unknown
Fade-In (1968) - really Jud Taylor
Death Of A Gunfighter (1967) - really Don Siegel and Robert Totten

THE HOLLYWOOD SIGN

The famous Hollywood sign was put up in the Hollywood hills in 1923 at a cost of $21,000. The letters were 30ft wide, 50ft high, built from 3ft x 9ft sheet metal, and each letter was studded with 20-watt light bulbs at eight-inch intervals. It fell to Albert Koethe, a man who lived in a hut behind the L, to change the bulbs when they burned out. The first suicide from the sign was starlet Peg Entwhistle, who nosedived off the top in 1932. Since then, the original sign was replaced in 1973 after a fund had been established by the likes of Alice Cooper, Gene Autry and Hugh Hefner. A group called The Environmental Pranksters used black sheets to cover up letters for satirical value: to mark the Pope's visit in 1987, they rechristened the sign HOLYWOOD; to mark the relaxation of laws regarding marijuana, they changed the sign to HOLLYWEED; and they doctored the sign to read OLLYWOOD as a tribute to Oliver North's Irangate hearings.

ROCK HUDSON & DORIS DAY* ROMCOMS

Pillow Talk (1959); Lover Come Back (1961); Send Me No Flowers (1964)

* real names Roy Harold Scherer and Doris Mary Ann Von Kappelhoff

SELECTED MOVIE TITLES THAT ARE JUST YEARS

1776 (1972); 1871 (1989); 1900 (1976); 1941 (1979); '68 (1988); 1969 (1988); 1984 (1955/1984); 2010 (1984)

DISNEY TRUE-LIFE ADVENTURES

A series of nature documentaries produced by the Mouse House. A cinema anthology, The Best Of Disney True Life Adventures, was theatrically released in 1976. The brand was resurrected on video in 2000 to little acclaim.

Features

The Living Desert (1953)*

The Vanishing Prairie (1954)

The African Lion (1955)

Secrets Of Life (1956)

White Wilderness (1958)*

Jungle Cat (1960)

* Academy Award winners for Best Documentary

Shorts

On Seal Island (1949)·

Beaver Valley (1950)·

Nature's Half Acre (1951)·

Olympic Elk (1952)

Water Birds (1952)·

Bear Country (1953)·

Prowlers Of The Everglades (1953)

· Academy Award winners for Best Short Subject

SELECTED FEATURE FILMS BASED ON SONGS

Alice's Restaurant (Arlo Guthrie)

Convoy (CW McCall)

Eskimo Nell (trad)

Frankie And Johnny (trad)

The Indian Runner (Bruce Springsteen's 'Highway Patrolman')

Ode To Billy Joe (Bobbie Gentry)

Purple People Eater (Sheb Woolley)

DAVID MAMET INSULTS

'I want this guy dead! I want his family dead! I want his house burned to the ground! I want to go there in the middle of the night and piss on his ashes!' Al Capone (Robert De Niro), The Untouchables

'I'm from the United States Of Kiss-my-ass.' Mike (Joe Mantegna), House Of Games

'Fuck you, that's my name.' Blake (Alec Baldwin), Glengarry Glen Ross

'I want you to kill the cocksucker! I want you to stuff his arms up his ass, that's what I fuckin' want!' Jimmy Hoffa (Jack Nicholson), Hoffa

BLAXSPLOITATION TAGLINES

'He's got The Man on the pan … and he's gonna fry him good!' Black Jack

'Women so hot with desire they melt the chains that enslave them!' The Big Bird Cage

'Hail Caesar, Godfather of Harlem … the Cat with the .45 Caliber Claws!' Black Caesar

'Every brother's friend. Every mother's enemy.' Black Samson

'6 feet 2 inches and all of it Dynamite!' Cleopatra Jones

'The Baddest One-Chick Hit-Squad that ever hit town!' Coffy

'Super sisters on cycles … better move your butt when these ladies strut!' Darktown Strutters

'She's brown sugar and spice but if you don't treat her nice she'll put you on ice!' Foxy Brown

'Wham! Bam! Here comes Pam!' Friday Foster (starring Pam Grier)

'The Brother Man in the Motherland … Shaft is stickin' it … all the way.' Shaft In Africa

'He's got a plan to stick it to The Man!' Super Fly

'She's a One Mama Massacre Squad!' TNT Jackson

'Men call him SAVAGE … Women call him all the time.' Savage!

'Get back Jack – give him no jive … he is the baaad'est cat in '75.' The Candy Tangerine Man

THREE COLOURS TRILOGY

Krzysztof Kieslowski's Three Colours trilogy is based on the themes of liberty, equality and fraternity, as represented by the tricolour of the French flag.

Film	Main character	Theme
Blue (1993)	Julie (Juliette Binoche)	Liberty
White (1994)	Dominique (Julie Delpy)	Equality
Red (1994)	Valentine (Irene Jacob)	Fraternity

THE BRAT PACK*

Emilio Estevez, Rob Lowe, Ally Sheedy, Demi Moore, Andrew McCarthy, Mare Winningham, Judd Nelson

*the term was coined by David Blum in *New York* magazine

HOLLYWOOD STUDIOS

Universal

Founded: 1912

Founder: Carl Laemmle

CEO: Jeff Zucker

Current owner: NBC

Biggest commercial hit: Jurassic Park ($920 million)

Warner Bros

Founded: 1923

Founders: Jack Warner, Harry Warner, Albert Warner, Sam Warner

CEO: Alan Horn

Current owner: Time-Warner AOL

Biggest commercial hit: Harry Potter And The Philosopher's Stone ($976 million)

MGM

Founded: 1924

Founders: Marcus Loew, Sam Goldwyn, Louis B Mayer

CEO: Harry Sloan

Current owner: Providence Equity Partners, Texas Pacific Group, Sony Corporation of America, Comcast Corporation, DLJ Merchant Banking Partners and Quadrangle Group

Biggest commercial hit: Die Another Day ($425 million)

Paramount

Founded: 1912

Founder: Adolph Zukor

CEO: Brad Grey

Current owner: Viacom
Biggest commercial hit: Forrest Gump ($679 million)

Columbia
Founded: 1924
Founders: Harry Cohn, Jack Cohn, Joseph Brandt
CEO: Michael Lynton
Current owner: Sony
Biggest commercial hit: Spider-Man ($821 million)

Twentieth Century Fox
Founded: 1935
Founders: Darryl F Zanuck, Joseph M Schenk
CEO: Peter Chernin
Current owner: News Corporation
Biggest commercial hit: Titanic ($1,835 million)

The Walt Disney Company
Founded: 1923
Founders: Walt Disney, Roy Disney
CEO: Robert A Iger
Current owner: Disney
Biggest commercial hit: The Lion King ($789 million)

DreamWorks SKG
Founded: 1994
Founders: Steven Spielberg, Jeffrey Katzenberg, David Geffen
CEO: Stacey Snider
Current owners: Viacom
Biggest commercial hit: Shrek 2 ($920 million)

DINING AT PANGKOT PALACE*

Roast boar (choose from a whole black boar skewered with arrows, tiny foetal boars impaled on the arrows' shafts, or a rafter of broiled baby boars suckling on overcooked teats)

Snake Surprise (steaming poached boa constrictor, with a garnish of fries and - the surprise - a selection of live squirming baby eels)

Baked black beetles

Sheep's eyeball soup

Chilled monkey brains

* see Indiana Jones And The Temple Of Doom

CELEBRITY IQS

Jodie Foster	132
Nicole Kidman	132
Steve Martin	135
Arnold Schwarzenegger	135
Geena Davis	140
Madonna	140
Jayne Mansfield	149
Sharon Stone	154
Sylvester Stallone	160
Quentin Tarantino	160
Courtney Love	160
James Woods	180

THE FEDERICO FELLINI/NINO ROTA COLLABORATIONS*

The White Sheik (1952); I, Vitelloni (1953); La Strada (1954); Il Bidone (1955); Nights Of Cabiria (1957); La Dolce Vita (1960); Boccaccio '70 (1962); 8½ (1963); Juliet Of The Spirits (1965); Tales Of Mystery And Imagination (1968, a segment in an anthology of three); Fellini Satyricon (1970); The Clowns (1971, TV); Roma (1972); Amarcord (1973); Fellini's Casanova (1976); Orchestra Rehearsal (1978)

* famous Italian director/composer partnership

OCEAN'S ELEVEN X 2

1960	2002
Frank Sinatra (Danny Ocean)	George Clooney (Danny Ocean)
Dean Martin (Sam Harmon)	Brad Pitt (Rusty Ryan)
Sammy Davis Jr (Josh Howard)	Matt Damon (Linus Caldwell)
Peter Lawford (Jimmy Foster)	Don Cheadle (Basher Tarr)
Richard Conte (Anthony Bergdorff)	Scott Caan (Turk Malloy)
Joey Bishop (Mushy O'Connors)	Casey Affleck (Virgil Malloy)
Akim Tamiroff (Spyros Acebos)	Elliott Gould (Reuben Tishkoff)
Henry Silva (Roger Corneal)	Carl Reiner (Sam Bloom)
Buddy Lester (Vince Massler)	Bernie Mac (Frank Catton)

WORKING TITLES

Scary Movie became Scream

Best Performance became All About Eve

The American became Citizen Kane

Red Line became The Fast And The Furious

Not Tonight Josephine became Some Like It Hot

People Like Us became Philadelphia

The Babysitter Murders became Halloween

Watch The Skies became Close Encounters Of The Third Kind

The Greatest Gift became It's A Wonderful Life

Would I Lie To You became Tootsie

Harry, This Is Sally became When Harry Met Sally

Anhedonia became Annie Hall

Journey Beyond The Stars became 2001: A Space Odyssey

$3000 became Pretty Woman

Star Beast became Alien

This Boy's Life became E.T. The Extra-Terrestrial

Eight Arms To Hold You became Help!

The Adventures Of Luke Starkiller became Star Wars

THE GIMMICKS OF WILLIAM CASTLE

A prolific B-movie director from the early 1940s, William Castle cornered the market in cheesy stunts designed to enliven the dullest horror flick. Here are his key ruses:

Film	Gimmick
Macabre (1958)	A $1,000 life insurance voucher from Lloyds - in case anyone in the audience died of fright.
House On Haunted Hill (1958)	A process called Emergo - a projectionist shot out a skeleton on a wire during a fright scene.
The Tingler (1958)	Select viewers received an electric shock at the scary bit through wires in the seat.
13 Ghosts (1960)	Illusion-O - a pair of filtered glasses that allowed audiences to see the invisible ghost.
Homicidal (1961)	A 'Fright Break', where Castle interrupted the action and told nervy viewers to go to Coward's Corner.

12 ANGRY MEN

Juror No. 1 (Martin Balsam), Juror No. 2 (John Fielder), Juror No. 3 (Lee J Cobb), Juror No. 4 (EG Marshall), Juror No. 5 (Jack Klugman), Juror No. 6 (Ed Binns), Juror No. 7 (Jack Warden), Juror No. 8 (Henry Fonda), Juror No. 9 (Joseph Sweeney), Juror No. 10 (Ed Begley), Juror No. 11 (George Voskovec), Juror No. 12 (Robert Webber)

SELECTED COLOUR/B&W MOVIES

Dixiana (1930), Victoria The Great (1937), The Wizard Of Oz (1939), The Blue Bird (1940), The Moon And Sixpence (1942), A Matter Of Life And Death (1946), Portrait Of Jennie (1948), I'll Never Forget You (1951), Jack And The Beanstalk (1953), The Solid Gold Cadillac (1956), The Tingler (1959), The Private Lives Of Adam And Eve (1960), A Man And A Woman (1966), If … (1968), And Now My Love (1975), Martin (1978), Stalker (1979), Zelig (1983), 19/19 (1985), Kiss Of The Spider Woman (1985), Mishima (1985), She's Gotta Have It (1986), Made In Heaven (1987), Wings Of Desire (1988),

D.O.A. (1988), The Navigator (1988), Transylvania Twist (1989), Schindler's List (1993), Pleasantville (1998)

THE BIGGEST MOVIE HITS FROM THE CAST OF FRIENDS

Cast	Movie	Gross
Jennifer Aniston (Rachel Green)	Bruce Almighty	$242m
David Schwimmer (Ross Geller)	Madagascar	$193m
Matt LeBlanc (Joey Tribbiani)	Charlie's Angels	$125m
Lisa Kudrow (Phoebe Buffay)	Dr Doolittle	$112m
Courteney Cox (Monica Geller Bing)	Scream	$103m
Matthew Perry (Chandler Bing)	Disney's The Kid	$69m

THE CARS OF CARS*

Name	Model
Lightning McQueen (Owen Wilson)	Dodge Charger (LX)
Doc Hudson (Paul Newman)	Fabulous Hudson Hornet
Mater (Larry The Cable Guy)	Chevrolet One-Ton Wrecker Tow Truck
Sally Carrera (Bonnie Hunt)	2022 Porsche 911 Carrera
Chick Hicks (Michael Keaton)	1980s Buick Regal
The King (Richard Petty)	1970 Plymouth Superbird
Ramone (Cheech Marin)	1959 Chevy Impala Lowrider
Fillmore (George Carlin)	1960 VW Bus
Sarge (Paul Dooley)	Jeep
Flo (Jenifer Lewis)	1957 Motorama show car
Luigi (Tony Shalhoub)	1959 Fiat 500
Guido (Guido Quaroni)	Isetta Forklift
Sheriff (Michael Wallis)	1949 Mercury Club Coupe
Mack (John Ratzenberger)	1985 Mack Superliner
Lizzie (Katherine Helmond)	1923 Ford Model T
Red (Joe Ranft)	1960s fire truck

* From John Lassetter's 2006 animated road movie

WHAT'S THE FILM WHERE THE HOUSE FALLS ON BUSTER KEATON?

Steamboat Bill Jr (1928)

AGES OF SEAN CONNERY COMPARED TO LOVE INTEREST

Title	His age*	Co-star's age*	Age gap (years)
Another Time, Another Place (1958)	27	37 (Lana Turner)	-10
Dr No (1962)	31	25 (Ursula Andress)	6
From Russia With Love (1963)	32	20 (Daniela Bianchi)	12
Goldfinger (1964)	33	36 (Honor Blackman)	-3
Thunderball (1965)	34	22 (Claudine Auger)	12
A Fine Madness (1966)	35	35 (Joanne Woodward)	0
You Only Live Twice (1967)	36	23 (Mie Hama)	13
Shalako (1968)	37	33 (Brigitte Bardot)	4
The Anderson Tapes (1971)	40	33 (Dyan Cannon)	7
Diamonds Are Forever (1971)	40	30 (Jill St John)	10
Zardoz (1974)	43	28 (Charlotte Rampling)	15
Murder On The Orient Express (1974)	43	36 (Vanessa Redgrave)	7
The Man Who Would Be King (1975)	44	27 (Shakira Caine)	17
Robin And Marian (1976)	45	46 (Audrey Hepburn)	-1
The First Great Train Robbery (1978)	48	24 (Lesley-Anne Down)	24
Five Days One Summer (1982)	51	26 (Betsy Brantley)	25
Never Say Never Again (1983)	52	30 (Kim Basinger)	22
Indiana Jones And The Last Crusade (1989)	58	22 (Alison Doody)	36
The Russia House (1990)	59	31 (Michelle Pfeiffer)	28
Medicine Man (1992)	61	36 (Lorraine Bracco)	25
Rising Sun (1993)	62	25 (Tia Carrere)	37
Just Cause (1995)	64	42 (Kate Capshaw)	22
First Knight (1995)	64	29 (Julia Ormond)	35

Entrapment (1999)	68	29 (Catherine Zeta-Jones)	39
The League Of Extraordinary Gentlemen (2003)	72	33 (Peta Wilson)	39

Age at the time of the shoot

STUNT DOUBLES

Keith Campbell – Tom Cruise

John Alden – Harrison Ford

Billy D Lucas – Arnold Schwarzenegger

Lance Gilbert – Mel Gibson

Terry Jackson – Bruce Willis

Randolph LeRoi – Will Smith

Troy Robinson – George Clooney/Vin Diesel

David Leitch – Brad Pitt

Tabitha Hanson – Julia Roberts

Chad Stahelski – Keanu Reeves

WHAT'S THE FILM WHERE HAROLD LLOYD HANGS OFF A CLOCK FACE?

Safety Last (1923)

BENJAMIN WILLARD

Captain Benjamin Willard – character played by Martin Sheen in Apocalypse Now

Ben (1972), Willard (1971) – a brace of films about killer rats

Benjamin and Willard – Harrison Ford's oldest sons

THE MARTINI SHOT

This is Hollywood-speak for the last shot of the day before everybody goes home and has a Martini. The shot is also referred to as the Abby Singer shot, named after an assistant director at Universal Studios during the 1950s who was constantly promising that only a single shot remained before the crew could knock off.

THE FILMS OF ANTOINE DOINEL

François Truffaut's Antoine Doinel cycle saw the director follow the same character, Antoine Doinel, played by the same actor, Jean-Pierre Léaud, over a twenty-year period. The films break down as follows:

Les Quatre Cents Coups (The Four Hundred Blows), 1959

L'Amour À Vingt Ans (Love At Twenty), 1962

Baisers Volés (Stolen Kisses), 1968

Domicile Conjugal (Bed And Board), 1970

L'Amour En Fuite (Love On The Run), 1979

STARS AND PRODUCTS THEY HAVE ADVERTISED

Star	Product
Ronald Reagan	Chesterfield cigarettes
Michael J Fox	Diet Pepsi
Samuel L Jackson	Barclays Bank
Rutger Hauer	Guinness
Laurence Olivier	Polaroid
Spike Lee	Nike
Darth Vader	Duracell

ROGUES GALLERY OF BRIT BADDIES

Joss Ackland (Lethal Weapon 2), Rowan Atkinson (Scooby-Doo), Lionel Atwill (Mystery Of The Wax Museum), Sean Bean (GoldenEye), Steven Berkoff (Beverly Hills Cop; Rambo: First Blood, Part 2; Octopussy), Doug Bradley (Hellraiser), Michael Caine (On Dangerous Ground), Robert Carlyle (The World Is Not Enough), Brian Cox (Manhunter; LIE; X-Men 2), Peter Cushing (Star Wars), Charles Dance (Last Action Hero), Christopher Ecclestone (Gone In 60 Seconds), Michael Gambon (Mobsters), Luke Goss (Blade II), Richard E Grant (Hudson Hawk), Charles Gray (Diamonds Are Forever), Nigel Hawthorne (Demolition Man), Ian Holm (Alien), Anthony Hopkins (The Silence Of The Lambs), Jason Isaacs (The Patriot), Jeremy Irons (Die Hard With A Vengeance; The Lion King), Boris Karloff (The Mummy; The Raven [Frankenstein's Monster is a tragic victim rather than a baddie]), Christopher Lee (The Lord Of The Rings trilogy; Star Wars Episode II: Attack Of The Clones; The Three Musketeers),

Art Malik (True Lies), James Mason (North By Northwest), Sir Ian McKellen (X-Men; X-Men 2), Gary Oldman (True Romance; Air Force One; The Fifth Element; Leon), Sir Laurence Olivier (Marathon Man), Donald Pleasence (You Only Live Twice), Jonathan Pryce (Tomorrow Never Dies), Claude Rains (The Adventures Of Robin Hood), Basil Rathbone (The Mark Of Zorro; The Adventures Of Robin Hood), Ian Richardson (Dark City), Alan Rickman (Die Hard; Robin Hood: Prince Of Thieves), Tim Roth (Planet Of The Apes), Richard Roxburgh (Van Helsing), George Sanders (Rebecca; All About Eve), Fiona Shaw (Super Mario Brothers), Terence Stamp (Superman 2), David Suchet (Executive Decision), Patrick Stewart (Conspiracy Theory), David Thewlis (Dragonheart), Stuart Wilson (The Mask Of Zorro), George Zucco (The Mummy's Hand)

WITHNAIL AND I DRINKING LIST

4 minutes	wine
12 minutes	lighter fluid
14 minutes	a gin and a cider with ice
24 minutes	several large sherries
29 minutes	whisky (for approximately six minutes)
50 minutes	more whisky
64 minutes	sherry over breakfast
65 minutes	beer
68 minutes	sherry
84 minutes	wine
87 minutes	scotch
94 minutes	'More whisky'
103 minutes	Chateau Margaux '53 ('The finest year of the century')

THE SCHÜFFTAN PROCESS

Invented by German cinematographer Eugene Schüfftan, the Schüfftan process was a photographic technique that allowed a full-scale studio set to be combined with artwork or miniatures into a single shot by use of a mirror. The mirror is placed at a 45-degree angle before the camera, reflecting into the lens a painting or miniature from the side of the field of view. Portions of the silver are subsequently scraped away, allowing the camera to photograph through the clear areas, thus combining the actual set behind the mirror with the reflected image. The technique was most notably employed in Fritz Lang's German silent films Die Nibelungen (1924) and Metropolis (1927).

THE USUAL SUSPECTS IN LEFT-TO-RIGHT ORDER OF POSTER APPEARANCE

Todd Hockney (Kevin Pollak)

Mcmanus (Stephen Baldwin)

Fred Fenster (Benicio Del Toro)

Dean Keaton (Gabriel Byrne)

Roger 'Verbal' Kint (Kevin Spacey)

SELECTED A-Z OF STARS WHO'VE POSED FOR PLAYBOY

Pamela Anderson (Feb '80, July '92, Aug '93, Nov '94, Jan '96, Sept '97, June '98, Feb '99), Ursula Andress (June '65, July '66, Nov '73, April '76, Jan '82), Rosanna Arquette (Sept '90), Barbara Bach (June '77, Jan '81), Brigitte Bardot (March '58, Nov '58, Dec '59, July '64, April '69, Jan '75), Kim Basinger (Feb '83, Jan '88), Claudia Cardinale (Feb '62, Sept '63), Rae Dawn Chong (May '82), Maryam d'Abo (Sept '87), Catherine Deneuve (Oct '65), Shannen Doherty (March '94), Erika Eleniak (July '89, Aug '90, Dec '93), Sherilyn Fenn (Dec '90), Jane Fonda (Oct '66, March '68), Robin Givens (Sept '94), Melanie Griffith (Dec '75, Jan '86), Mariel Hemingway (April '82, Jan '84), Nastassja Kinski (Aug '79), Sophia Loren (Nov '57, Aug '60), Madonna (Sept '85, July '92), Jayne Mansfield (Feb '55, Feb '57, Feb '58, Feb '60, June '63), Marilyn Monroe (Dec '53, Dec '60, Jan '64), Brigitte Nielsen (Sept '85, Aug '86, Dec '87), Carrie Otis (June '90), Victoria Principal (Sept '73), Charlotte Rampling (Mar '74), Vanessa Redgrave (April '69), Sharon Stone (July '90), Sharon Tate (Mar '67), Elizabeth Taylor (Mar '63), Raquel Welch (Dec '79), Tuesday Weld (Oct '60), Susannah York (June '64), Pia Zadora (Mar '82)

THE DEAN MARTIN/JERRY LEWIS MOVIES

My Friend Irma (1949), My Friend Irma Goes West (1950), At War With The Army (1950), That's My Boy (1951), Sailor Beware (1951), Jumping Jacks (1952), Road To Bali

(1952), The Caddy (1953), The Stooge (1953), Scared Stiff (1953), 3 Ring Circus (1954), Money From Home (1954), Living It Up (1954), Artists And Models (1955), You're Never Too Young (1955), Pardners (1956), Hollywood Or Bust (1956)

THE FELLOWSHIP OF THE RING

Character (actor)	Type
Gandalf (Ian McKellen)	Istari
Frodo Baggins (Elijah Wood)	Hobbit
Samwise Gamgee (Sean Astin)	Hobbit
Meriadoc 'Merry' Brandybuck (Dominic Monaghan)	Hobbit
Peregrin 'Pippin' Took (Billy Boyd)	Hobbit
Aragorn, a.k.a. Strider (Viggo Mortensen)	Human
Boromir (Sean Bean)	Human
Legolas Greenleaf (Orlando Bloom)	Elf
Gimli (John Rhys-Davies)	Dwarf

THE EIGHT ROLES ALEC GUINNESS PLAYS IN KIND HEARTS AND CORONETS

The Duke, The Banker, The Parson, The General, The Admiral, Young Ascoyne, Young Henry, Lady Agatha

FAMOUS VOICE TALENT IN TRANSFORMERS: THE MOVIE (1986)

Based on the popular 1980s toy ('robots in disguise'), Transformers: The Movie is centred around the battle between the heroic Autobots and the evil Decepticons.

Voice	Character
Robert Stack	Ultra Magnus
Judd Nelson	Rodimus Prime/Hot Rod
Leonard Nimoy	Galvatron
Scatman Crothers	Jazz
Jack Angel*	Astrotrain
Eric Idle	Wreck-Gar

Casey Kasem	Cliffjumper
Clive Revill	Kickback
Lionel Stander	Kup
Orson Welles	Unicron

* Also provides the voice of Teddy in A.I.: Artificial Intelligence (2001)

CHARLES FOSTER KANE'S DECLARATION OF PRINCIPLES

In Orson Welles' Citizen Kane (1941), young idealistic newspaper editor Charles Foster Kane dreams up a manifesto to put on the front cover of the *New York Inquirer* as a way to make his newspaper matter to the people. Needless to say, his idealism comes back to haunt him.

I

I will provide the people of this city with a daily paper that will tell all the news honestly.

II

I will also provide them with a fighting and tireless champion of their rights as citizens and as human beings, Signed … Charles Foster Kane

CHOCOLATE SAUCE

Chocolate sauce is often used as blood in black-and-white movies. The most famous examples are Psycho (1960) and Raging Bull (1980).

TEN STARS WHO HAVE STAYED AT THE BETTY FORD CLINIC*

Gary Busey, Chevy Chase, Tony Curtis, William Hurt, Don Johnson, Liza Minnelli, Robert Mitchum, Sean Penn, Richard Pryor, Elizabeth Taylor

* US drug and alcohol rehabilitation centre

HITCHCOCK CAMEOS

Film	Cameo
The Lodger	Man in newsroom
Easy Virtue	Man beside tennis court
Blackmail	Man on Underground train being tormented by obnoxious child
Murder!	Man walking by
The 39 Steps	The return of man walking by
Young And Innocent	Man taking photographs outside court
The Lady Vanishes	Man at railway station
Rebecca	Man outside telephone box
Foreign Correspondent	Man reading newspaper
Mr And Mrs Smith	It's that man walking by again
Suspicion	Man posting letter
Saboteur	Man at newsstand
Shadow Of A Doubt	Man playing bridge on a train
Lifeboat	Man in the 'Reduco' weight-loss programme ad, before and after (seen in newspaper)
Spellbound	Man walking out of lift in the Empire State Building
Notorious	Man drinking champagne
The Paradine Case	Man with cello at railway station
Rope	Man whose profile is part of neon sign
Under Capricorn	Man outside Government House
Stage Fright	Man walking by IV: this time, he stares at heroine
Strangers On A Train	Man getting on a train with a double bass (sequel to The Paradine Case?)
I Confess	Man walking across top of steps
Dial M For Murder	Man at school reunion dinner (seen only in photograph)
Rear Window	Man winding clock
To Catch A Thief	Man on bus
The Trouble With Harry	Man walking by - but on a country road
The Man Who Knew Too Much	Man in crowd watching acrobats
The Wrong Man	Man introducing film (uniquely, playing himself and talking)

Vertigo	Man carrying horn case
North By Northwest	Man who misses bus
Psycho	Man in cowboy hat standing outside office
The Birds	Man coming out of pet shop with two terriers
Marnie	Man in hotel corridor
Torn Curtain	Man holding baby in Copenhagen hotel lobby
Topaz	Man in wheelchair at airport
Frenzy	Man in crowd at political speech
Family Plot	Man registering two deaths, or giving an American official a British insulting gesture (seen only in silhouette)

GIMMICK COP PARTNERSHIPS

White and black (Running Scared, Miami Vice), insane white and boring black (Lethal Weapon and sequels), straight and gay (Partners), American and British (Brannigan – John Wayne and Richard Attenborough), American and Japanese (Black Rain), honest white and crooked black (Training Day), honest Hispanic and crooked white (Internal Affairs), honest white and slightly crooked but all right in the end Asian (The Corruptor), straight white and comedy black (Showtime), white and Latino (Freebie And The Bean), white and Asian (Showdown In Little Tokyo), black and Asian (Rush Hour), black woman and intelligent dinosaur (Theodore Rex), black and white who would like to be Asian (Rising Sun), civilian and military (The Presidio), paralysed black and woman (The Bone Collector), contemporary and futuristic (Out Of Time), slightly futuristic man and more futuristic woman (Demolition Man), living and dead (Dead Heat), capitalist and communist (Red Heat), cowboy and New Yorker (Coogan's Bluff), cop and crook (48 Hrs), cop and actor (The Hard Way), cyborg and woman (RoboCop), cop and little old lady (Stop! Or My Mom Will Shoot), scruffy and smart (Tango And Cash), male and female (The Enforcer, Cat And Dog), sexually abusive crack addict and his faith in Jesus (Bad Lieutenant), human and dog (K9, Turner And Hooch), human and 'toon (Who Framed Roger Rabbit), human and alien (Alien Nation, The Hidden), human and vampire (The Breed), human and ghost (The Border), human and robot (Holmes And Yoyo, Future Cop), human and gnome (Upworld)

A CINEMATOGRAPHY GLOSSARY

BABY LEGS - a tripod with short legs for low-angle shots

CHIAROSCURO - the arrangement of light and dark in pictorial patterns (seen in film noir)

DEEP FOCUS - a style of cinematography that keeps the foreground, middleground and background in focus (e.g. Citizen Kane)

DEPTH OF FIELD - the area of acceptable focus that extends both in front of and behind the primary plane of focus

DOLLY - a mobile platform that allows the camera to move in a short area

DUTCH ANGLES - a camera angle deviating from the normal vertical/horizontal

FILL LIGHT - a soft light that fills in the unlit areas or shadows created by the key light

F-STOP - the measurement for calculating the opening of the lens aperture in order to regulate the amount of light

HANDHELD - a cinematography style that eschews the tripod and has the camera held by the camera operator

HIGH CONTRAST - sharp contrast in an image between the light and dark areas with little intermediary areas

KEY LIGHT - the major source of illumination for a scene

KICKER - a light to the rear or side of the subject a.k.a. back light or rim light - the opposite of the key light

LOUMA CRANE - a flexible, mobile crane allowing the camera to be operated by remote control

LOW CONTRAST - little contrast between light and dark areas (e.g. in most comedies)

PAN - a shot where the camera moves horizontally across a scene or following a character (i.e. panoramic) - if done very quickly it is called a Swish Pan

STEADICAM - trade name for a device allowing the camera operator to keep the camera steady

TILT - a vertical pan

THE DTV (DIRECT TO VIDEO) DIRECTORY

To save you the hassle of watching the entire filmographies of the second-string action men (and women), here's an easy cheat guide so you can skip straight to their best or, if you're in the mood, worst. We also list their trademarks so you can tell them apart.

Actor	Best film	Worst film	Trademark
Brian Bosworth	Stone Cold	Spill	skunk hairdo
David Bradley	Total Reality	Blood Warriors	poor man's Jeff Speakman
Mark Dacascos	Brotherhood Of The Wolf	Kickboxer	amazing martial arts moves
Michael Dudikoff	Midnight Ride	American Ninja 4	poor man's Steven Seagal
Robert Ginty	Scarab	White Fire	wobbly chin
Thomas Ian Griffith	Ulterior Motive	Excessive Force	also writes his scripts, just like Stallone
Olivier Gruner	Savage Velocity	Trap	French
David Hasselhoff	Bridge Across Time	Gridlock	big in Germany
Rutger Hauer	The Hitcher	Omega Doom	will do any film for money
Hulk Hogan	Suburban Commando	Mr Nanny	very bad hairdo
Ice-T	R Xmas	Leprechaun In The Hood	slight lisp
Sho Kosugi	Ninja III: The Domination	Black Eagle	Ninja moves
Christopher Lambert	Highlander	Beowolf	would make scripts Rutger Hauer passes on
Brandon Lee	Rapid Fire	Legacy Of Rage	heir to an action dynasty

Dolph Lundgren	Showdown In Little Tokyo	Cover Up	hulking shoulders, lantern jaw
Sasha Mitchell	Kickboxer II: The Road Back	Class Of 1999 II: The Substitute	makes sequels to rip-offs
Chuck Norris	Code Of Silence	Top Dog	beard, ass-kicking moves
Philip Rhee	Best Of The Best	Best Of The Best: Without Warning	fancy footwork and clawing hands
Cynthia Rothrock	Blonde Fury	Outside The Law	bubbly blonde kickboxer
Steven Seagal	Under Siege	The Foreigner	ponytail, viciousness
Jeff Speakman	The Perfect Weapon	Hot Boyz	poor man's Michael Dudikoff
Shannon Tweed	Piranha Women In The Avocado Jungle Of Death	Shadow Warriors II	long blonde hair tossed back during simulated sex
Jean-Claude Van Damme	Sudden Death	Knock Off	can do the splits in midair
Carl Weathers	Action Jackson	Hurricane Jones	conservative clothes for a black action hero
Shannon Whirry	Animal Instincts	Hollywood Madam	natural breasts
Fred Williamson	Black Caesar	Warrior Of The Lost World	big cigar
Don 'The Dragon' Wilson	Bloodfist V: Human Target	The Prophet	genuine martial arts moves

EMPIRE MOVIE MISCELLANY

THE COPPOLA CLAN

The following family tree shows the frankly frightening talent of the Coppola clan. Please note, for the most part, only the members of the family in the entertainment industry are depicted.

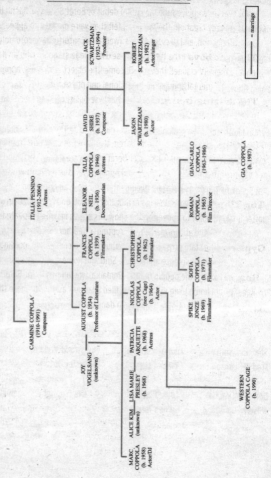

= marriage

CARMINE COPPOLA (1910–1991) Composer

ITALIA PENNINO (1912–2004) Actress

JACK SCWARTZMAN (1932–1994) Producer

AUGUST COPPOLA (b. 1934) Professor of Literature

FRANCIS COPPOLA (b. 1939) Filmmaker

ELEANOR NEIL (b. 1936) Documentarian

TALIA COPPOLA (b. 1946) Actress

DAVID SHIRE (b. 1937) Composer

ROBERT SCWARTZMAN (b. 1982) Actor/singer

JASON SCWARTZMAN (b. 1980) Actor

JOY VOGELSANG (unknown)

MARC COPPOLA (b. 1958) Actor/DJ

ALICE KIM (unknown)

LISA MARIE PRESLEY (b. 1968)

NICOLAS COPPOLA (see Cage) (b. 1964)

PATRICIA ARQUETTE (b. 1968) Actress

CHRISTOPHER COPPOLA (b. 1962) Filmmaker

GIAN-CARLO COPPOLA (1963–1986)

ROMAN COPPOLA (b. 1965) Film Director

SOFIA COPPOLA (b. 1971) Filmmaker

SPIKE JONZE (b. 1969) Filmmaker

GIA COPPOLA (b. 1987)

WESTERN COPPOLA CAGE (b. 1990)

PEOPLE WHO SUED BORAT

Not everyone enjoyed the moviefilm debut of Borat Sagdiyev, Sacha Baron Cohen's comedy creation. The following felt they were duped into appearing in the production, and decided to sue Twentieth Century Fox accordingly:

The frat boys - the three racist, sexist college students who invite Borat aboard their RV claimed they had become 'the object of ridicule, humiliation, mental anguish and emotional and physical distress'.

The driving instructor - Michael Psenicska claimed he risked his life by getting into the car with Borat, who at one point drives on the wrong side of the road.

The etiquette coach - Cindy Streit, the owner of Etiquette Training Service, claimed mistreatment and fraud after Borat attended a dinner party and subjected her and the other guests to 'ridicule and humiliation'. She maintained she agreed to be filmed as part of a documentary for Belarus television only.

The TV producer - Dharma Arthur lost her job on Mississippi network WAPT after booking Borat to appear on the show. His antics included repeatedly kissing the anchorman and disrupting a weather forecast.

Gypsies - the state prosecutor in Hamburg filed a complaint, accusing Cohen of inciting violence against the Sinti and Roma gypsy groups.

Romanians - the people of Glod, Romania, which filled in for Borat's scuzzy Kazahkstani home town in the movie, filed a lawsuit asking for more than $30 million in damages.

THE MOVIE AA

Car	Driver	Movie
Rolls-Royce	Paula Powers (Nancy Morgan)	Grand Theft Auto (1977)
Porsche 911	Mike Lowrey (Will Smith)	Bad Boys (1995)
3.8l Mk III Jaguar	Paul Clifton (Stanley Baker)	Robbery (1967)
Dodge Charger	Larry Rayder (Peter Fonda)	Dirty Mary, Crazy
	Sommers (Adam Roarke)	Larry Deke (1974)
Valiant	David Mann (Dennis Weaver)	Duel (1971)
1949 Mercury	Lt Marion Cobretti	Cobra (1986)
	(Sylvester Stallone)	

Ford Mustang Mach One	Maindrian Pace (HB Halicki)	Gone In 60 Seconds (1974)
Dodge Challenger	Kowalski (Barry Newman)	Vanishing Point (1971)
Citroën 2CV	James Bond (Roger Moore)	For Your Eyes Only (1981)
Ford Mustang	Frank Bullitt (Steve McQueen)	Bullitt (1968)
'55 Chevy	The Driver (James Taylor) The Mechanic (Dennis Wilson)	Two Lane Blacktop (1971)
Ford Capri	Lt Jim Brannigan (John Wayne)	Brannigan (1978)
Pontiac Trans Am	Stroker Ace (Burt Reynolds)	Stroker Ace (1983)
Rover SDI	Bob (George Costigan)	Rita, Sue And Bob Too (1986)
'61 Ford Thunderbird	Thelma (Geena Davis) Louise (Susan Sarandon)	Thelma And Louise (1991)
Ferrari 275GTB NART	Vicki Anderson (Faye Dunaway)	The Thomas Crown Affair (1968)
Alfa Romeo 1750 Spyder	Benjamin Braddock (Dustin Hoffman)	The Graduate (1967)
'59 Cadillac ambulance	Dr Peter Venkman (Bill Murray)	Ghostbusters (1984)
'58 Plymouth Fury	Arnie Cunningham (Keith Gordon)	Christine (1983)
'32 Ford Deuce Coupe	John Milner (Paul Le Mat)	American Graffiti (1973)

THE VICTIMS OF THEATRE OF BLOOD

Mad tragedian Edward Lionheart (Vincent Price) kills off the members of the London Critics' Circle who have humiliated him with persistent bad reviews, using apt methods based on the Shakespeare plays he staged in his last season:

George Maxwell (Michael Hordern) - stabbed by squatters (*Julius Caesar*)

Horace Sprout (Arthur Lowe) - decapitated in bed (*Cymbeline*)

Oliver Larding (Robert Coote) -drowned in butt of malmsey (*Richard III*)

Solomon Psaltery (Jack Hawkins) - tricked into murdering his wife (*Othello*)

Trevor Dickman (Harry Andrews) - has his heart carved out (*The Merchant Of Venice*); 'It must be Edward Lionheart. Only he would have the temerity to rewrite Shakespeare!'

Hector Snipe (Dennis Price) -catapulted into a killer mob and dragged by a horse through a cemetery (*Troilus And Cressida*)

Chloe Moon (Coral Browne) - electrocuted in a hairdresser's chair (it's supposed to represent the burning of Joan Of Arc in *Henry VI, Part I*)

Meredith Merridew (Robert Morley) - force-fed his beloved poodles until he chokes ('Some old queen is made to eat her children,' *Titus Andronicus*)

Peregrine Devlin (Ian Hendry) - threatened with eye-gouging (*King Lear*)

44 STARS WHO NEVER FINISHED SCHOOL

Danny Aiello

Brigitte Bardot

Drew Barrymore

Robert Blake

Ellen Burstyn

Nicolas Cage

Michael Caine

Jim Carrey

Cher

Sean Connery

Tom Cruise

Gérard Depardieu*

Johnny Depp

Bo Derek

Robert Downey Jr

Laurence Fishburne

James Garner

Cary Grant

Gene Hackman

Jerry Lewis

Sophia Loren*

Rob Lowe

Dean Martin

Lee Marvin

Steve McQueen

Robert Mitchum

Demi Moore

Roger Moore

Olivia Newton-John

Peter O'Toole

Al Pacino

Joe Pesci

Sidney Poitier*

Richard Pryor

Anthony Quinn

Keanu Reeves

Rene Russo

Charlie Sheen

Frank Sinatra

Rod Steiger

Quentin Tarantino

Uma Thurman

John Travolta

Peter Ustinov

*Dropped out of grammar school

FRUIT CART!

Invented by US critic Roger Ebert (of Siskel & Ebert fame), Fruit Cart is a rule of movies that decrees any chase scene taking place in a foreign/ethnic locale will at some point include a fruit cart overturned during a chase followed by an angry peddler running into the street, shaking his fist at the departing vehicle. Ebert has identified a James Bond variation where Bond ploughs his vehicle through a wedding reception buffet – an illustration of Bond's cavalier attitude to monogamy.

UNITED ARTISTS

A production company formed in 1919 by Charlie Chaplin, DW Griffith, Mary Pickford and Douglas Fairbanks.

THE MUPPET MOVIES

The Muppet Movie (1979)

The Great Muppet Caper (1981)

The Muppets Take Manhattan (1984)

The Muppet Christmas Carol (1992)

Muppet Treasure Island (1996)

Muppets From Space (1999)

THE RAZZIES: WORST PICTURE AWARDS

Held the night before the Academy Awards, The Golden Raspberry Awards, inaugurated in 1981, were set up by film advertising/promotion man John Wilson to honour the worst achievements in filmmaking. Affectionately known as The Razzies, the role call of dross reads like this:

Ceremony	Film	Director
1981	Can't Stop The Music	Nancy Walker
1982	Mommie Dearest	Frank Perry
1983	Inchon	Terence Young
1984	Lonely Lady	Peter Sasdy
1985	Bolero	John Derek
1986	Rambo: First Blood Part 2	George Pan Cosmatos
1987	Howard The Duck/Under A Cherry Moon	Willard Huyck/Prince
1988	Leonard Part 6	Paul Weiland
1989	Cocktail	Roger Donaldson
1990	Star Trek: The Final Frontier	William Shatner
1991	The Adventures Of Ford Fairlane/	Renny Harlin/John Derek
	Ghosts Can't Do It	
1992	Hudson Hawk	Michael Lehmann
1993	Shining Through	David Seltzer

87

1994	Indecent Proposal	Adrian Lynne
1995	Color Of Night	Richard Rush
1996	Showgirls	Paul Verhoeven*
1997	Striptease	Andrew Bergman
1998	The Postman	Kevin Costner
1999	Burn Hollywood Burn	Alan Smithee
2000	Wild, Wild West	Barry Sonnenfeld
2001	Battlefield Earth	Roger Christian
2002	Freddy Got Fingered	Tom Green*
2003	Swept Away	Guy Ritchie
2004	Gigli	Martin Brest
2005	Catwoman	Pitof
2006	Dirty Love	John Mallory Asher
2007	Basic Instinct 2	Michael Caton-Jones

* Only directors to pick up Razzies in person

THE LADY WITH THE TORCH

Draped in a toga and holding a torch, the lady in the Columbia logo made her first appearance in 1924. While actress Claudia Dell, model Amelia Batchler and extra Jane Bartholomew have all been mooted as the original inspiration for the logo, Columbia Pictures deny any claims that the lady is modelled after any one person. In the 1993 logo revamp, she was designed by illustrator Michael Deas and the body was based on Louisiana housewife Jenny Joseph – rather than using Joseph's face, a composite face was created digitally.

THE LOST BOYS VS. THE NEAR DARK GANG

Lost Boys - Jason Patric (Michael*), Kiefer Sutherland (David), Jami Gertz (Star*), Billy Wirth (Dwayne), Alex Winter (Marko), Chance Michael Corbitt (Laddie*), Brooke McCarter (Paul)

Near Dark - Lance Henriksen (Jesse), Jenny Wright (Mae*), Adrian Pasdar (Caleb*), Bill Paxton (Severen), Jenette Goldstein (Diamondback), Joshua John Miller (Homer)

* betrays the pack by reverting to human at the end

DIMINUTIVE HOLLYWOOD STARS

Height	Star
5ft 6in	Woody Allen, Peter Falk, Dustin Hoffman
5ft 5in	Michael J Fox, Peter Lorre, Rod Serling
5ft 4½in	Alan Ladd, Mel Brooks, Roman Polanski
5ft 3in	Sammy Davis Jr, Mickey Rooney
5ft 2in	Linda Blair, Sally Field, Natalie Wood
5ft 1in	Bette Midler, Carrie Fisher, Debbie Reynolds
5ft	Danny DeVito, Janet Gaynor, Pia Zadora
4ft 11in	Estelle Getty, Gloria Swanson
4ft 7in	Gary Coleman
3ft 11in	Herve Villechaize
2ft 8in	Verne Troyer

COMMONLY MADE FACTUAL ERRORS IN FILMS

1   In the airless vacuum of outer space, explosions would be silent and spaceships wouldn't bank against the wind like World War II Spitfires. See: Star Wars etc. The rare film that gets it right: 2001: A Space Odyssey.

2   In America and England, witches were hanged, not burned. See: City Of The Dead, Witchcraft, Love At Stake, I Married A Witch. The rare film that gets it right: The Crucible.

3   If you meet someone to whom you are attracted in an amusing but slightly irritating manner and then proceed to work your way into his or her life at every opportunity, wrecking their current romantic involvement and persistently pitching woo, this is not considered cute. In fact, it's called stalking and you're liable to get a restraining order stuck on you. See: Bringing Up Baby, Top Hat, Notting Hill, etc. The rare film that gets it right: Play Misty For Me.

4   If a heroine is thrown off a building and a superhero swoops by to catch her in midair, the force of inertia would still break her neck. See: Superman, Spider-Man. The rare comic that gets it right: The Amazing Spider-Man #121 ('The Night Gwen Stacy Died').

5   At the time of the Jack The Ripper murders (1888), London's famous Tower Bridge had not yet been built. And yet, in The Lodger, the Ripper dies falling off it, and many other Ripper films (Murder By Decree) include cityscapes showing the bridge.

6   Dinosaurs and cavemen existed at vastly different eras of prehistory. See: One Million Years BC, The Flintstones, When Dinosaurs Ruled The Earth, Caveman. The rare film that gets it right: Quest For Fire.

7   London fog, which periodically blighted the city until the Clean Air Acts of the 1950s, was greenish-yellow (hence the term 'peasouper'). Naturally, this makes fog white in black-and-white movies (e.g. Hangover Square), but most colour films set in Victorian London (e.g. From Hell) pass off white dry-ice smoke as fog.

8   A .45 calibre Magnum, the most powerful handgun in the world, cannot be fired one-handed without Dirty Harry breaking his wrist and probably discharging the bullet straight up in the air and thus well away from the punk he wants to kill.

9   Women in the Wild West were unlikely to win any beauty contests, and certainly didn't have access to modern cosmetics See: Calamity Jane, Belle Starr, almost every Western ever made. The rare film that gets it right: The Ballad Of Little Jo.

10   The following are twentieth-century phenomena, and yet they turn up in many, many films set in earlier eras. See how often you can spot them: inoculation scars, zip-fasteners, jet trails in the sky, tyre tracks in the desert, elaborate dental work, rock music, politically correct attitudes to racial and sexual equality, bikini-tan lines.

72–23–36

The vital statistics of cult actress Chesty Morgan, real name Lillian Wilczkowsky.

CRITICS ON FILM

Since filmmakers are interested in critics primarily because critics are interested in them, it's intriguing that whenever critics appear as characters in films, they are represented in a very limited, frankly inaccurate manner. Note that films may present filmmakers – unethical producers like Kirk Douglas and Tim Robbins in The Bad And The Beautiful and The Player, megalomaniac directors like Peter O'Toole and Peter Coyote in The Stunt Man and Strangers Kiss – as unsympathetic, but always as big, powerful bastards who get laid all the time. Their depictions of critics are no more realistic, but are at least consistent …

Character (actor)	Film
Parker Ballantine (Bob Hope)	Critic's Choice
Richter Boudreau (Eric Stoltz)	Keys To Tulsa
Mortimer Brewster (Cary Grant)	Arsenic And Old Lace
Peregrine Devlin (Ian Hendry)	Theatre Of Blood
Addison DeWitt (George Sanders)	All About Eve
Harry Farber (Bob Balaban)	Lady In The Water
Allan Felix (Woody Allen)	Play It Again, Sam
F Holmes Harmon (Alan Napier)	House Of Horrors
Paul Hatcher (Charles Dance)	The McGuffin
Trevor Dickman (Harry Andrews)	Theatre Of Blood
Oliver Larding (Robert Coote)	Theatre Of Blood
Jedediah Leland (Joseph Cotten)	Citizen Kane
Franklyn Marsh (Christopher Lee)	Dr Terror's House Of Horrors
Lawrence Mackay (David Niven)	Please Don't Eat The Daisies
George Maxwell (Michael Hordern)	Theatre Of Blood
Meredith Merridew (Robert Morley)	Theatre Of Blood
Chloe Moon (Coral Browne)	Theatre Of Blood
Solomon Psaltery (Jack Hawkins)	Theatre Of Blood
Jay Sherman (Jon Lovitz)	The Critic
Hector Snipe (Dennis Price)	Theatre Of Blood
Horace Sprout (Arthur Lowe)	Theatre Of Blood
Sheridan Whiteside (Monty Woolley)	The Man Who Came To Dinner

THE LEPRECHAUN FRANCHISE

Created by Mark Jones, the Leprechaun franchise centres on Warwick 'Wicket off Return Of The Jedi' Davis as a leprechaun who goes on the rampage after his pot of gold is stolen. From Leprechaun 3 onwards, the series switched to video.
Leprechaun (1993), Leprechaun 2 (1994), Leprechaun 3 (1995), Leprechaun 4: In Space (1996), Leprechaun In The Hood (2000), Leprechaun: Back 2 Tha Hood (2003)

NATIONAL LAMPOON'S ANIMAL HOUSE FRATS
Delta Tai Chai

John Blutarsky ('Bluto') – John Belushi

Kent Dorfman ('Flounder') – Stephen Furst

Larry Kroger ('Pinto') – Tom Hulce

Eric Stratton ('Otter') – Tim Matheson

Daniel Simpson Day ('D-Day') – Bruce McGill

Donald Schoenstein ('Boon') – Peter Riegert

Full name unknown ('Stork') – Douglas Kenney

Full name unknown ('Hardbar') – Chris Miller

Full name unknown ('Mothball') – Joshua Daniel

Robert Hoover – James Widdoes

Alpha Omega

Greg Marmalad – James Daughton

Doug Neidermeyer – Mark Metcalf

Chip Diller – Kevin Bacon

THE DISNEY NINE OLD MEN

President Franklin D Roosevelt called his Supreme Court the 'nine old men'. In homage, Walt Disney dubbed his nine key animators by the same sobriquet. Below are the original nine:

Les Clark (1907-79), Marc Davis (1913-2000), Ollie Johnston (b. 1912), Milt Kahl (1907-87), Ward Kimball (1914-2002), Eric Larson (1905-88), John Lounsberry (1911-76), Wolfgang 'Woolie' Reitherman (1909-85), Frank Thomas (1912-2004)

THE KULESHOV EXPERIMENT

The experiments of Russian film pioneer Lev Kuleshov in the late teens and early 1920s are touchstones in any Film Studies 101 course. Kuleshov's most famous experiment saw him juxtapose a neutral close-up of actor Ivan Mozhukhin with a shot of a bowl of soup; then the same close-up with a dead woman in a coffin; then again with a little girl playing with a doll. Audiences apparently raved at the actor's sensitive projection of hunger, grief and paternal pride, proving Kuleshov's theory that two individual shots projected in succession are always integrated into one whole by the viewer so that A+B = C. While certain film scholars have disputed Kuleshov's findings - the footage no longer exists - the influence of his experiment paved the way for all film grammar to come.

HOTELS

Tariff per night for a double room, as of May 2007.

Film	Hotel	Price
Lost In Translation	Park Hyatt, Tokyo	£310
Pretty Woman	Regent Beverly Wilshire, LA	£560
Ocean's Eleven	Bellagio, Las Vegas	£305
The Shining	Timberline Lodge, Oregon	£130
Notting Hill	The Ritz, London	£380

THIS IS SPINAL TAP

David St Hubbins (Michael McKean) - Lead guitar/lead singer

Nigel Tufnel (Christopher Guest) - Lead guitar

Derek Smalls (Harry Shearer) - Bass guitar

Viv Savage (David Kaff) - Keyboards

SELECTED SPINAL TAP DRUMMERS AND CAUSES OF DEATH

John 'Stumpy' Pepys (Ed Begley Jr) died in bizarre gardening accident

Eric 'Stumpy Joe' Childs (Russ Kunkel) choked to death on vomit, not his own

Peter 'James' Bond spontaneously combusted on stage

Mick Shrimpton (RJ Parnell) exploded on stage at the end of the comeback tour, in a puff of green smoke

Joe 'Mama' Besser disappeared under mysterious circumstances, presumed dead

SPINAL TAP 'FAMILY TREE'

The Creatures (David St Hubbins) + The Lovely Lads (Nigel Tufnel)

= The Originals

= The New Originals

= The Thamesmen (r&b)

= Spinal Tap* (psychedelic pop, 'evolving' into heavy metal)

* Rejected band names: the Ravebreakers, the Doppel Gang, the Silver Service

A TAXONOMY OF T-SHIRTS WORN BY STILES* IN TEEN WOLF

Colour	Slogan
Yellow	'Life sucks and then you die'
Blue	'Obnoxious: The Movie'
Black	'What are you looking at Dicknose?'
Grey	'Drunken State Florida'
Pink	No slogan
Black	Unreadable
White	'Wolf Buddy'
White	'Teen Wolf'

* Sidekick character played by Jerry Levine

COUPLES ON THE RUN

Kit Carruthers (Martin Sheen) and Holly Sargis (Sissy Spacek) – Badlands

Bonnie Parker (Faye Dunaway)* and Clyde Barrow (Warren Beatty) –
Bonnie And Clyde

Billy (Dennis Hopper)* and Wyatt a.k.a. Captain America (Peter Fonda)*# – Easy Rider

Bart Tare (John Dall)* and Annie Laurie Starr (Peggie Cummins)* –
Deadly Is The Female

Bowie (Farley Granger)* and Keechie (Cathy O'Donnell) – They Live By Night

Mickey (Woody Harrelson) and Mallory (Juliette Lewis) – Natural Born Killers

Clovis (William Atherton) and Lou Jean (Goldie Hawn) – The Sugarland Express

Thelma (Geena Davis) and Louise (Susan Sarandon)# – Thelma And Louise

Bowie (Keith Carradine)* and Keechie (Shelley Duvall) – Thieves Like Us

Thunderbolt (Clint Eastwood) and Lightfoot (Jeff Bridges)# -
Thunderbolt And Lightfoot
Clarence (Christian Slater) and Alabama (Patricia Arquette) - True Romance
Eddie (Henry Fonda)* and Joan (Sylvia Sidney)* - You Only Live Once

* Mown down by bullets at the end

Not actually lovers, though there's certainly a gay reading

POTENTIAL TABLOID HEADLINE MOVIE TITLES
Bring Me The Head Of Alfredo Garcia
Children Shouldn't Play With Dead Things
8 Dead Gay Guys
Headless Body In Topless Bar
I Am A Fugitive From A Chain Gang
I Bought A Vampire Motorcycle
I Died A Thousand Times
I Escaped From Devil's Island
I Married A Monster From Outer Space
I Shot Andy Warhol
I Was A Communist For The FBI
I Was A Male War Bride
I Was A Teenage Werewolf
Let's Scare Jessica To Death
Mondo Topless
Strip Nude For Your Killer
What Are Those Strange Drops Of Blood Doing On Jennifer's Body?
Who's Afraid Of Virginia Woolf?
Would You Kill A Child?

THE NATIVE-AMERICAN NAMES FROM DANCES WITH WOLVES

Character	Actor
Dances With Wolves	Kevin Costner
Stands With A Fist	Mary McDonnell

Kicking Bird	Graham Greene
Wind In His Hair	Rodney A Grant
Ten Bears	Floyd 'Red Crow' Westerman
Black Shawl	Tantoo Cardinal
Stone Calf	Jimmy Herman
Smiles A Lot	Nathan Lee Chasing His Horse
Otter	Michael Spears

SELECTED LIVE-ACTION FILMS BASED ON CARTOONS/PUPPET SHOWS

The Adventures Of Rocky & Bullwinkle, Dudley Do-Right, The Flintstones, George Of The Jungle, The Grinch, Inspector Gadget, Josie And The Pussycats, Scooby-Doo, Thunderbirds, Garfield, He-Man, Transformers, The Simpsons Movie

IMAGINARY FRIENDS

Anthony (Toby Kebbell) - Dead Man's Shoes
Ben Loman (Louis Zorich) - Death Of A Salesman
Bruce Lee (Kim Tai Chong) - No Retreat, No Surrender
Cain/Nix (John Lithgow) - Raising Cain
Charles Herman (Paul Bettany) - A Beautiful Mind
Elvis/Mentor (Val Kilmer) - True Romance
Humphrey Bogart (Jerry Lacy) - Play It Again, Sam
Ivan (John Sharian) - The Machinist
John Shooter (John Turturro) - Secret Window
Julie (Ludivine Sagnier) - Swimming Pool
The Killer (Philippe Nahon) - Switchblade Romance
Lucy (Britt Ekland) - Asylum
Sigmund Freud (Alec Guinness) - Lovesick
Tyler Durden (Brad Pitt) - Fight Club

TITLES THAT WERE JUST ASKING FOR IT ...

Bad, Can't Stop The Music, Don't Do It, The Greatest, No Escape, Nothing But Trouble, Nuts, Swept Away, Very Bad Things

OUTRAGEOUS B-MOVIE TAGLINES

'Their bodies were caged, but not their desires. They would do anything for a man – or to him.' – The Big Doll House

'In the year 2000 hit and run driving is no longer a felony. It's the national sport!' – Death Race 2000

'Bullets … won't kill it! Flames … can't burn it! Nothing … can stop it!' – Earth Versus The Spider

'Every man its prisoner … every woman its slave!' – It Conquered The World

'Some have to dance … Some have to kill!' – Rock All Night

'Growing … ! Growing … ! Growing … ! To a giant! To a monster! When will it stop?' – The Amazing Colossal Man

'Hypnotized! Reincarnated as a monster from hell!' – The She-Creature

'She dropped out of high school this morning … Tonight she's a Times Square hooker.' – Streetwalkin'

'They transplanted a white bigot's head on a soul brother's body!' – The Thing With Two Heads

'Raw and rough as today's billion-dollar whiskey war!' – Thunder Road

'An entire town bathed in pulsing human blood! Madmen crazed for carnage!' – Two Thousand Maniacs

'Their credo is violence … Their God is hate …' – The Wild Angels

ACTORS WHO HAVE WRITTEN SCRIPTS

Actor	Film
Joseph Cotton	Journey Into Fear
Alan Cumming and Jennifer Jason Leigh	The Anniversary Party
Matt Damon and Ben Affleck	Good Will Hunting
Julian Fellowes	Gosford Park, Vanity Fair
Carrie Fisher	Postcards From The Edge
Alec Guinness	The Horse's Mouth
Tommy Lee Jones	The Good Old Boys
William H Macy	A Slight Case Of Murder
Ian McKellen	Richard III
Robert Mitchum	Thunder Road

Paul Newman	Harry And Son
Jack Nicholson	The Trip, Head
Anthony Perkins (and Stephen Sondheim)	The Last Of Sheila
Sylvester Stallone	Rocky
Mickey Rourke	Homeboy
Robert Shaw	Figures In A Landscape
Emma Thompson	Sense And Sensibility
Billy Bob Thornton	The Gift
Owen Wilson	Rushmore

THE CHILDREN OF WHO WILL LOVE MY CHILDREN?*

Carl Fray (Patrick Brennan), Linda Fray (Soleil Moon Frye), Pauline Fray (Tracey Gold), Warren Fray (Joel Graves), Joyce Fray (Rachel Jacobs), Frank Fray (Robby Kiger), Virginia Fray (Cady McClain), Joann Fray (Hallie Todd), Ivan Fray Jr (Cory 'Bumper' Yothers)

Classic 1983 made-for-TV weepie

HOGWARTS' HOUSES*
Gryffindor

Harry Potter, Hermione Granger, Ron Weasley, George Weasley, Fred Weasley, Ginny Weasley, Percy Weasley, Neville Longbottom

Mascot: Griffin

Slytherin

Draco Malfoy, Vincent Crabbe, Gregory Goyle

Mascot: Snake

Hufflepuff

Cedric Diggory, Justin Finch-Fletchley

Mascot: Badger

Ravenclaw
Cho Chang, Roger Davies
Mascot: Raven

THE SKIPPING RHYME FROM A NIGHTMARE ON ELM STREET

One, two, Freddy's coming for you,
Three, four, better lock your door,
Five, six, grab a crucifix,
Seven, eight, better stay up late,
Nine, ten, never sleep again!

STARS WHO HAVE CAMEOED IN REMAKES OF THEIR TV/FILM HITS

Kirk Alyn (the serial Superman), Noel Neill (the TV Lois Lane) (Superman)
Joanna Barnes (The Parent Trap)
Michael Caine (Get Carter)
Virginia Christine (The Killers)
Bruce Davison (Willard)
Angie Dickinson, Henry Silva (Ocean's Eleven)
Faye Dunaway (The Thomas Crown Affair)
Buddy Ebsen (The Beverly Hillbillies)
Lou Ferrigno (Hulk)
Steve Forrest (S.W.A.T.)
John Forsythe (Charlie's Angels)
James Garner (Maverick)
Paul Michael Glaser, David Soul (Starsky & Hutch)
Juliette Gréco (Belphégor)
Florence Henderson, Ann B Davis (The Brady Bunch)
Charlton Heston (Planet Of The Apes)
Jimmy Hunt (Invaders From Mars)
June Lockhart, Angela Cartwright, Marta Kristen, Mark Goddard (Lost In Space)
Patrick MacNee (The Avengers)

Kevin McCarthy (Invasion Of The Body Snatchers)
Marc McClure (Freaky Friday)
Burgess Meredith (Twilight Zone: The Movie)
Robert Mitchum, Gregory Peck, Martin Balsam (Cape Fear)
Roger Moore (The Saint)
Harry Morgan (Dragnet)
Christopher Reeve (Smallville)
Richard Roundtree (Shaft)
Tom Savini, Ken Foree, Scott Reiniger (Dawn Of The Dead)
Jaclyn Smith (Charlie's Angels: Full Throttle)
Jean Vander Pyl (the original Wilma) (The Flintstones)
Ray Walston (My Favorite Martian)
Alan Young (The Time Machine)

SELECTED ACME PRODUCTS*

Adding Machine, Airdrop, All-Purpose Farm Implement, Animal Delivery Service, Anti-Nightmare Machine, Anvil, Artificial Rock, Aspirin, Atom Re-Arranger, Axle Grease, Baby Sitting Service, Balloon, Basket, Bat-Man's Outfit, Bed Springs, Billboard, Birdseed, Blasting Powder Co., Bomb, Boomerang, Breakfast Cereals, Buck Shot, Building And Wrecking Co. Inc., Building Disintegrators, Bumble Bees, Car, Christmas Packaging Machine, Corks, Cube Sugar, Dehydrated Boulders, Detonator, Disintegrating Pistol, Do-It-Yourself Tornado Kit, Earthquake Pills, Electric Eye, Elephant Bullets, Eye Test Chart, Female Road Runner Costume, Flour, Flypaper, Foods, Gas, Giant Kite Kit, Giant Rubber Band, Glass Cutter, Glue, Grease, Hair Grower, Handlebars, Hen, Hi-Speed Tonic, Hitchhiker's Thumb, Indestructo Steel Ball, Instant Awakener, Instant Feathers, Instant Girl, Instant Icicle Maker, Integrating Pistol, Invisible Paint, Iron Bird Seed, Iron Carrot, Iron Pellets, Jet Motor, Jet-Propelled Pogo Stick, Jet-Propelled Unicycle, Jim-Dandy Wagon, Junior Explosive Kit, Little Giant Do-It-Yourself Rocket-Sled Kit, Matches, Mouse Snare; Nitroglycerin, Oil, Out-Board Motor, Railroad Ties, Railroad Track, Rocket-Powered Roller Skates, Rocket Sled, Roller Skis, Smokescreen Bomb, Spikes, Stove Lid, Stove Lid Lifter, Strait-Jacket Ejecting Bazooka, Street Cleaners Wagon, Super Outfit, Super Speed Vitamins, Suspenders, Time Space Gun, Toaster, Toothpicks, Trick Balls, Trick Bone,

Triple-Strength Battleship Steel Armor Plate, Triple-Strength Fortified Leg Muscle Vitamins, Ultimatum Dispatcher, Water Pistol, Wild-Cat, Whipped Cream Dispenser, X-Ray.

* The ACME Corporation is a fixture of Road Runner cartoons, acting as suppliers of every kind of explosive device and other novelties to the dastardly Wile E Coyote. The word acme is derived from the Latin 'high point' or 'best'.

THE GANGS IN GREASE
T-Birds
Danny Zuko (John Travolta), Kenickie (Jeff Conaway), Doody (Barry Pearl), Sonny (Michael Tucci), Putzie (Kelly Ward)

Pink Ladies*
Betty Rizzo (Stockard Channing), Frenchy (Didi Conn), Jan (Jamie Donnelly), Marty Maraschino (Dinah Manoff)
Couples by the end: Rizzo and Kenickie, Frenchy and Sonny

* Sandy is not a Pink Lady

STARS WITH TATTOOS
The waiting rooms of Hollywood tattoo parlours must be permanently crammed with A-list actors, judging by the number who have got inked up. Here's a selection:

Mark Wahlberg - his surname and initials (right shoulder), Bob Marley's face (left shoulder), 'In God I Trust' (chest), rosary (neck)

Angelina Jolie* - tiger (lower back), dragon (left arm), Arabic phrase meaning 'strength of will' (inside right forearm), Buddhist Pali incantation (left shoulder blade), three sets of geographical co-ordinates indicating birthplaces of her children (left shoulder), numeral 13 (inside left forearm), 'Know Your Rights' (back of neck), letter H (inside left wrist), black cross and Latin phrase meaning 'what nourishes me, destroys me' (front of left hip)

Ben Affleck - barbed wire (right arm), cross (right arm), others unconfirmed

Charlize Theron - flower (right foot)

Lucy Liu - tiger (lower back)

Michael Madsen - winged design (right bicep)

Penelope Cruz – number 883 (right ankle)

Winona Ryder – S-like symbol (left arm)

Kurt Russell – letter G (leg)

Sandra Bullock – tribal tattoo (navel)

Julia Roberts – heart with Japanese kanji for strength (left shoulder), butterfly (small of back)

Jessica Alba – flower and ladybug (back of neck), Sanskrit character for lotus flower (wrist), bow (small of back)

Christina Ricci – lion (back), bouquet of sweet peas (lower back)

Halle Berry – flower (right buttock)

Robert De Niro – panther (right shoulder)

Jessica Biel – dove (stomach)

Sean Connery – 'Scotland Forever', 'Mum & Dad' (forearm)

Nicolas Cage – monitor lizard with top hat (upper back)

Colin Farrell – 'Millie' (left ring finger), 'Carpe Diem' (left forearm), black cross (left forearm), large design featuring fish (right forearm)

Johnny Depp* – 'Wino forever' (right bicep), Native American face (right bicep), inverted triangle (left bicep), heart engraved with 'Betty Sue' (left bicep), three small rectangles (right index finger), number 3 (left hand), skull and crossbones plus 'Death is certain' (lower right leg), 'Lily Rose' (over heart), 'Jack' and bird in flight (right forearm), plus others unconfirmed

Ewan McGregor – heart and dagger tattoo with names of daughters and wife (right arm)

Elijah Wood – Elvish symbol for nine (right hipbone)

Sean Astin – Elvish symbol for nine (right ankle)

Billy Boyd – Elvish symbol for nine (foot)

Viggo Mortensen – Elvish symbol for nine (shoulder), fist and barbed wire (left arm), crescent moon (left hip), letter H (right wrist), others unconfirmed

Sean Bean – Elvish symbol for nine (right arm), '100% Blade' (left arm)

Ian McKellen – Elvish symbol for nine (right arm)

Dominic Monahan – Elvish symbol for nine (right shoulder), 'Living is easy with eyes closed' (left arm), two stars (right foot)

Orlando Bloom – Elvish symbol for nine (right forearm), sun (navel)

Peter Jackson, Bernard Hill - Elvish symbol for ten

Sarah Michelle Gellar - Chinese symbol for integrity (small of back), Celtic symbol (left hip), heart with dagger above it (right ankle)

Drew Barrymore - three cherubs holding cross with mother's name (lower back), another cherub (back), butterfly (navel), flower (stomach), cross with vine around it (right ankle), moon (big toe of right foot)

* Ink-addicts Jolie and Depp add and remove tats on an almost daily basis, so their entries probably need updating already

ELVIS IMPERSONATORS

Actor	Film
Simon Babbs	Twister: A Musical Catastrophe
Bruce Campbell*	Bubba Ho-Tep
Peter Dobson	Forrest Gump
Lele Dorazio	Elvis! Elvis!
Rob Fenton	Ricky Nelson: Original Teen Idol
Károly Gesztesi	A Titkos Hely
Paul Hipp	Liberace: Behind The Music
Don Johnson#	Elvis And The Beauty Queen
David Keith	Heartbreak Hotel
Val Kilmer	True Romance
Pieter Kuijpers	Elvis Lives!
Dana MacKay	This is Elvis
Gil McKinney	Elvis Has Left The Building
Dale Midkiff#	Elvis And Me
Rick Peters#	Elvis Meets Nixon
Todd Petersen	Shake, Rattle And Roll: An American Love Story
Kurt Russell#	Elvis
Michael St Gerard	Great Balls Of Fire!
Jeff Yagher*	The Twilight Zone: The Once And Future King

* also plays an Elvis impersonator

singing dubbed by Ronnie McDowell

THE PINK PANTHER/INSPECTOR CLOUSEAU SERIES

The Pink Panther (1963)

A Shot In The Dark (1964)

Inspector Clouseau* (1968)

The Pink Panther Show+

The Return Of The Pink Panther (1975)

The Pink Panther Strikes Again (1976)

Revenge Of The Pink Panther (1978)

Trail Of The Pink Panther~ (1982)

Curse Of The Pink Panther# (1983)

Son Of The Pink Panther^ (1993)

The Pink Panther@ (2005)

* without Peter Sellers but with Alan Arkin as Clouseau

+ the TV cartoon series, with Pat Harrington Jr voicing Clouseau (and Sergeant Deux Deux)

~ without Peter Sellers except in old footage

without Peter Sellers except in old footage, but with Turk Thrust II (Roger Moore) as Clouseau

^ without Peter Sellers, but with Roberto Benigni as Clouseau's son

@ without Peter Sellers, but with Steve Martin as Clouseau

THE MAJOR GANGS IN THE WARRIORS

The Warriors:

Ajax (James Remar), Cleon (Dorsey Wright), Cochise (David Harris), Cowboy (Tom McKitterick), The Fox (Thomas G Waites), Rembrandt (Marcelino Sánchez), Snow (Brian Tyler), Swan (Michael Beck), Vermin (Terry Michos)

Vs:

The Turnbull AC's, The Orphans, The Baseball Furies, The Lizzies, The Punks, The Rogues, The Gramercy Riffs, The Boppers, The High Hats, The Electric Eliminators, The Savage Huns, The Moonrunners, The Satan's Mothers, The Saracens, The Zodiacs, The Firetasters, The Blackjacks

DIRECTORS WHO HAVE COMPOSED THEIR OWN SCORES

John Carpenter, Robert Rodriguez, Mike Figgis, Alejandro Amenábar, Charlie Chaplin, John Ottman, Frank LaLoggia, Clint Eastwood, Dario Argento

20 CINEMATOGRAPHERS TURNED DIRECTORS

Cinematographer	Shot	Directed
Jack Cardiff	The Red Shoes	Girl On A Motorcycle
Janusz Kaminski	Schindler's List	Lost Souls*
Barry Sonnenfeld	Raising Arizona	Men In Black
Haskell Wexler	One Flew Over The Cuckoo's Nest	Medium Cool
Chris Menges	Kes	The Lost Son
Ernest Dickerson	Do The Right Thing	Juice
Mikael Salomon	The Abyss	Hard Rain
Vilmos Zsigmond	The Deer Hunter	The Long Shadow*
László Kovács	Easy Rider	Napfényes Oszkár
John Seale	Cold Mountain	Till There Was You*
Gordon Willis	The Godfather	Windows*
Jan De Bont	Basic Instinct	Speed
Andrzej Bartkowiak	Speed	Romeo Must Die
Nic Roeg	Fahrenheit 451	Don't Look Now
Néstor Almendros	Days Of Heaven	Improper Conduct
William A Fraker	Bullitt	The Legend Of The Lone Ranger
Freddie Francis	The Elephant Man	Tales From The Crypt
Freddie Young	Lawrence Of Arabia	Arthur's Hallowed Ground*
Michael Chapman	Raging Bull	All The Right Moves
Gregg Toland	Citizen Kane	December 7th@*

* their only directorial venture

@ co-directed by John Ford

THE EIGHT BASIC STORY TYPES

Certain narrative theorists have argued that all stories fit into at least one of the following story types. Most movies use a combination of these plots:

Achilles: The fatal flaw that leads to the destruction of the previously flawless individual. This plotline is also the basis of most whodunnit flicks, with the fatal flaw belonging to the criminal, not the cop. Some famous filmic flaws include Samson And Delilah (haircut), Superman (kryptonite), Fatal Attraction (keeping dick in pants), Jagged Edge (falling for Glenn Close).

Candide: The indomitable hero who cannot be put down - often produces franchise flicks (Van Helsing, Indiana Jones, James Bond, Die Hard, Rocky, Billy Elliot, Erin Brockovich, Amélie).

Cinderella: The dream-come-true scenario where virtue is rewarded in the end (Pretty Woman, Pretty In Pink, Strictly Ballroom, Shrek, My Big Fat Greek Wedding).

Faust: The selling-your-soul-to-the-Devil motif where fate eventually catches up with you (Wall Street, The Red Shoes, The Devil's Advocate).

Orpheus: The gift that is taken away - this could take the form of the tragedy of the loss, or the journey that follows the loss (Love Story, Born On The Fourth Of July, Doctor Zhivago, Rain Man, Signs).

Romeo And Juliet: Self-explanatory. Boy meets girl. Boy loses girl. Boy finds girl again - or doesn't (West Side Story, Wimbledon, Titanic, practically all romcoms).

Circe: The spider and the fly, the innocent and the victim (Duel, Double Indemnity, The Terminator, The Last Seduction).

Tristan: Triangles - man loves woman but a third party intervenes (Jules Et Jim, The Graduate, Gone With The Wind).

MOVIE HITLERS

Actor	Film
Luther Adler*	The Desert Fox
Günther Bader	Schtonk!
Richard Basehart	Hitler
Steven Berkoff	War And Remembrance

Larry J Blake	The Road Back
Mel Blanc*	Herr Meets Hare
Robert Carlyle	Hitler – The Rise Of Evil
Christopher Carroll	Little Nicky
Ludwig Donath*	The Strange Death Of Adolf Hitler
Carl Ekberg*	Man Hunt
Frank Finlay	The Death Of Adolf Hitler
Bill Freed	They Saved Hitler's Brain
Bruno Ganz	The Downfall: Hitler And The End Of The Third Reich
Roy Goldman	To Be Or Not To Be
Gilbert Gottfried	Highway To Hell
Kenneth Griffith	The Two-Headed Spy
Ludwig Haas	Shining Through
Anthony Hopkins	The Bunker
Derek Jacobi	Inside The Third Reich
Ernst Jacobi	Hamsun
Colin Jeavons	Hitler's SS: Portrait In Evil
Udo Kier	100 Years Of Adolf Hitler
Ira Lewis	Loose Cannons
Ian McKellen	Countdown To War
Günter Meisner*	The Winds Of War
Sidney Miller	Which Way To The Front?
Michael Moriarty	Hitler Meets Christ
Armin Mueller-Stahl	Conversation With The Beast
Kurt Raab	Mussolini: The Decline and Fall of Il Duce
Norman Rodway	The Empty Mirror
Maurice Roëves	Journal Of Bridget Hitler
Billy Russell*	Night Train To Munich
Peter Sellers	Soft Beds, Hard Battles
Michael Sheard*	Indiana Jones And The Last Crusade
Antony Sher	Churchill: The Hollywood Year
Rolf Stiefel	Battle Of Britain

Ken Stott	Uncle Adolf
Noah Taylor	Max
Bobby Watson*	The Hitler Gang

frequently cast as Hitler

ACTRESSES WHO HAVE INCLUDED THEIR HUSBAND'S NAME IN THEIR CREDITS

Roseanne Arnold#* (born Roseanne Barr, billed as Roseanne after divorce from Tom Arnold), Meredith Baxter-Birney*, Courteney Cox Arquette, Sammi Davis-Voss*, Patty Duke Astin* Jada Pinkett-Smith, Rebecca Romijn-Stamos*, Susan Sarandon#* (born Susan Tomalin, once married to Chris Sarandon), Joanne Whalley-Kilmer*, Robin Wright Penn

* subsequently divorced

\# dropped maiden name

FILMS WITHIN A FILM

Film	Within A Film
Snow White And The Seven Dwarfs	Gremlins
The Sorrow And The Pity	Annie Hall
The Evil Dead	Donnie Darko
Dumbo	1941
The Tomb Of Ligeia	Mean Streets
The Swedish Marriage Manual	Taxi Driver
Goldfinger	Catch Me If You Can
Seven	The Butterfly Effect
Problem Child	Cape Fear
Duck Soup	Hannah And Her Sisters
The Shining	Twister
A Summer Place	Diner
The Three Faces Of Eve	Far From Heaven
This Gun For Hire	Foul Play
Sleepless In Seattle	How To Lose A Guy In Ten Days
Myrt And Marge	O Brother, Where Art Thou?

Goofy Gymnastics	Who Framed Roger Rabbit
Casablanca	Play It Again, Sam
Shakespeare In Love	Scary Movie
Salaam Bombay!	Scenes From A Mall
The Street Fighter	True Romance
Now, Voyager	Summer Of '42
The Wizard Of Oz	Sky Captain And The World Of Tomorrow

THE LINGO OF BRICK*

Blow - to leave, depart: 'Did she blow last night?'

Bulls - cops

Burg (or burgh) - town, city: 'He knew every two bit toker in the burg'

Copped - stole

Dose - to take drugs: 'He dosed off the bad junk'

Duck soup - easy pickings

Gat - gun

Gum - to mess things up: 'Bulls would only gum it'

Hop, jake, junk - drugs

Pick - a ride in a car: 'Did she get a pick?'

Reef worm - a stoner

Scape - a patsy to take the blame (origin - scapegoat)

Shamus - A private detective

Shine - to wield, as in weapon: 'He shines a blade'

Sprang - originated: 'His gat sprang from Tugger's gang'

* Rian Johnson's 2006 film noir in a high school

BIG-SCREEN NAPOLEONS

Film	Napoleon
Napoleon (1927)	Albert Dieudonne
Waterloo (1970)	Rod Steiger
Love And Death (1975)	James Tolkan
The Emperor's New Clothes (2001)	Ian Holm
War And Peace (1955)	Herbert Lom

Conquest (1937)	Charles Boyer
Devil May Care (1929)	William Humphrey
Adieu Bonaparte (1985)	Patrice Chereau
Monsieur N (2003)	Phillippe Torneton
Le Destin Fabuleux De Desiree Clary (1942)	Jean-Louis Barrault
Austerlitz (1960)	Pierre Mondy
Hearts Divided (1936)	Claude Rains
Sabotage (2000)	David Suchet
Et Budskab Til Napoleon Paa Elba (1909)	Viggo Larsen
Time Bandits (1981)	Ian Holm
Voyna I Mir (1968)	Vladislav Strzhelchik

* Holm played Napoleon again in TV mini-series Napoleon And Love

LANDMARK RELEASE DATES

The Arrival Of The Mail Train – 28 December 1895

The Jazz Singer – 6 October 1927

The Wizard Of Oz – 17 August 1939

Gone With The Wind – 14 December 1939

Citizen Kane – 1 May 1941

Casablanca – 26 November 1942

It's A Wonderful Life – 20 December 1946

Singin' In The Rain – 27 March 1952

The Seven Samurai – 26 April 1954

Plan 9 From Outer Space – 2 July 1959

À Bout De Souffle – 16 March 1960

Psycho – 16 June 1960

Easy Rider – 8 May 1969

The Godfather – 15 March 1972

Jaws – 20 June 1975

Star Wars – 25 May 1977

E.T. The Extra-Terrestrial – 11 June 1982

Reservoir Dogs – 2 September 1992

Toy Story – 22 November 1995
Titanic – 1 November 1997

WHAT'S THE SPANISH SHORT FILM WHERE THE BLOKE GETS TRAPPED IN A TELEPHONE BOX?

La Cabina (1972) – it was made for TV

JELLY

1 Wobbly dessert favoured by children's parties in the 1970s
2 Colloquial term for gelatin, a diffuser placed in front of a light to soften it or change colour

HOLLYWOOD VEGETARIANS

Casey Affleck, Rosanna Arquette, Alec Baldwin, Brigitte Bardot, Kim Basinger, Elizabeth Berkley, Orlando Bloom, Dan Castellaneta, Julie Christie, Doris Day, Danny DeVito, David Duchovny, Corey Feldman, Michael J Fox, Edward Furlong, Richard Gere, Josh Hartnett, Dustin Hoffman, Jude Law, Cloris Leachman, Téa Leoni, Madonna, Tobey Maguire, Steve Martin, Leonard Nimoy, Guy Pearce, Natalie Portman, Eric Stoltz, Liv Tyler, Reese Witherspoon

AND HOLLYWOOD VEGANS

Gillian Anderson, Pamela Anderson, Bea Arthur, Drew Barrymore, Jessica Biel, Linda Blair, James Cromwell, Daryl Hannah, Woody Harrelson, Gwyneth Paltrow, Joaquin Phoenix, River Phoenix, Summer Phoenix, Alicia Silverstone, Dominique Swain, Keenan Ivory Wayans, Betty White

THE HOLLYWOOD WALK OF FAME

Established in 1958 by the Hollywood Chamber Of Commerce, the three-and-a-half mile Hollywood Walk Of Fame now plays home to well over 2,200 stars (which cost around $15,000 each, including the public unveiling ceremony). Below are some of the street numbers to help you find your favourites:

Hollywood Boulevard

6,153	Gene Kelly
6,263	Kirk Douglas
6,284	Katharine Hepburn
6,322	Humphrey Bogart
6,329	Grace Kelly
6,355	John Belushi
6,355	Kevin Costner
6,368	Lassie
6,506	Alfred Hitchcock
6,600	Jamie Lee Curtis
6,777	Elvis Presley
6,801	Kevin Spacey
6,801	Harrison Ford
6,801	Steven Spielberg
6,814	Spencer Tracy
6,912	Tom Cruise
6,925	Mickey Mouse
7,000	Tom Hanks
7,018	David Hasselhoff
7,083	Pierce Brosnan
7,060	Paul Newman

Vine Street

1,541	John Wayne
1,637	Frank Sinatra
1,708	James Stewart
1,765	Marlon Brando

THEY WOULD HAVE GOTTEN AWAY WITH IT IF IT WEREN'T FOR ...

The fact that middle-aged men are suckers for childlike women and will sell out their comrades to keep Marilyn Monroe in their lives (The Asphalt Jungle)

The little girl who won't exchange her Eiffel Tower souvenir for a new one and a ten-shilling note (The Lavender Hill Mob)

The cheap second-hand suitcase (The Killing)

The ingrained treachery of the underworld (Rififi)

'Mrs Lopsided' (Katie Johnson) (The Ladykillers)

The little boy who collects number-plate numbers (The League Of Gentlemen)

The pesky audience who make *Springtime For Hitler* a hit (The Producers)

The answerphone message picked up by Gina Mckee, not Clive Owen (Croupier)

Ray Milland putting the wrong latch-key in Grace Kelly's purse (Dial M For Murder)

The undercover cop in the gang (White Heat, Reservoir Dogs, The Fast And The Furious)

KNOW YOUR ANIMATED ANIMAL MOVIES

If it's underwater and funny, you're watching Finding Nemo

If it's underwater and not funny, you're watching Shark Tale

If there's a blue ant, you're watching Bug's Life

If there's an ant-sized boy, you're watching The Ant Bully

If there's a neurotic ant, you're watching Antz

If there's a neurotic giraffe, you're watching Madagascar

If there's a neurotic chicken, you're watching Chicken Little

If there's a rat that looks like plasticine, you're watching Flushed Away

If there's a rat touching food and you're OK with it, you're watching Ratatouille

If it looks prehistoric and you're laughing, you're watching Ice Age

If it looks prehistoric and you're laughing a little less you're watching Ice Age 2: The Meltdown

If it looks prehistoric and you're bored, you're watching Dinosaur

If there are penguins singing and dancing, you're watching Happy Feet

If there are penguins surfing, you're watching Surf's Up

If there are pigeons, you're watching Valiant

If there's a racoon that sounds like John McClane, you're watching Over The Hedge

If every other word is 'Dude', you're watching TMNT

BABETTE'S FEAST

In Gabriel Axel's 1987 Best Foreign Language Oscar winner, acclaimed Parisian chef Babette (Stéphane Audran) whips up a sumptous meal that rejuvenates a remote religious community in 1870s Denmark. The menu breaks down like this:

Potage à la Tortue (Turtle Soup)

Blini Demidoff au Caviar (Buckwheat Cakes with Caviar)

Caille en Sarcophage avec Sauce Perigourdine (Quail in Puff Pastry Shell with Foie Gras and Truffle Sauce)

La Salade (Salad Course)

Les Fromages (Cheese and Fresh Fruit)

Baba au Rhum avec les Figues (Rum Cake with Dried Figs)

Wine

Clos de Vougeot

THE FREED UNIT

Below is a list of musicals created by The Freed Unit, headed up by producer/ songwriter Arthur Freed (1894-1973) at MGM after the success of The Wizard Of Oz. Freed was a brilliant spotter/nurturer of talent – Fred Astaire, Gene Kelly, Judy Garland and directors such as Vincente Minnelli and George Sidney all flourished under his aegis – and when people think of the Golden Age of the MGM musical, they are really thinking of The Freed Unit's astonishing output.

Babes In Arms (1939), Strike Up The Band (1940), Little Nellie Kelly (1940), Lady Be Good (1941), Babes On Broadway (1941), Panama Hattie (1942), For Me And My Gal (1942), Cabin In The Sky (1943), Best Foot Forward (1943), Du Barry Was A Lady (1943), Girl Crazy (1943), Meet The People (1944, uncredited), Meet Me In St Louis (1944), Yolanda And The Thief (1945), The Harvey Girls (1946), Ziegfeld Follies (1946), Till The Clouds Roll By (1946), Good News (1947), Summer Holiday (1948), The Pirate (1948), Easter Parade (1948), Words And Music (1948), Take Me Out To The Ball Game (1949), The Barkleys Of Broadway (1949), Any Number Can Play (1949), On The Town (1949), Annie Get Your Gun (1950), Pagan Love Song (1950), Royal Wedding (1951), Show Boat (1951), An American In Paris* (1951), The Belle Of New York (1952), Singin' In The Rain (1952), The Band Wagon (1953), Brigadoon

(1954), It's Always Fair Weather (1955), Kismet (1955), Invitation To The Dance (1956), Silk Stockings (1957), Gigi* (1958)

* Best Picture Academy Award Winners

OLDER MEN, YOUNGER WOMEN

Couple	Age difference
Jack Haley Jr and Liza Minnelli	12 years
Humphrey Bogart and Lauren Bacall	16 years
Kevin Kline and Phoebe Cates	16 years
Richard Gere and Cindy Crawford	17 years
Peter Sellers and Britt Ekland	17 years
Warren Beatty and Annette Bening	21 years
Carlo Ponti and Sophia Loren	21 years
Mike Todd and Elizabeth Taylor	23 years
Dudley Moore and Nicole Rothschild	28 years
Robert Duvall and Sharon Brophy	30 years
Dennis Hopper and Victoria Duffy	31 years
Roy Boulting and Hayley Mills	32 years
Rod Steiger and Paula Ellis	34 years
Clint Eastwood and Dina Ruiz	35 years
Charlie Chaplin and Oona O'Neill	36 years
Tony Curtis and Lisa Deutsch	37 years
Woody Allen and Soon-Yi Previn	39 years
Glenn Ford and Jeanne Baus	40 years

OLDER WOMEN, YOUNGER MEN

Sharon Stone and Dweezil Zappa	12 years*
Susan Sarandon and Tim Robbins	12 years*
Cher and Val Kilmer	13 years*
Jackie Domac and Edward Furlong	13 years*
Linda Evans and Yanni	15 years*
Demi Moore and Ashton Kutcher	16 years*
Juliet Mills and Maxwell Caulfield	18 years

Joan Collins and Peter Holm		20 years
Elizabeth Taylor and Larry Fortensky		20 years

* dated but never married

SHORT FILMS BY BIG DIRECTORS

Director	Short Film	Big Film
Steven Spielberg	Amblin	Jurassic Park
Martin Scorsese	It's Not Just You, Murray	GoodFellas
Robert Zemeckis	Field Of Honor	Forrest Gump
Spike Lee	Joe's Bed Stuy Apartment; We Cut Heads	Do The Right Thing
Kevin Reynolds	Proof	Robin Hood Prince Of Thieves
David Lynch	The Grandmother	Mulholland Dr.
Jane Campion	Passionless Moments	The Piano
Steven Soderbergh	Winston	Ocean's Eleven
Peter Jackson	The Valley	The Lord Of The Rings Trilogy
Tim Burton	Vincent	Edward Scissorhands
Ridley Scott	Boy On A Bicycle	Gladiator
Christopher Nolan	Doodlebug	Batman Begins
Edgar Wright	Dead Right	Shaun Of The Dead
Oliver Stone	Last Year In Vietnam	Platoon
Michael Mann	17 Days Down The Line	Heat
Alexander Payne	Carmen	About Schmidt
Sam Raimi	Within The Woods	Spider-Man
Gore Verbinski	The Ritual	Pirates Of The Caribbean
Robert Rodriguez	Bedhead	Sin City
Bryan Singer	Lion's Den	Superman Returns

THE RULES OF SUPER SIZE ME

For his 2004 documentary Super Size Me, Morgan Spurlock lived on nothing but McDonald's for an entire month, obeying the following three simple rules:

1 No options: he could only eat what was available over the counter (water included)
2 No super-sizing unless offered the deal by a McDonald's employee
3 No excuses: he had to eat every item on the menu at least once

MTA'S*

Maude Adams, Stephen Baldwin, Alec Baldwin, Antonio Banderas, Kim Basinger, Candice Bergen, Halle Berry, Joanna Cassidy, Courteney Cox, Geena Davis, Cameron Diaz, James Garner, Melanie Griffith, Mariel Hemingway, Natasha Henstridge, Elizabeth Hurley, Lauren Hutton, Milla Jovovich, Jessica Lange, Kelly Lynch, Andie MacDowell, Ali MacGraw, Eva Mendes, Sienna Miller, Demi Moore, Chris O'Donnell, Michelle Pfeiffer, Rene Russo, Susan Sarandon, Cybill Shepherd, Brooke Shields, Sharon Stone, Rebecca Romijn-Stamos, Uma Thurman, Charlize Theron, Liv Tyler

* model-turned-actor

FILM ... PRESENTERS

Starting in 1971, *Film* [insert year here] has remained Britain's premier TV film-review show. While everybody knows Bazza and Wossy, below is the list of presenters in full (FYI, the eminently catchy theme tune is 'I Wish I Knew How It Felt To Be Free', by Billy Taylor):

Maria Aitken, Joan Bakewell, Tina Brown, Jacky Gillott*, Russell Harty, Iain Johnstone, Miles Kington, Barry Norman, Philip Oakes, Michael Parkinson, Frederic Raphael, Jonathan Ross, Glyn Worsnip

* first presenter

MOVIE POSTER DESIGNERS

Designer	Classic poster(s)
John Alvin	E.T. The Extra-Terrestrial, Blade Runner
Richard Amsel	Raiders Of The Lost Ark
Ben Barenholtz	Eraserhead
Saul Bass	Vertigo, West Side Story, Anatomy Of A Murder
Reynold Brown	Attack Of The 50 Foot Woman
Philip Castle	A Clockwork Orange
Howard Chaykin	1976 Star Wars teaser poster

Pat Olbert	M*A*S*H
Thomas Eckersley	Whisky Galore
Steve Frankfurt	Rosemary's Baby, Alien
Bill Gold	Casablanca, Unforgiven
Richard Kastel	The Empire Strikes Back
Tom Martin	Jurassic Park
Bob Peak	Superman: The Movie, Star Trek
Roger Silver	The Truman Show
Peter Strausfeld	Seven Samurai (Posters for London's Academy cinema)
Drew Struzan	Star Wars Episode I: The Phantom Menace

FICTIONAL COMPANIES

Company	Film	Business
Ace Tomato Company	Spies Like Us	Front for the CIA
Axis Chemical Co	Batman	Chemical factory
Benthic Petroleum	The Abyss	Deep core mining
BLAND Corporation	Dr Strangelove	Think tank (weapons)
Cloverleaf Industries	Who Framed Roger Rabbit	Highway construction
CompuTech	The Stepford Wives	Technology
Con-Am	Outland	Off-world mining
Cyberdyne Systems	The Terminator franchise	Robotics
Engulf And Devour Corporation	Silent Movie	Holding company
Genco Olive Oil Company	The Godfather	Front for shady dealings
Ghostbusters	Ghostbusters	Ghostbusting
Hudsucker Industries	The Hudsucker Proxy	Toy maufacturers
InGen	Jurassic Park	Theme park construction
Initech/Initrode	Office Space	Software technology
Kane Foods	Citizen Kane	Grocery store chain
Lacuna Inc.	Eternal Sunshine Of The Spotless Mind	Memory management
LesterCorp	Being John Malkovich	Filing
Life Extension	Vanilla Sky	Cryogenics

Metacortex	The Matrix	Software development
Montague Construction	William Shakespeare's Romeo + Juliet	Construction
Monumental Pictures	Singin' In The Rain	Film studio
Nakatomi Trading Corp	Die Hard	Bankers
NorthAm Robotics	Bicentennial Man	Robot servants
Oscorp Industries	Spider-Man	Military contractor
Pacific Courier*	Speed	Courier company
Pan Universe Airlines	Airplane II: The Sequel	Moon-Earth airline
Paper Street Soap Company	Fight Club	Premium soap
Rekall, Inc.	Total Recall	Memory implant vendors
Ryan Entertainment	Mulholland Dr.	Film studio
Scolex Industries	Inspector Gadget	Front for nefarious activity
Shields Pictures	The Bad And The Beautiful	Film studio
Tyrell Corporation	Blade Runner	Replicant construction
Umbrella Corporation	Resident Evil: Apocalypse	Rejuvenating medication
The Very Big Corporation Of America	The Meaning Of Life	Amorphous conglomerate
Wally World	National Lampoon's Vacation	Amusement park
Weyland-Yutani	Alien franchise	Bio-weaponry
Wolfgang And Marx	The Producers	Money lenders
Yoyodyne Propulsion Systems	The Adventures Of Buckaroo Banzai Across The 8th Dimension	Front for aliens
Zap-Em	Men In Black	Pest control
Zorin Industries	A View To A Kill	Microchip technology

FIRST TITLES TO BE RELEASED ON BLU-RAY

Blu-Ray is the next evoolution of home viewing format. Listed below are the first titles to be released:

20 June 2006
50 First Dates
Hitch

The Fifth Element
House of Flying Daggers
The Terminator
Underworld: Evolution
xXx

27 June 2006
Crash
Lord of War
Muriel Anderson: A Guitarscape Planet*
The Punisher
Saw
Terminator 2: Judgment Day
Ultraviolet

* Classical guitarist Muriel Anderson released the first music Blu-Ray disc with this combination of live music and nature scenes

THE PRIME DIRECTIVES OF ROBOCOP
1   Serve the public trust
2   Protect the innocent
3   Uphold the law
4   Cannot harm any officer of OCP (Omni Consumer Products)*

* classified

STARS AND THEIR PHOBIAS
Woody Allen – Showers with drains in the middle
Drew Barrymore – Insomnia, claustrophobia
Kim Basinger – Agoraphobia
Charles Bronson – Claustrophobia
Chevy Chase – Snakes
Cher – Flying
Joan Crawford – Germs

Tony Curtis - Flying
Whoopi Goldberg - Flying
Betty Grable - Crowds
Daryl Hannah - Insomnia
Katharine Hepburn - Fire
Alfred Hitchcock - Policemen
Stanley Kubrick - Flying, fast driving
Burt Lancaster - Hydrophobia
Robert Mitchum - Crowds
Peter O'Toole - Insomnia
Roseanne - Her toes
Steven Spielberg - Elevators
Liv Ullman - Flying
Joanne Woodward - Flying
Billy Bob Thornton - Antiques
Johnny Depp - 'Little tiny babies with their little heads rolling', clowns

STAR WARS CALL SIGNS

In A New Hope, the call designations belong to the rebel fleet attacking the Death Star. In The Empire Strikes Back, they refer to the Battle Of Hoth.

Call Sign	Character	Actor
Red Leader*	Dave	Drewe Henley
Red Two*	Wedge Antilles	Denis Lawson
Red Three*	Biggs Darklighter	Garrick Hagon
Red Four*	John D	Jack Klaff
Red Five*	Luke Skywalker	Mark Hamill
Red Six*	Porkins	William Hootkins
Gold Leader*		Angus MacInnes
Gold Two*		Jeremy Sinden
Gold Three*		Graham Ashley
Rogue Two•	Zev Senesca	Christopher Malcolm

| Rogue Three· | Wedge Antilles | Denis Lawson |
| Rogue Four· | Derek 'Hobbie' Klivian | Richard Oldfield |

* A New Hope

· The Empire Strikes Back

HEATHERS*

Heather Duke (Shannen Doherty), Heather McNamara (Lisanne Falk), Heather Chandler (Kim Walker), Veronica Sawyer (Winona Ryder)

* High school clique in Michael Lehmann's 1989 black comedy

MILLER'S CROSSING: A GLOSSARY

The Coen brothers' 1990 gangster epic drips with its own 1920s language. Below are some of the more frequently used phrases:

Chisel - To cheat, or a cheater (chiseller)

Dangle - To leave

Drift - 'Let it drift' meaning 'Forget about it' or to ignore

Flop - Sleep, or stay

Flunky - Someone who will never be the boss

High Hat - The 'brush-off', to disrespect

Poop - To kill

Potato Eater - Offensive term for someone of Irish descent

Sheeny - Offensive term for someone of Jewish descent

Shmatteh - Yiddish for 'rag', anything worthless

Twist - A girl

'What're you chewing over?' - 'What are you thinking about?'

'What's the rumpus?' - 'What's up?'/'How are you?'

Yegg - General term for a thug or gangster

SELECTED FILMS BASED ON MAGAZINE ARTICLES

Calling Northside 777, Gentlemen's Agreement, Bigger Than Life, On The Waterfront, Dog Day Afternoon, Saturday Night Fever, Fast Times At Ridgemont High, The Best Little Whorehouse In Texas, Top Gun, Perfect, Pushing Tin, Proof Of Life, Article 99,

The Insider, The Fast And The Furious, City By The Sea, Blue Crush, Biker Boyz, Shattered Glass

WHICH CARRY ON FILM ARE YOU WATCHING?

Carry On	The one where ...
Sergeant	Sergeant Grimshawe (William Hartnell) whips his National Service foul-ups into a crack platoon
Nurse	Wilfrid Hyde-White gets a daffodil shoved up his bum
Teacher	Kenneth Williams tries to teach a rowdy class Romeo and Juliet
Constable	Kenneth Connor plays Constable Constable
Regardless	The gang run an employment agency
Cruising	The veiled gay reference is in the title but very few of the onscreen gags
Cabby	Hattie Jacques undercuts Sid James' sexist bloke cab company by starting Glamcabs, staffed only by dollybirds
Jack	The series first goes historical, with Kenneth Williams, Bernard Cribbins, Juliet Mills and Charles Hawtrey serving under Lord Nelson
Spying	The series' first genre spoof, with Charles Hawtrey as Bondian superspy Charlie Bind, Agent 000 (pronounced 'double-oh ooh!')
Cleo	Kenneth Williams' Caesar cries, 'Infamy, infamy, they've all got it in for me!'
Cowboy	Sid James plays The Rumpo Kid
Screaming!	Fenella Fielding smokes
Don't Lose Your Head	Sid James plays Sir Rodney Ffing, a.k.a. The Black Fingernail
Follow That Camel	Phil Silvers plays a Bilko type in the Foreign Legion
Doctor	Jim Dale plays Dr Kilmore
Up The Khyber	Sid James and Joan Sims have a very British tea party in the middle of a big battle
Camping	Barbara Windsor's bra flies off during the keep-fit class
Again Doctor	The future Mrs Michael Caine (Shakira Baksh) plays a native girl called Scrubba

Up The Jungle	Terry Scott's Tarzan type loses his loincloth
Loving	Sid James and Hattie Jacques run a dating service
Henry	Sid plays Henry VIII and Charles Hawtrey is Sir Roger de Lodgerley
At Your Convenience	The producers' desire to be nasty about unions eclipses even the nonstop toilet jokes
Matron	All the jokes from Carry On Nurse, Carry On Doctor and Carry On Again Doctor show up again
Abroad	The gang go on holiday to a resort called Elsbels
Girls	June Whitfield plays a humourless feminist (they were called Women's Libbers in 1973) called Augusta Prodworthy
Dick	Sid James plays the Reverend Flasher, identifiable as highwayman Dick Turpin by an 'amazing birthmark on his diddler'
Behind	Windsor Davies fails to replace Sid James
England	Kenneth Connor plays 'Captain S Melly' – guess what his nickname is?
Emmannuelle	Kenneth Williams enthusiastically does a nude scene
Columbus	Barbara Windsor doesn't appear because she read the script and decided to do end-of-the-pier theatre in Blackpool instead

EYEPATCH WEARERS

Character	Actor	Film
Valentin	Henry Brandon	Three Comrades
Caldwell*	John Carradine	Drums Along The Mohawk
Emilio Largo*	Adolfo Celi	Thunderball
Mrs Taggart*	Bette Davis	The Anniversary
Pechet	Warwick Davis	Prince Valiant
Fearless Leader*	Robert De Niro	The Adventures Of Rocky And Bullwinkle
Patch#	Monica Gayle	Switchblade Sisters
Elle Driver~	Daryl Hannah	Kill Bill
Alex Cutter#	John Heard	Cutter's Way
Young May Dove Canady	Chandler Riley Hecht	May

Captain Franky Cook#	Angelina Jolie	Sky Captain And The World Of Tomorrow
Rochefort~	Christopher Lee	The Three Musketeers
Chad Palomino	James LeGros	Living In Oblivion
Black Fox	Brigitte Lin	Amazon Commando
Frigga/Madeleine#	Christina Lindberg	They Call Her One Eye
Peter Gatien	Dylan McDermott	Party Monster
Nick Fury#	David Hasselhoff	Nick Fury: Agent Of Shield
Fearless Leader*	Christopher Neame	Boris And Natasha
Eye Patch~	Milton Reid	Number One Of The Secret Service
Snake Plissken#	Kurt Russell	Escape From New York
Number Two~	Robert Wagner/ Rob Lowe	Austin Powers
Moshe Dayan	Yossi Graber	A Woman Called Golda

* flamboyant villain

\# gritty anti-hero

~ minion villain

THE MOVIE DICTIONARY

Below is a selection of words derived from or made popular by movies, which have gone on to enter common usage. The year indicates its first appearance in dictionaries.

Big chill (1983): a period of despondency; also death. Usage influenced by The Big Chill.

Bunny boiler (2002): a woman who is vindictive after being spurned by her lover. From Fatal Attraction.

Dorothy (1972): a homosexual man. Used in phrases such as a 'friend of Dorothy'. An allusion to the lead character in The Wizard Of Oz.

Drack (1945): unattractive; an unattractive person. Australian slang - a reference to Dracula's Daughter.

Gaslight (1944): the practice of making someone question their sanity. An allusion to the George Cukor film.

RUNNING TIMES OF DIRECTOR'S CUTS

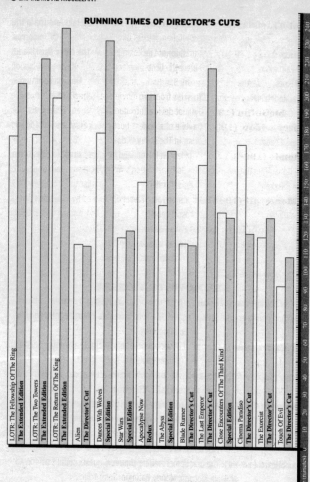

LOTR: The Fellowship Of The Ring
The Extended Edition
LOTR: The Two Towers
The Extended Edition
LOTR: The Return Of The King
The Extended Edition
Alien
The Director's Cut
Dances With Wolves
Special Edition
Star Wars
Special Edition
Apocalypse Now
Redux
The Abyss
Special Edition
Blade Runner
The Director's Cut
The Last Emperor
The Director's Cut
Close Encounters Of The Third Kind
Special Edition
Cinema Paradiso
The Director's Cut
The Exorcist
The Director's Cut
Touch Of Evil
The Director's Cut

Length (minutes) 0 10 20 30 40 50 60 70 80 90 100 110 120 130 140 150 160 170 180 190 200 210 220 230 240

126

Lollo biondo; lollo rosso (1953): types of lettuce. In reference to the hairstyle worn by Italian actress Gina Lollobrigida.

Mae West (1940): an inflatable life jacket, named by Allied troops in World War II after the busty film actress.

Majita (1963): a guy; a man. South African urban slang – an allusion to the black petty-thief character from the movie The Magic Garden.

McGuffin (1939): a plot device. Introduced by Alfred Hitchcock.

Merry widow (1952): a style of strapless bustier or corset, as worn by Lana Turner in The Merry Widow.

Mondo (1966): something bizarre. Introduced into English as an allusion to the Italian film documentary Mondo Cane (A Dog's World; English title A Dog's Life) of 1961.

Money pit (1984): a drain on resources. Popularised by the movie The Money Pit.

Munchkin (1976): a small person. From The Wizard Of Oz.

Paparazzo (1961): reference to the photographer character in La Dolce Vita.

Ramboesque (1985): typified by mindless brutality. From the hero of First Blood (1982) and its sequels.

Sabrina neckline (1959): as worn by Audrey Hepburn in Sabrina.

Shirley Temple (1966): a non-alcoholic cocktail. Named after the film actress.

Stepford wife (1981): a subservient, 'perfect' woman. From The Stepford Wives.

Up to 11 (2002): up to maximum volume. From Spinal Tap.

Valentino (1927): a lover. After the film actor Rudolph Valentino.

Zelig (1983): a chameleon; someone who adapts their personality to their surroundings.

GENDER-CONFUSED STAR NAMES

Glenn Close, Alice Cooper, Cameron Diaz, James King, Michael Learned, Marilyn Manson, Mandy Patinkin, Sean Young

PLANETS VISITED

Acheron - formerly LV-426 (Alien, Aliens)

Altair-IV (Forbidden Planet)

Arrakis (Dune)

Counter-Earth - mirror-image planet (Journey To The Far Side Of The Sun)

Dagobah (The Empire Strikes Back)

Earth (Planet Of The Apes~)

Europa - moon of Jupiter (2010)

Fiorina 161 (Alien³)

Giedi Prime (Dune)

Gor - another Counter-Earth (Outlaw Of Gor)

Helion Prime (The Chronicles Of Riddick)

Hoth (The Empire Strikes Back)

Io - moon of Jupiter (Outland)

Jupiter (Fire Maidens From Outer Space, 2001: A Space Odyssey)

Klendathu (Starship Troopers)

Krypton (Superman)

Mars (Aelita, Flash Gordon's Trip To Mars, Rocketship X-M, Flight To Mars, Conquest Of Space, It!, The Terror From Beyond Space, The Angry Red Planet, Robinson Crusoe On Mars, Thunderbirds Are GO, Mission To Mars, Red Planet, Contamination, Species 2)

Mercury (surprisingly unvisited in movies - though a Mercurian shows up in the 1951 version of The Mysterious Island)

Metaluna (This Island Earth)

Miranda (Serenity)

Mongo (Flash Gordon)

The Moon - moon of Earth (A Voyage To The Moon, Frau Im Mond, Destination: Moon, Cat Women Of The Moon, Project Moonbase, The First Men In The Moon, Countdown, 2001: A Space Odyssey)

Mustafar - Revenge Of The Sith

Neptune (Invasion Of The Neptune Men)

Planet X (Duck Dodgers In The 24½th Century, The Strange World Of Planet X, The Man From Planet X)

Plutonium (The Road To Hong Kong)

Pyrine IV (Enemy Mine)
Rehton (The Phantom Planet)
Saturn (Buck Rogers, The Incredible Melting Man, Saturn 3)
Skaro (Dr Who And The Daleks)
Solaris (Solaris)
Tatooine (Star Wars)
Uranus (Journey To The Seventh Planet, Sex Trek: The Next Generation)
Venus (20 Million Miles To Earth, Abbott And Costello Go To Mars, Queen Of
Outer Space)
Vulcan (Star Trek)

YABBA DABBA...

To coincide with the release of the live-action version of The Flintstones (1994),
newspaper critics went into overdrive on 'yabba dabba doo' puns. To wit:

'Yabba Dabba Dud' - *New York Daily News*
'Yabba Dabba Don't' - *USA Today*
'Yabba Dabba Boo'- *Washington Post*
'Yabba Dabba Dumb' - *Boston Globe*
'Yabba Dabba Doo-doo' - *Philadelphia Enquirer*

ROCKY BALBOA FIGHT CARD

Fighter	Film	Result
Spider Rico	Rocky	Rocky wins (knockout in second round)
Apollo Creed*	Rocky	Rocky loses (split decision in 15th round)
Apollo Creed*	Rocky II	Rocky wins (knockout in 15th round)
Joe Czak@	Rocky III	Rocky wins
Big Yank Ball@	Rocky III	Rocky wins
Vito Soto@	Rocky III=	Rocky wins
Thunderlips (wrestling champion)	Rocky III	The charity match spills out of the ring and ends in a draw
Clubber Lang@	Rocky III	Lang wins (knockout in second round)
Clubber Lang*	Rocky III	Rocky wins (knockout in third round)
Ivan Drago@	Rocky IV	Rocky wins (knockout in 15th round)

Tommy 'Machine' Gunn	Rocky V	Rocky pummels Gunn to the ground, then the police arrive and arrest Gunn
Mason 'The Line' Dixon	Rocky Balboa	Rocky loses (split decision in 15th round)

* World Heavyweight Championship challenge

@ World Heavyweight Championship defence

= includes seven title defences against unnamed fighters

THE GOOD ...

Companions (1933 & 1956)

Die First (1967)

Die Young (1954)

Earth (1937)

Fairy (1935)

Father (1986)

German (2006)

Girl (2001)

Guys And The Bad Guys (1969)

Old Naughty Days (2002)

Son (1993)

Shepherd (2006)

The Bad And The Ugly (1966)

Thief (2002)

Wife (1986)

Woman Of Bangkok (1991)

FILMS ON TELEVISION IN FILMS

Film On TV	In
The Beast From 20,000 Fathoms, Dracula	Innocent Blood (1931) and Dracula (1958)
Bride Of Frankenstein	Bride Of Chucky, Gods And Monsters
The Brides Of Dracula	The Matrix Reloaded
The Criminal Code (1931)	Targets
The Dead Zone	Cat's Eye
Duck Dodgers In The 24½th Century	Close Encounters Of The Third Kind

Frankenstein (1931)	Shocker, Scream
Frankenstein Meets The Wolf Man	AvP
Freejack	True Romance
A Guy Named Joe	Poltergeist
Halloween	Halloween III: Season Of The Witch, Scream
Hellraiser	Basic Instinct
It's A Wonderful Life, Night Of The Living Dead	976-EVIL 2: The Astral Factor
It's A Wonderful Life, Invasion Of The Body Snatchers, To Please A Lady	Gremlins
Night Of The Lepus	The Matrix
Night Of The Living Dead	Halloween II
Octaman, Rambo III	Gremlins 2: The New Batch
Plague Of The Zombies	Fright
Rio Bravo	Get Shorty
The Quiet Man	E.T. The Extra-Terrestrial
Shogun Assassin	Kill Bill Vol. 2
Stagecoach	The Apartment
Summer Of '42	The Shining
The Thing From Another World, Forbidden Planet	Halloween
The Third Man, Billy Budd	The Man Who Fell To Earth
The Vampire Lovers	The Return Of Count Yorga
White Zombie	Ed Wood
The Wolf Man	The Howling

THX-1138 REFERENCES*

George Lucas has consistently paid homage to his directorial debut, THX-1138.
Return Of The Jedi is a notable omission.

American Graffiti - On the number-plate of John Milner's (Paul Le Mat) Deuce Coupe

Star Wars - Han and Luke transfer Chewie from Cell Block 1138

The Empire Strikes Back - On Hoth, General Rieekan says, 'Send Rogues 10 and 11 to station 38.'

The Phantom Menace - 1138 appears on the back of a battle droid destroyed by Jar Jar Binks

Attack Of The Clones – The tiny LED on the back of CloneTrooper helmets reads 1138
Revenge Of The Sith – Clone commander Bacara is identified in the script as
Commander 1138

* references are also included in Sesame Street: Follow That Bird (Big Bird arrives on flight 1138), Swingers (Trent's licence plate), Ocean's Eleven (Matt Damon punches '1138' into an elevator keypad) and Sky Captain And The World Of Tomorrow (on Dr Jennings' door)

SPECTACULARLY WRONG REVIEWS

'I thought the photography quite good but nothing to write to Moscow about, the acting middling and the whole thing a little dull.' – James Agate on Citizen Kane

'So mincing as to border on baby talk.' – Bosley Crowther on It's A Wonderful Life

'The old master has turned out another Hitchcock and bull story, in which the mystery is not so much who done it as who cares.' – *Time* magazine on Vertigo

'I sat cringing before Oz, which displays no trace of imagination, good taste or ingenuity.' – The *New Yorker* on The Wizard Of Oz

'The jokes are tired and can often be seen dragging their feet towards us a mile off; when they finally arrive, we are more apt to commiserate than laugh.' – John Simon on Annie Hall

'The only really satisfactory way to dispose of Peeping Tom would be to shovel it up and flush it swiftly down the nearest sewer. Even then, the stench would remain.' – Derek Hill on Peeping Tom

'For all of its good choices, there's something deeply wanting about Jackson's vision.' – Jason Clark on LOTR: The Fellowship Of The Ring

'Here is the ideal date movie, assuming you're dating a psychopath sadist with a high tolerance for dilly-dallying … The younger actors all seem fresh off the campus of the James Woods-Willem Dafoe Institute For Acting Surly, Nervous And Dishevelled.' – Ralph Novak on Reservoir Dogs

'Disappointing. There is a feeling that it could have been so much more. Overlong and repetitive, there are subtleties in the basically simple story that are not adequately explained.' – *Variety* on The Searchers

'No comedy dependent on men impersonating women can make friends and influence laughter for very long, certainly not for two hours.' – The *Daily Mail* on Some Like It Hot

HERBIE

Based on Gordon Buford's story 'Car-Boy-Girl', The Love Bug made an international star of Herbie, a VW Beetle with a mind of its own. Three features followed, plus two TV outings. A Lindsay Lohan update appeared in 2005. The full list:

The Love Bug (1968), Herbie Goes To Monte Carlo (1977), Herbie Goes Bananas (1980), Herbie, The Love Bug (1982, TV series), The Love Bug (1997, TV), Herbie: Fully Loaded (2005)

INNOVATIVE TRIPLE BILLS

Candy, Mandy and Gandhi

Basic, Instinct and Basic Instinct

When Harry Met Sally, Bob & Carol & Ted & Alice, and Hannah And Her Sisters

Sleeper, Slacker and Slither

Blow, Blow-Up and Blow Out

MOVIE Q&A

What Ever Happened To Baby Jane?

… She got old and went mad after her sister tried to kill her

Who Slew Auntie Roo?

… Christopher (Mark Lester) and Katy (Chloe Franks)

Dude, Where's My Car?

… Like, parked somewhere

Who's Harry Crumb?

… John Candy

Who Framed Roger Rabbit?

… Judge Doom (Christopher Lloyd)

What Makes Daffy Duck?

… Elmer Fudd during duck season

Guess Who's Coming To Dinner?
... Dr John Wade Prentice (Sidney Poitier)

Car 54, Where Are You?
... Bypassing even video and turning up late at night on television

Who Is Harry Kellerman And Why Is He Saying Those Terrible Things About Me?
... You are, and you've got a self-hating split personality

Who's That Girl?
... Nikki Finn (Madonna)

Who's Afraid Of Virginia Woolf?
... George (Richard Burton)

What's The Worst That Could Happen?
... Another Martin Lawrence movie

Will Success Spoil Rock Hunter?
... For a little while but not by the end

What's Eating Gilbert Grape?
... His big fat mum

Are You Being Served?
... No, because they've all buggered off to Spain in a terrible spin-off

Shall We Dance?
... Are you asking?

FAMOUS MONSTERS OF FILMLAND MAGAZINE

This seminal periodical, created (and edited) by Forrest J Ackerman in 1958, was launched at the time of a mini-monster craze during which 1930s horror films appeared on TV just as drive-ins were filling with Hammer and Corman pictures. It became a touchstone for a whole generation of youngsters like Steven Spielberg, Stephen King, Joe Dante (published in *Famous Monsters Of Filmland* at fourteen!) and John Landis, who devoured Forry's dreadful puns ('You axed for it!'), 'filmbooks' (illustrated synopses of movies), lengthy coming-soon announcements (many for films we're still waiting to see) and sheaves of small ads for novelties (rubber spiders!) from the Captain Company.

MOVIE COUPLES WHO GOT MARRIED AFTER MEETING AT WORK

Couple	Film
Lew Ayres and Ginger Rogers	Don't Bet On Love (1933)
Alec Baldwin and Kim Basinger	The Marrying Man (1991)
Ellen Barkin and Gabriel Byrne	Siesta (1987)
Warren Beatty and Annette Bening	Bugsy (1991)
Luc Besson and Milla Jovovich	The Fifth Element (1997)
Humphrey Bogart and Lauren Bacall	To Have And Have Not (1944)
Ernest Borgnine and Katy Jurado	The Badlanders (1958)
Richard Burton and Elizabeth Taylor	Cleopatra (1963)
James Cameron and Linda Hamilton	Terminator 2: Judgment Day (1991)
Tom Cruise and Nicole Kidman	Days Of Thunder (1990)
Tony Curtis and Christine Kaufmann	Taras Bulba (1962)
Brian De Palma and Nancy Allen	Carrie (1976)
Howard Deutch and Lea Thompson	Some Kind Of Wonderful (1987)
Howard Duff and Ida Lupino	Woman In Hiding (1950)
Blake Edwards and Julie Andrews	Darling Lili (1970)
Errol Flynn and Patrice Wymore	Rocky Mountain (1950)
Jeff Goldblum and Geena Davis	The Fly (1986)
Stewart Granger and Jean Simmons	Adam And Evelyne (1949)
Cary Grant and Betsy Drake	Every Girl Should Be Married (1948)

Tom Hanks and Rita Wilson	Volunteers (1985)
Danny Huston and Virginia Madsen	Mr North (1988)
Harry James and Betty Grable	Springtime In The Rockies (1942)
Stanley Kubrick and Christiane Harlan	Paths Of Glory (1957)
Tony Martin and Cyd Charisse	Till The Clouds Roll By (1946)
Malcolm McDowell and Mary Steenburgen	Time After Time (1979)
Pat O'Connor and Mary Elizabeth Mastrantonio	The January Man (1989)
Laurence Olivier and Vivien Leigh	Fire Over England (1937)
George Peppard and Elizabeth Ashley	The Carpetbaggers (1964)
Dennis Quaid and Meg Ryan	Innerspace (1987)
Ronald Reagan and Jane Wyman	Brother Rat (1938)
Nicolas Roeg and Theresa Russell	Bad Timing (1980)
Roy Rogers and Dale Evans	Cowboy And The Senorita (1944)
Roberto Rossellini and Ingrid Bergman	Stromboli (1950)
Ron Shelton And Lolita Davidovich	Blaze (1989)
Kate Winslet and James Threapleton	Hideous Kinky (1998)

SPORTSFOLK TURNED ACTORS

Joe Bugner* (boxing)
Sonny Chiba (gymnastics)
Larry 'Buster' Crabbe (swimming)#
Roosevelt 'Rosey' Grier (American football)
Sonja Henie (skating)#
Karim Abdul-Jabbar (basketball)
Thomas Kretschmann (swimming)
Strother Martin (diving)#
Shaquille O'Neal (basketball)#
Nat Pendleton (wrestling)*
David Prowse (weight-lifting)
The Rock (wrestling)
Arnold Schwarzenegger (body-building)
OJ Simpson (American football)
Renée Soutendijk (gymnastics)

Bud Spencer (swimming)#
Jason Statham (diving)#
Woody Strode (decathlon/American football)
Dennis Weaver (track and field)
Johnny Weissmuller (swimming)#
Cornel Wilde (fencing)#
Fred Williamson (American football)
Rick Yune (tae kwon do)

* what do you mean, you've not seen any of his films? – he was in I'm For The Hippopotamus and The Sheriff And The Satellite Kid!

competed in the Olympics

CLASSICAL MUSIC MADE FAMOUS BY THE MOVIES

Piece	Composer	Film
Also Sprach Zarathustra	Strauss	2001: A Space Odyssey
Bolero	Ravel	10
Canon In D	Pachelbel	Ordinary People
Die Valkyrie	Wagner	Apocalypse Now
Piano Concerto No. 2	Rachmaninov	Brief Encounter
Presto Symphony No. 3	Saint-Saëns	Babe
Adagietto (from *Symphony No. 5*)	Mahler	Death In Venice
Musica Poetica	Orff/Keetman	Badlands
Rhapsody In Blue	Gershwin	Manhattan
Adagio For Strings	Barber	Platoon
Intermezzo (from *Cavalleria Rusticana*)	Mascagni	Raging Bull
'Chi Il Bel Sogno Di Doretta' (from *La Rondine*)	Puccini	Room With A View
Duettino – Sull'aria (from *The Marriage Of Figaro*)	Mozart	The Shawshank Redemption
Mad Scene (from *Lucia Di Lammermoor*)	Donizetti	The Fifth Element
Allegro (from *Water Music*)	Handel	Dead Poets Society

Night On Bald Mountain	Mussorgsky	Fantasia
Hungarian Rhapsody No. 2	Liszt	Who Framed Roger Rabbit
'La Mamma Morta' (from	Giordano	Philadelphia
Andrea Chénier)		

ACTORS WHO STARTED THEIR CAREERS AS EXTRAS

Michael Caine, Gary Cooper, Marlene Dietrich, Clint Eastwood, Clark Gable, Stewart Granger, Melanie Griffith, Jean Harlow, Harold Lloyd, Sophia Loren, Peter Lorre, Fred MacMurray, Robert Mitchum, Marilyn Monroe, Roger Moore, David Niven, Ramon Novarro, Lana Turner, Rudolph Valentino, Loretta Young

LEMON POPSICLE

Produced by Cannon Films moguls Menahem Golan and Yoram Globus, this Israeli series of teen sex comedies proved so popular in Europe that an American remake, The Last American Virgin, was produced in 1981. The full list:

Lemon Popsicle (1978)

Lemon Popsicle II (a.k.a. Greasy Kid Stuff) (1979)

Lemon Popsicle III: Let's Go To Paris (a.k.a. Hot Bubblegum) (1981)

Lemon Popsicle IV (a.k.a. Private Popsicle) (1982)

Lemon Popsicle V (a.k.a. Baby Love) (1983)

Lemon Popsicle VI (a.k.a. Up Your Anchor) (1985)

Lemon Popsicle VII (a.k.a. Young Love) (1987)

Summertime Blues: Lemon Popsicle VIII (1988)

Lemon Popsicle 9: The Party Goes On (2001)

ERIC ROHMER FRANCHISES

French film critic-turned-filmmaker Eric Rohmer often liked to fashion his low-key stories of love and loss into collections. Below are the films that make up his three best-known cycles – Moral Tales, Comedies and Proverbs, and Tales Of Four Seasons.

Moral Tales

La Boulangerie De Monceau (1962)

La Carrière De Suzanne (Suzanne's Profession) (1963)

La Collectionneuse (1967)

Ma Nuit Chez Maud (My Night At Maud's) (1969)

Claire's Knee (Le Genou De Claire) (1970)

L'Amour, L'Après-Midi (Love In The Afternoon) (1972)

Comedies and Proverbs

La Femme De L'Aviateur (The Aviator's Wife) (1981)

La Beau Mariage (The Perfect Marriage) (1982)

Pauline Sur La Plage (Pauline On The Beach) (1982)

Les Nuits De La Pleine Lune (Full Moon In Paris) (1984)

Le Rayon Vert (The Green Ray) (1986)

L'Ami De Mon Amie (My Girlfriend's Boyfriend) (1987)

Tales of Four Seasons

Conte De Printemps (A Tale Of Springtime) (1990)

Conte D'Hiver (A Winter's Tale) (1992)

Conte D'Été (A Summer's Tale) (1996)

Conte D'Autoumne (An Autumn Tale) (1998)

THE WILHELM SCREAM

First used in the Western Distant Drums (1951) as three Injuns are shot, the Wilhelm Scream is arguably cinema's most famous sound effect. Absent from movies for many years, the effect came back into fashion after sound designer Ben Burtt tracked down the original recording (the effect was labelled 'Man being eaten by alligator') and put it into Star Wars. Burtt dubbed the effect the Wilhelm Scream after a minor character who emitted it in The Charge At Feather River. Since then, the Wilhelm Scream has become an in-joke amongst modern sound designers (particularly at Skywalker Sound), who try to interpolate it wherever possible.

Below are some of the most notorious usages:

Distant Drums - Three Injuns are shot, one after the other.

The Charge At Feather River - Wilhelm is struck in the leg by an arrow.

Them! - Ben Peterson is throttled to death by a giant ant.

Star Wars - A stormtrooper falls into the chasm before Luke and Leia swing across.

The Empire Strikes Back – A rebel soldier screams when his laser-gun dish is hit during the battle of Hoth.

Raiders Of The Lost Ark – A Nazi soldier is thrown from the back of a truck.

Poltergeist – Carol Anne watches a soldier killed in a war movie.

Return Of The Jedi – A victim of Luke's lightsaber falls into the Sarlacc pit.

Indiana Jones And The Temple Of Doom – (i) Indy shoots the driver of Lao Che's car.

(ii) Mola Ram is eaten by alligators.

Howard The Duck – A duck hunter is knocked out of his boat.

Indiana Jones And The Last Crusade – A soldier is blown down a hill by a grenade blast.

Batman Returns – Batman punches a clown and throws him out of the way.

Aladdin – The Genie lifts the palace into the air.

Reservoir Dogs – Mr Brown is shot in his car.

A Goofy Movie – Goofy's car hits scaffolding.

Toy Story – Buzz is knocked out of the bedroom window.

Die Hard: With A Vengeance – John McClane nearly runs over a mime artist.

Titanic – A man in the engine room is hit by a jet of water.

Star Wars Episode I: The Phantom Menace – Two security guards are shot in the Naboo hangar.

Planet Of The Apes – General Thade hurls two humans into the air.

Star Wars Episode II: Attack Of The Clones – The opening starship explosion on Coruscant.

LOTR: The Two Towers – A soldier falls during the Helm's Deep battle.

Revenge Of The Sith – A CloneTrooper is sent flying during the opening dogfight.

Fantastic Four – As Dr Doom picks up and throws a bus.

King Kong – A sailor is knocked off a cliff by the brontosaurus stampede.

Cars – One of the cars in Lightning McQueen's dream sequence.

STARS WHO USE THEIR MIDDLE NAME AS THEIR FIRST ONE

William Clark Gable

Edward Montgomery Clift

Henry Warren Beatty

Robert Oliver Reed

Dorothy Faye Dunaway
Charles Robert Redford
Michael Sylvester Stallone
Maria Debra Winger
William Bradley Pitt

MOVIE MEMORABILIA AUCTION PRICES

Film	Item	Price
2001: A Space Odyssey	Bowman's grey jumpsuit	£2,200
Aliens	Hicks' Perspex dog tags	£345
Aliens	Alien egg	£920
Back To The Future Part II	Hoverboard	£2,640
Batman Returns	Batman's cowl	£5,625
Braveheart	William Wallace costume	£27,000
Charlie Chaplin	Bowler hat and cane	£44,750
Citizen Kane	Rosebud sled	£233,500
A Clockwork Orange	Alex's bowler hat	£1,980
Conan The Barbarian	Serpent-entwined dagger	£805
Die Hard	Kalashnikov 9mm	£345
The Empire Strikes Back	Luke's lightsaber	£3,000-4,000
Excalibur	The principal sword	£1,380
Forrest Gump	'Russell Stover Candies' choc box	£460
From Russia With Love	Lotte Lenya's knuckle-duster	£1,495
Goldfinger	Aston Martin DB5	£162,000
Goldfinger	Oddjob's bowler hat	£62,000
Gone With The Wind	David O. Selznick's Oscar	£907,000
Hellraiser	Wooden cube	£600-800
Hook	Hook's hook	£2,500-3,000
Lawrence Of Arabia	Lawrence's desert robe	£12,375
The Magnificent Seven	Chris Adams' black Stetson	£5,175
The Maltese Falcon	The Maltese Falcon statuette	£234,111
Moonraker	Space-marine laser gun	£1,150
One Flew Over The Cuckoo's Nest	Straitjacket signed by Jack	£2,070

Raiders Of The Lost Ark	Indy's bullwhip	£2,000-3,000
RoboCop	RoboCop costume	£2,300
The Spy Who Loved Me	1977 Lotus Esprit shell	£29,900
Star Wars	Ceremonial medallion	£54,000
Supergirl	Four-piece Supergirl outfit	£4,025
Superman	A piece of Kryptonite	£920
The Terminator	Sunglasses	£800-1,200
Terminator 2: Judgment Day	Leather jacket	£3,500-4,500
Thunderball	007's dinner jacket	£30,900
The Wizard Of Oz	Dorothy's ruby slippers	£391,764
Zulu	Two prop shields and spears	£250

CINEMAS IN KAZAKHSTAN ...

... are oval, as the shape resembles the traditional yurts in which nomadic Kazakhs lived.

THE LONGEST ACCEPTANCE SPEECH IN OSCAR HISTORY

Five minutes and 30 seconds - Greer Garson picking up Best Actress for Mrs Miniver (1943)

THE TOP 10 HIGHEST-GROSSING R-RATED MOVIES

1 The Passion Of The Christ (2004) - $370,274,604

2 The Matrix Reloaded (2003) - $281,576,461

3 Beverly Hills Cop (1984) - $234,760,478

4 The Exorcist (1973) - $232,671,011

5. Saving Private Ryan (1998) - $216,540,909

6. Wedding Crashers (2003) - $209,255,921

7. Terminator 2: Judgment Day (1991) - $204,843,345

8. Gladiator (2000) - $187,705,427

9. 300 (2007) - $179,941,919*

10. Pretty Woman (1990) - $178,406,268

*Still on release at the time of writing

6,469,952
The total number of spots drawn by Disney animators during 101 Dalmatians (1961).

THE STUDENT FILMS OF GEORGE LUCAS*
Look At Life (1965), Freheit (1965), Herbie (1966), 1:42:08: A Man And His Car (1966),
The Emperor (1967), THX 1138: 4EB (1967), Anyone Lived In A Pretty (How) Town (1967)

* made at The University of Southern California Cinema School

AMERICAN DODGEBALL* ASSOCIATION OF AMERICA
FINALISTS 2004
The Average Joes
Peter LaFleur (Vince Vaughn) – Captain
Kate Veatch (Christine Taylor) – Striker
Dwight (Chris Williams) – Striker
Gordon (Stephen Root) – Returner/Beserker
Justin (Justin Long) – Catcher/Cheerleader
Steve The Pirate (Alan Tudyk) – Outer Court
Owen (Joel Moore) – Outer Court
Honorary mention: Patches O'Houlihan (Rip Torn)

The Purple Cobras
White Goodman (Ben Stiller) – Captain
Fran Stalinofskivich (Missi Pyle) – Striker
Blade (Rusty Joiner) – Outer Court
Laser (Kevin Porter) – Striker
Blazer (Brandon Molale) – Returner
Me'Shell Jones (Jamal Duff) – Striker/Receiver

* The Five Ds of Dodgeball: Dodge. Duck. Dip. Dive. Dodge.

ODDBALL MTV AWARD WINNERS
Best Kiss
1998	Adam Sandler & Drew Barrymore (The Wedding Singer)
1999	Gwyneth Paltrow & Joseph Fiennes (Shakespeare In Love)

2000	Sarah Michelle Gellar & Selma Blair (Cruel Intentions)
2001	Julia Stiles & Sean Patrick Thomas (Save The Last Dance)
2002	Jason Biggs & Seann William Scott (American Pie 2)
2003	Tobey Maguire & Kirsten Dunst (Spider-Man)
2004	Owen Wilson & Carmen Electra & Amy Smart (Starsky & Hutch)
2005	Rachel McAdams & Ryan Gosling (The Notebook)
2006	Jake Gyllenhaal & Heath Ledger (Brokeback Mountain)

Best Fight Scene

1998	Will Smith vs. Cockroach (Men In Black)
1999	Ben Stiller vs. Puffy the Dog (There's Something About Mary)
2000	Keanu Reeves vs. Laurence Fishburne (The Matrix)
2001	Zhang Ziyi vs. Entire Bar (Crouching Tiger, Hidden Dragon)
2002	Chris Tucker and Jackie Chan vs. The Hong Kong Gang (Rush Hour)
2003	Yoda vs. Christopher Lee (Star Wars: Episode II – Attack Of The Clones)
2004	Uma Thurman vs. Chiaki Kuriyama (Kill Bill: Vol. 1)
2005	Uma Thurman vs. Daryl Hannah (Kill Bill: Vol. 2)
2006	Angeline Jolie vs Brad Pitt (Mr & Mrs Smith)

SUGGESTED RENTALS FOR ESTATE AGENTS*

House Of A Thousand Dolls (1967), House Of America (1997), House Of Angels (1992), House Of Angels: The Second Summer (1994), House Of Bamboo (1955), The House Of Bernarda Alba (1987), House Of Blackmail (1953), House Of Cards (1968), House Of Games (1993), House Of Dark Shadows (1970), House Of Dracula (1945), House Of Evil (1968), House Of Evil (1983), The House Of Fear (1945), House Of Flying Daggers (2004), House Of Frankenstein (1944), House Of Games (1987), The House Of Mirth (2000), House Of Mortal Sin (1975), House Of Mystery (1961), House Of Numbers (1957), House Of 1000 Corpses (2003), The House Of Rothschild (1934), House Of Sand And Fog (2003), House Of Secrets (1956), The House Of Seven Corpses (1974), House Of Strangers (1949), House Of The Long Shadows (1983), The House Of The Seven Gables (1940), The House Of The Seven Hawks (1959), The House Of The Spirits

(1993), The House Of Usher (1988), House Of Wax (1953), House Of Whipcord (1974), House Of Women (1962), The House Of Yes (1997)

* selected films with the title House Of …

THE WRIGHT STUFF

A selection of movie references in Shaun Of The Dead and Hot Fuzz, the films to date of Edgar Wright:

Shaun Of The Dead

The title is a pun on the George A Romero zombie classic, Dawn Of The Dead. The synth music over the studio logo at the start is from DOTD. Also, Shaun (Simon Pegg) works at Foree Electronics, Ken Foree being one of the stars of that film. The boss of Foree Electronics (who's off sick) is named Ash, after the hero in The Evil Dead. The restaurant called Fulci is a reference to Lucio Fulci, the Italian horror director. The shot that looks through a hole in one zombie's body is a riff on Fulci's The Beyond. At the end, 'bio-hazard' troops show up. Bio-Hazard was the Japanese title for the game Resident Evil. The tie around Shaun's head is a nod to The Deerhunter.

Hot Fuzz

Nicholas Angel (Pegg) and Danny Butterman (Frost) watch Point Break and Bad Boys II on DVD, and later re-create scenes from both films. The mid-film foot-chase is also based on the chase in Point Break. The town play spoofs Baz Luhrmann's Romeo + Juliet. Angel's 'tool-up' sequence spoofs films including Commando and Rambo: First Blood Part II. Angel looks after a plant, à la Leon. Place-name references in Sandford include Norris Avenue (after Chuck Norris), Callahan Park (after Dirty Harry's surname) and Spencer Hill (after Bud Spencer and Terence Hill, pseudonyms for Italian action-movie stars).

When the guys find the horde of guns, the music that plays is a cue from Lethal Weapon. Dialogue references include The Shining ('You've always been here'), Chinatown ('Forget it, Nick. It's Sandford') and He-Man ('By the power of Grayskull!'). One of the big reveals is a direct homage to The Wicker Man (1973).

There are several references to Shaun Of The Dead, including the familiar jingle on a pub slot machine, Cornetto cameos, the fence gag and a conversation in a pub featuring the word 'cunt'. The SOTD DVD is even glimpsed in the bargain bin of the supermarket.

FAVOURITE FILMS OF FAMOUS FIGURES

Queen Victoria	The Pillow Fight (1898)
Tsar Nicholas II	The Exploits Of Elaine (1914)
Queen Alexandra	True Heart Susie (1919)
Stalin	Lady Hamilton (1942)
Adolf Hitler	The Blue Angel (1930), The Rebel (1933), Mazurka (1935)
Dwight Eisenhower	Angels In The Outfield (1951), Rear Window (1954)
Ronald Reagan	Friendly Persuasion (1956)
John F Kennedy	Spartacus (1960)
Richard Nixon	Patton: Lust For Glory (1969)
Nicolas Ceausescu	The Great Gatsby (1974)
Leonid Brezhnev	Dirty Harry (1971), Magnum Force (1973), Taxi Driver (1976)
Yuri Andropov	The Godfather (1972), the James Bond series
Princess Diana	Rain Man (1988)
Bill Clinton	High Noon (1952)

FICTIONAL EDUCATIONAL ESTABLISHMENTS

Adam's College	Revenge Of The Nerds
Bates High School	Carrie
Biblioll College	Jude
Camden College	The Rules Of Attraction
Empire State University	Spider-Man
Hamilton High	Prom Night II: Hello Mary Lou
Herrington High	The Faculty
Hickory High School	Hoosiers
Hogwarts	Harry Potter franchise
Lakewood High School	10 Things I Hate About You
Marion Barry High School	High School High

Rancho Carne High School	Bring It On
Robert E Lee High School	Dazed And Confused
Rydell High	Grease
The Tanz Akademie	Suspiria
St Trinian's	The Belles Of St Trinian's
Salem Academy For Girls	Satan's School For Girls
School Of Lifemanship	School For Scoundrels
Shermer High School	The Breakfast Club
Taft And Adams High School*	Screwballs
Welton Academy	Dead Poets Society
Westerberg High School	Heathers
Xavier's School For Gifted Youngsters	X-Men

* 'Let's hear it for T&A!'

FICTIONAL PERIODICALS

Title	Film
The Back Bay Mainline	Between The Lines
The Center City Examiner	The Front Page
*Chunky Asses**	The Golden Child
Crimeways	The Big Clock
The Daily Bugle	Spider-Man
The Daily Planet	Superman
Dysentery·	Annie Hall
Know	Down With Love
The Ledger	Not For Publication
The Morning Post	His Girl Friday
The New York Inquirer	Citizen Kane
The New York Sun	The Paper
*Playbirds**	The Playbirds
The Tally Ho	The Prisoner
The National Tattler	Manhunter/Red Dragon

* porno magazine

· formed when *Dissent* and *Commentary* merged

147

THE CARTOON LAWS OF PHYSICS*

I: Any body suspended in space will remain in space until made aware of its situation.

So, Daffy Duck steps off a cliff, expecting further pastureland. He loiters in midair, soliloquising flippantly, until he chances to look down. At this point, the familiar principle of 32 feet per second takes over.

II: Any body in motion will tend to remain in motion until solid matter intervenes suddenly.

Whether shot from a cannon or in hot pursuit on foot, cartoon characters are so absolute in their momentum that only a telephone pole or an outsize boulder retards their forward motion absolutely. Sir Isaac Newton called this sudden termination of motion the stooge's surcease.

III: Any body passing through solid matter will leave a perforation conforming to its perimeter.

Also called the silhouette of passage, this phenomenon is the speciality of victims of directed-pressure explosions and of reckless cowards who are so eager to escape that they exit directly through the wall of a house, leaving a cookie-cutout-perfect hole. The threat of skunks or matrimony often catalyses this reaction.

IV: The time required for an object to fall twenty storeys is greater than or equal to the time it takes for whoever knocked it off the ledge to spiral down twenty flights to attempt to capture it unbroken.

Such an object is inevitably priceless, the attempt to capture it inevitably unsuccessful.

V: All principles of gravity are negated by fear.

Psychic forces are sufficient in most bodies for a shock to propel them directly away from the earth's surface. A spooky noise or an adversary's signature sound will induce motion upward, usually to the cradle of a chandelier, a treetop, or the crest of a flagpole. The feet of a character who is running or the wheels of a speeding auto need never touch the ground, especially when in flight.

VI: As speed increases, objects can be in several places at once.

This is particularly true of tooth-and-claw fights, in which a character's head may be glimpsed emerging from the cloud of altercation at several places simultaneously. This effect is common as well among bodies that are spinning or being throttled. A 'wacky' character has the option of self-replication only at manic high speeds and may ricochet off walls to achieve the velocity required.

VII: Certain bodies can pass through solid walls painted to resemble tunnel entrances; others cannot.

This trompe l'oeil inconsistency has baffled generations, but at least it is known that whoever paints an entrance on a wall's surface to trick an opponent will be unable to pursue him into this theoretical space. The painter is flattened against the wall when he attempts to follow into the painting. This is ultimately a problem of art, not of science.

VIII: Any violent rearrangement of feline matter is impermanent.

Cartoon cats possess even more deaths than the traditional nine lives might comfortably afford. They can be decimated, spliced, splayed, accordion-pleated, spindled, or disassembled, but they cannot be destroyed. After a few moments of blinking self-pity, they reinflate, elongate, snap back, or solidify.

Corollary 1: A cat will assume the shape of its container.

Corollary 2: Cartoon cats have the uncanny ability to emit piano sounds when their teeth are transformed into piano keys after having a piano dropped on them.

IX: Everything falls faster than an anvil.

See examples too numerous to mention from the Roadrunner cartoons.

X: For every vengeance there is an equal and opposite revengeance.

This is the one law of animated cartoon motion that also applies to the physical world at large. For that reason, we need the relief of watching it happen to a duck instead.

* Originally 'O'Donnell's Laws of Cartoon Motion', *Esquire*, 6/80

TEN MOVIE DJS

DJ	Actor	Film
Wolfman Jack	Wolfman Jack	American Graffiti
Alan 'Dickie' Bird	Bill Paterson	Comfort And Joy
Howard Stern	Howard Stern	Private Parts
Hard Harry	Christian Slater	Pump Up The Volume
Barry Champlain	Eric Bogosian	Talk Radio
Abby	Janeane Garofalo	The Truth About Cats & Dogs
Adrian Cronauer	Robin Williams	Good Morning, Vietnam

| Dave Garver | Clint Eastwood | Play Misty For Me |
| Jack Lucas | Jeff Bridges | The Fisher King |

THE CAMERON CROWE SONGBOOK

Song: 'She Sells Sanctuary' by The Cult

Film: Singles

Where to find it: Linda (Kyra Sedgwick) tells Steve (Campbell Scott) about old boyfriends.

Song: 'Free Falling' by Tom Petty And The Heartbreakers

Film: Jerry Maguire

Where to find it: Jerry's (Tom Cruise) driving song.

Song: 'In Your Eyes' by Peter Gabriel

Film: Say Anything

Where to find it: At the end, on a held-aloft beatbox.

Song: 'Everything In Its Right Place' by Radiohead

Film: Vanilla Sky

Where to find it: At the opening when David Aames (Tom Cruise) wakes up.

Song: 'Secret Garden' by Bruce Springsteen

Film: Jerry Maguire

Where to find it: As Jerry and Dorothy (Renée Zellweger) leave the house for their first date.

Song: 'Waiting For Somebody' by Paul Westerberg

Film: Singles

Where to find it: Openng credits/Janet (Bridget Fonda) on her own.

Song: 'Tiny Dancer' by Elton John

Film: Almost Famous

Where to find it: The tour bus sing-a-long.

MR MOTO

Based on JP Marquand's books, the Mr Moto series of films saw Peter Lorre assaying a Japanese supersleuth. The franchise came to an abrupt end in 1939 when the US became distrustful of Japan's activities in the lead-up to World War II. The series was revived in 1965 for one film, with Henry Silva as Moto, but it flopped.

The only other actor to play Mr Moto was Porky Pig in the 1939 cartoon 'Porky's Movie Mystery'. The full list:

Think Fast, Mr Moto (1937), Mr Moto's Gamble (1938), Mr Moto Takes A Chance (1938), The Mysterious Mr Moto (1938), Thank You, Mr Moto (1938), Mr Moto On Danger Island (1939), Mr Moto's Last Warning (1939), Mr Moto Takes A Vacation (1939), The Return Of Mr Moto (1965)

THE WISDOM OF PAULINE KAEL

Pauline Kael was the film critic for the *New Yorker* from 1967 to 1991 and her jazzy, subjective style is generally considered to have invented modern film criticism. She died on 3 September 2001.

On Chaplin's Limelight: 'Slimelight.'

On Rain Man: 'A wet piece of kitsch.'

On Dances With Wolves: 'A nature-boy movie … Costner has feathers in his hair and feathers in his head.'

On Top Gun: 'Top Gun is a recruiting poster that isn't concerned with recruiting but with being a poster.'

On The Exorcist: 'Shallowness that asks to be taken seriously – shallowness like William Peter Blatty's – is an embarrassment. When you hear him on TV talking about communicating with his dead mother, your heart doesn't bleed for him, your stomach turns for him.'

On Dial M For Murder: 'A mystery more dark than any propounded by the film: why does Hitchcock persist in using actors as unattractively untalented as Robert Cummings?'

On A Man For All Seasons: 'Perhaps people think it is so great because, unlike the usual movie which is aimed at twelve-year-olds, this one is aimed at twelve-year-old intellectuals and idealists.'

On The Band Wagon: 'When the bespangled Cyd Charisse wraps her phenomenal legs around Astaire, she can be forgiven everything – even the fact that she reads her lines as if she learned them phonetically.'

On Return Of The Jedi: 'The battle between good and evil, which is the theme of just about every big fantasy adventure film, has become a flabby excuse for a lot of dumb tricks and noise.'

On Diner: 'With luck, Mickey Rourke could become a major star: he has an edge and a magnetism, and a sweet pure smile that surprises you. He seems to be acting to you and no one else.'

On The Sound Of Music: 'Wasn't there perhaps one little Von Trapp who didn't want to sing his head off, or who screamed that he wouldn't act out little glockenspiel routines for Papa's party guests, or who got nervous and threw up if he had to get on a stage?'

FILM FOLK TURNED NOVELISTS

Star	Novel
Whoopi Goldberg	Alice
Julie Andrews	The Last Of The Really Great Whangdoodles
Tony Curtis	Kid Andrew Cody & Julie Sparrow
Joan Collins	Prime Time
Robert Shaw	The Sun Doctor
David Niven	Once Over Lightly
Dirk Bogarde	West Of Sunset
Simon Signoret	Adieu Volodia
Mae West	The Constant Sinner
Jean Harlow	Today Is Tonight
Orson Welles	Mr Arkadin
John Sayles	Union Dues
Jean Cocteau	Les Enfants Terribles
Gus Van Sant	Pink
Ethan Hawke	Ash Wednesday, The Hottest State
Peter Farrelly	Outside Providence, The Comedy Writer
Carrie Fisher	Postcards From The Edge, The Best Awful
Steve Martin	Shopgirl
Sophie Marceau	Telling Lies
Rupert Everett	Hello Darling, Are You Working?
Pamela Anderson	Star

SCREEN SNOGS

The first screen kiss - May Irwin and John Rice (The Widow Jones, 1896)

The first Hollywood French kiss - Natalie Wood and Warren Beatty (Splendor In The Grass, 1961)

The first Japanese kiss - Hatachi No Koi (1962)

The first same-sex kiss - the orgy scene in Cecil B DeMille's Manslaughter (1922)

The first explicit male kiss - Murray Head and Peter Finch (Sunday Bloody Sunday, 1971)

The most kisses in one movie - 127 bestowed by John Barrymore in Don Juan (1926)

THE FIRST TEN FILMS IN TECHNICOLOR

Technicolor is a colour process invented by Herbert T Kalmus and Daniel F Comstock. Initially a two-colour (red and green) process used successfully in The Black Pirate (1926), the full-blown three-colour process came out of merging negatives individually sensitive to red, green and blue. The process inaugurated lush, vibrant images that connote a 'movie-movieness', seen famously in Gone With The Wind and the films of Michael Powell and Emeric Pressburger (The Red Shoes and Black Narcissus). Here are the first feature films to use the three-colour process:

Becky Sharp (1935)

Captain Blue Blood (1935)

The Trail Of The Lonesome Pine (1936)

Dancing Pirate (1936)

Ramona (1936)

The Garden Of Allah (1936)

God's Country And The Woman (1937)

Wings Of The Morning (1937)

A Star Is Born (1937)

Vogues Of 1938 (1937)

JAMES BOND, 007 – TWAT!

Over the years, James Bond has become an icon of cool, charm and suavity. You remember the successful one-liners that bowled over exotic heroines in film after film; now reacquaint yourself with the Bond whose stupid, offensive, stuffy remarks would see him shot down in flames if he tried to chat up a desperate divorcee at a Midlands hen night:

Chatting up a bird
'Your mouth is the right size … for me, that is!' – From Russia With Love*

On drinking unchilled champagne
'That would be like listening to The Beatles without earmuffs!' – Goldfinger

After snogging a Chinese chick
'Why do Chinese girls taste different from all other girls?' – You Only Live Twice*

On the phone and on the job
'She's just coming, sir.' – The Man With The Golden Gun*

Ditto, when asked what he is doing
'Keeping the British end up, sir.' – The Spy Who Loved Me*

While paying an Indian
'That'll keep you in curry for a few weeks!' – Octopussy

To Barbara Carrera
'Going down, one should always be relaxed.' – Never Say Never Again*

Copping off with a character called Christmas in the country of Turkey
'I always wanted to have Christmas in Turkey.' – The World is Not Enough*

* imagine this followed by a Sid James 'fnarr-fnarr' laugh … and calculate the odds on Bond getting a drink in his face or a knee in the goolies

SPIKE JONZE* PROMOS
Beastie Boys (Time For Livin', Sabotage, Root Down (Live Version), Sure Shot, Ricky's Theme), Bjork (It's Oh So Quiet, It's In Our Hands), Blind (Days), The

Breeders (Divine Hammer, Cannonball), Chainsaw Kittens (High In High School), Chemical Brothers (Elektrobank), Daft Punk (Da Funk), Dinosaur Jr (Feel The Pain), Elastica (Car Song), Fatboy Slim (Praise You, Weapon Of Choice), Fatlip (What's Up Fatlip?), Luscious Jackson (Daughter Of The KAOS), Marxman (All About Eve), MC 900 feat. Jesus (If I Only Had A Brain), Mike Watt (Big Train, Liberty Calls), Notorious B.I.G. (Sky's The Limit feat. 112), Pavement (Shady Lanes), The Pharcyde (Drop), Puff Daddy (It's All About The Benjamins), R.E.M. (Crush With Eyeliner, Electrolite), Rocket From The Crypt (Ditch Digger), Sean Lennon (Home), Sonic Youth (The Diamond Sea, 100%), Teenage Fanclub (Hang On), Tenacious D (Wonderboy), That Dog (Old Timer), Velocity Girl (I Can't Stop Smiling), Wax (California, Who Is Next), Ween (Freedom Of '76), Weezer (Buddy Holly, Island In The Sun, The Sweater Song), X (Country At War)

* director of Being John Malkovich and Adaptation

FICTIONAL SPORTS TEAMS

Team	Sport	Movie
The Bad News Bears	Baseball	The Bad News Bears
California Crusaders	US Football	Any Given Sunday
Charlestown Chiefs	Ice Hockey	Slapshot
Cleveland Indians	Baseball	Major League
Dallas Felons	BASEketball	BASEketball
Dallas Knights	US Football	Any Given Sunday
Hickory High School Huskers	Basketball	Hoosiers
LA Riots	BASEketball	BASEketball
Leicester Forest	Football	Yesterday's Hero
LA Stallions	US Football	The Last Boy Scout
The Miami Gators	Baseball	Back To The Future Part II
Miami Sharks	US Football	Any Given Sunday
The Mighty Ducks	Ice Hockey	The Mighty Ducks
The Milwaukee Beers	BASEketball	BASEketball
New York Knights	Baseball	The Natural
North Dallas Bulls	US Football	North Dallas Forty
The Saints	Football	Yesterday's Hero

SCLSU	US Football	The Waterboy
Texas State Fighting Armadillos	US Football	Necessary Roughness
West Canaan Coyotes	US Football	Varsity Blues
Windsor United	Football	Yesterday's Hero

NINE STARS WHO DIED MID-SHOOT

Billy Mead – They Died With Their Boots On (1941)

Tyrone Power – Solomon And Sheba (1959)

Jean Harlow – Saratoga (1937)

John Candy – Wagon's East (1994)

River Phoenix – Dark Blood (1993)

Brandon Lee – The Crow (1994)

Marilyn Monroe – Something's Gotta Give (1962)

Anthony Perkins – Psycho V (1992)

Robert Walker – My Son John (1952)

THE GANGS OF GANGS OF NEW YORK

The Dead Rabbits, The Native Americans, The O'Connell Guards, The Plug Uglies, The Shirt Tails, The Chichesters, The Forty Thieves, The Daybreak Boys, The Swamp Angels, The Frog Hollows, The Night Walkers Of Ragpickers Row, The Little 40 Thieves*, The Slaughter Housers, The Broadway Twisters, The Lime Juicers, The True Blues, The Kerryonians, The American Guards, The Atlantic Guards

* run by 'One Lung' Curran

HEALERS PLAYED BY ROBIN WILLIAMS

Dr Malcolm Sayer – Awakenings (1990)

Dr Cozy Carlisle – Dead Again (1991)

Dr Kosevich – Nine Months (1995)

Sean Maguire – Good Will Hunting (1997)

Hunter 'Patch' Adams – Patch Adams (1998)

Dr Chris Nielsen – What Dreams May Come (1998)

TALENTS WHO NEVER WON AN OSCAR

Montgomery Clift, Peter O'Toole, Marlene Dietrich, Kirk Douglas, WC Fields, John Ford, Greta Garbo, Judy Garland, Jean Harlow, Rita Hayworth, Alfred Hitchcock, Steve McQueen, Robert Mitchum, Marilyn Monroe, Peter Sellers, Barbara Stanwyck, Gloria Swanson, Lana Turner, Orson Welles, Natalie Wood

MOVIES BASED ON THEME-PARK ATTRACTIONS

The Country Bears (2002), Pirates Of The Caribbean: The Curse Of The Black Pearl (2003), The Haunted Mansion (2003)

THE FALLS

Peter Greenaway's first full-length feature, The Falls (1980), takes the form of a *faux* filmed directory of the survivors of a Violent Unknown Event (VUE). Ninety-two short films cover the people in the directory whose surname begins with the letters FALL. Below is the list of FALLS detailed in the movie, containing some of the greatest character names ever to grace the cinema:

Orchard Falls, Constance Ortuist Fallaburr, Melorder Fallaburr, Appis (Arris) Fallabus, Standard Fallaby, Tasida Fallaby, Lacer Fallacet, Mashanter Fallack, Arris Fallacy, Squaline Fallaize, Carlos Fallantly, Muscus Fallantly, Wrallis Fallanway, Allia Fallanx, Starling Fallanx, Ipson & Pulat Fallari, Stachia Fallari, Aptesia Fallarme, Cornoptia Fallas, Aneto Fallapsy, Pandist Fallapsy, Sashi Fallaspy, Vyanine Fallaspy, Casternarm Fallast, Ardenaur Fallatter, Agropio Fallaver, Propine Fallax, Cash Fallaxy, Antopody Fallabatt, Coppice Fallbatteo, Agrendo Fallbazz, Cisgattern Fallbazz, Hasp Fallbazz, Canopy Fallbenning, Cole Fallbird, Castel Fallboys, Acataloope Fallbus, Astraham Fallbute, Loosely Fallbute, Betheda Fallbutus, Bwythan Fallbutus, Cathine Fallbutus, Menenome Fallbutus, Olivine Fallbutus, Vacete Fallbutus, Astra Fallcas, David Fallcash, Bewick Fallcaster, Catch-Hanger Fallcaster, Clasper Fallcaster, Felix Fallcaster, Max Fallcaster, Orion Fallcaster, Throper 'Castor' Fallcaster, Raskado Fallcastle, Appropinquo Fallcatti, Agrimany Fallchester, Sitrach Fallding, Ostler Falleaver, Edio Fallenby, Shey Fallenby, Affinado Falleur, Eric Fallfree, Thomax Fallfrex, Zachia Fallgilot, Joyan Fallicory, Bird Raspara Fallicutt, Obsian Fallicut, Wallis Fallinway, Ashile Fallko, Agostina Fallmutt, Anonymous*, Anonymous*, Polle Fallory, Afracious Fallows, Hearty Fallparco, Sallis Fallpinio, Crasstranger Fallqueue,

Romanese Fallracce, Ascrib Fallstaff, Armeror Fallstag, Combayne Fallstoward, Geoffrey Fallthuis, Merrium Falltrick, Stephany Falltrix, Tolley Falluger, Vassian Falluger, Erhaus Bewler Falluper, Grastled Falluson, Castral Fallvernon, Leasting Fallvo, Anthior Fallwaste

* these entries have been compiled by the Bird Foundation Industries (BFI)

STARS WHO APPEARED IN THE GHOSTBUSTERS MUSIC VIDEO

For the release of Ray Parker Jr's hit single, the cast of Ghostbusters roped in friends to cameo in the promo vid. It's an eclectic bunch ...

Chevy Chase

Irene Cara

John Candy

Nickolas Ashford

Melissa Gilbert

Jeffrey Tambor

George Wendt

Al Franken

Dannny DeVito

Carly Simon

Peter Falk

Teri Garr

ARNIE KISS-OFF LINES

'Don't disturb my friend, he's dead tired.' – After killing a man on a plane in Commando

'Consider that a divorce!' – Shooting his wife (Sharon Stone) in Total Recall

'Hasta la vista, baby!' – Shooting the T-1000 (Robert Patrick) in Terminator 2: Judgment Day

'Stick around.' – As he impales a baddie with a stake in Predator

'He was a pain in the neck!' – After garrotting a 'stalker' in The Running Man

'Soviet method is more economical.' – After torturing a criminal in Red Heat

'To be or not to be? Not to be.' – Playing Hamlet in The Last Action Hero

'You're fired!' – Firing a missile at a baddie in True Lies

'You're luggage!' – To a dead crocodile in Eraser

'I'm afraid my condition has left me cold to your pleas of mercy.' – Mr Freeze to a cop in Batman & Robin

'You are terminated!' – On killing the T-X in Terminator 3: Rise Of The Machines

TIM BURTON–DANNY ELFMAN COLLABORATIONS

Pee-Wee's Big Adventure (1985), Beetlejuice (1988), Batman (1989), Edward Scissorhands (1990), Batman Returns (1992), The Nightmare Before Christmas (1993), Family Dog (1993), Mars Attacks! (1996), Sleepy Hollow (1999), The World Of Stainboy (2000), Planet Of The Apes (2001), Big Fish (2003), Charlie And The Chocolate Factory (2005), The Corpse Bride (2005)

* famous director/producer and composer collaboration

JFK'S MAGIC BULLET THEORY*

In Oliver Stone's 1991 examination of President Kennedy's assassination, D. A. Jim Garrison (Kevin Costner) uses the diagram below to explain the 'magic bullet' theory, or how one bullet caused seven wounds on President Kennedy and Governor John Connally's bodies.

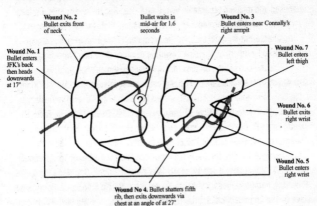

Wound No. 2
Bullet exits front of neck

Bullet waits in mid-air for 1.6 seconds

Wound No. 3
Bullet enters near Connally's right armpit

Wound No. 1
Bullet enters JFK's back then heads downwards at 17°

Wound No. 7
Bullet enters left thigh

Wound No. 6
Bullet exits right wrist

Wound No. 5
Bullet enters right wrist

Wound No 4. Bullet shatters fifth rib, then exits downwards via chest at an angle of at 27°

* The magic bullet theory, or the single bullet theory, is a crucial element of the Warren Commission's findings that 'assassin' Lee Harvey Oswald acted alone

TEN DIRECTORS WHO MADE ADVERTS AFTER THEY GOT FAMOUS

David Lynch	PlayStation 2
Spike Lee	Nike
Bill Forsyth	Foster's
Martin Scorsese	Armani, Revlon, Johnnie Walker
Wong Kar-Wai	BMW
Baz Luhrmann	Chanel No. 5
Luc Besson	L'Oreal, Chanel, Estée Lauder
John Woo	Nike
Michael Mann	Mercedes Benz
Quentin Tarantino	PerfecTV!

ANIMALS WERE HARMED IN THE MAKING OF THIS PRODUCTION

The American Humane Association has presided over movie sets since 1940 to make sure animals in movies are safe. While the majority of Hollywood films are supervised and deemed acceptable by the AHA – earning the end credits disclaimer 'No Animals Were Harmed …'™ – there are some films that are monitored as 'unacceptable', meaning that the production filmed 'an at-risk segment unauthorised by American Humane, resulting in injury or death of an animal'. Below is the current list of films that are categorised as unacceptable:

The Abyss, The Annihilation of Fish, Antarctica, Apocalypse Now, Arabian Nights, Big Bad John, Cannibal Holocaust, Conan The Barbarian, Conan The Destroyer, Crocodile, Crystal Eye, Curse Of The Starving Class, Deathstalker III, Faces Of Death, Faces Of Death 2, Ferryman, First Blood, Fist Of Fury II, Heart Of The Stag, Heartland, Heaven's Gate, In The Blood, Lawrence Of Arabia, The Legend Of The Lone Ranger, Lion Of The Desert, Lord Of The Flies, Moments of Truth, Mondo New York, Mountains Of The Moon, Mr Mike's Mondo Video, One Man's Hero, The Prophecy, Rambo III, Reds, Return To Snowy River, Rodeo Bloopers 2, Roger & Me, Slave Of The Cannibal God, Southern Comfort, Suburbia: You Wouldn't Want To Live There, The Black Cobra, Unknown, The Chisholms, The Field, The Lion Speaks,

The Long Riders, The Mountain Men, The Snake Fist Vs. The Dragon, Tom Horn, Tomcat, Triumphs Of A Man Called Horse, Tundra, Vampire's Kiss, Yellow Hair And The Fortress of Gold.

INCORRECT MOVIE TITLES

Krakatoa, East Of Java	... Krakatoa is actually 200 miles west of Java
Assault On Precinct 13	... is about an assault on Precinct 9
Frogs	... is about marauding toads
Remake	... is an original
Cremaster 4	... is the first in the cycle
The Bible	... has nothing to do with old or new testaments
Tracked By The Police	... stars Rin Tin Tin and has no cops in it
Big Deal At Dodge City	... is set in Laredo
Haunted Honeymoon	... ends with no honeymoon in sight
Special Effects	... is an effects-free zone
As You Like It	... is a Bulgarian film based on *Romeo And Juliet*
Her Twelve Men	... teacher Greer Garson taught thirteen school kids

SELECTED CINEMATIC CROSSDRESSERS

Michael Caine - Dressed To Kill (1980)
Dustin Hoffman - Tootsie (1982)
Cary Grant - I Was A Male War Bride (1949)
Debra Winger - Made In Heaven (1987)
Tony Curtis - Some Like It Hot (1959)
Tim Curry - The Rocky Horror Picture Show (1975)
Linda Hunt - The Year Of Living Dangerously (1982)
Julie Andrews - Victor/Victoria (1982)
Ed Wood Jr - Glen Or Glenda (1952)
Johnny Depp - Ed Wood (1994)
Robin Wiliams - Mrs Doubtfire (1993)
Rod Steiger - No Way To Treat A Lady (1968)
John Lithgow - The World According To Garp (1982)
Anne Heywood - I Want What I Want (1972)

Theresa Russell - Aria (1988)

Jaye Davidson - The Crying Game (1992)

Harvey Fierstein - Torch Song Trilogy (1988)

Patrick Swayze - To Wong Foo, Thanks For Everything! Julie Newmar (1995)

Robbie Coltrane - Nuns On The Run (1990)

Raquel Welch - Myra Breckinridge (1970)

Dudley Moore - Bedazzled (1967)

Bob Hope - The Princess And The Pirate (1944)

Alec Guiness - Kind Hearts And Coronets (1949)

Hilary Swank - Boys Don't Cry (2000)

Greta Garbo - Queen Christina (1933)

Marlene Dietrich - Morocco (1930)

Katharine Hepburn - Sylvia Scarlett (1935)

Dick Shawn - What Did You Do In The War, Daddy? (1966)

Bing Crosby - High Time (1960)

Gael García Benal - Bad Education (2004)

Peter Sellers - The Mouse That Roared (1959)

Lee J Cobb - In Like Flint (1967)

Jerry Lewis - Three On A Couch (1966)

Marlon Wayans - White Chicks (2004)

Cillian Murphy - Breakfast At Pluto (2005)

FIVE STARS WHO STARTED AS TEACHERS

George C Scott, Gabriel Byrne, Margaret Hamilton, Ramon Navarro, Sir Michael Redgrave

ENGLISH-LANGUAGE WINNERS OF THE PALME D'OR*

Othello - Orson Welles (1952)

Marty - Delbert Mann (1955)

Friendly Persuasion - William Wyler (1957)

The Knack... And How To Get It - Richard Lester (1965)

Blowup - Michelangelo Antonioni (1967)

If - Lindsay Anderson (1969)

M*A*S*H – Robert Altman (1970)

The Go-Between – Joseph Losey (1971)

The Hireling – Alan Bridges (1973)

Scarecrow – Jerry Schatzberg (1973)

The Conversation – Francis Ford Coppola (1974)

Taxi Driver – Martin Scorsese (1976)

Apocalypse Now – Francis Ford Coppola (1979)

All That Jazz – Bob Fosse (1980)

Paris, Texas – Wim Wenders (1984)

The Mission – Roland Joffé (1986)

Sex, Lies, And Videotape – Steven Soderbergh (1989)

Wild At Heart – David Lynch (1990)

Barton Fink – Joel Coen (1991)

The Piano – Jane Campion (1993)

Pulp Fiction – Quentin Tarantino (1994)

Secrets & Lies – Mike Leigh (1996)

Dancer In The Dark – Lars von Trier (2000)

The Pianist – Roman Polanski (2002)

Elephant – Gus Van Sant (2003)

Fahrenheit 9/11 – Michael Moore (2004)

* the 'Best Picture' award at the Cannes Film Festival

MONTY PYTHON* FILMOGRAPHY

And Now For Something Completely Different (1971), Monty Python And The Holy Grail (1975), Monty Python's Life Of Brian (1979), Monty Python Live At The Hollywood Bowl (1982), Monty Python's The Meaning Of Life (1983)

* comedy troupe consisting of John Cleese, Michael Palin, Graham Chapman, Eric Idle, Terry Jones and Terry Gilliam

'CLASSIC CINEMA' VERSUS 'COUNTER-CINEMA'

In response to Jean-Luc Godard's Le Vent D'Est (1972), renowned film theorist Peter Wollen devised a definition of that type of filmmaking which he dubbed 'counter-cinema'. Wollen argued that it stood in direct opposition to the aesthetics of dominant mainstream cinema.

Classic Cinema	Counter-Cinema
Narrative Transitivity	Narrative Intransitivity
Identification	Estrangement
Transparency	Foregrounding
Single Diegesis	Multiple Diegesis
Closure	Aperture
Pleasure	Unpleasure
Fiction	Reality

THE TRANSFORMERS OF TRANSFORMERS (2007) FILM AND WHAT THEY TRANSFORM INTO

Autobots

Optimus Prime – Peterbilt truck

Bumblebee – 1974 Chevrolet Camaro*

Jazz – Pontiac Solstice

Ironhide – GMC Topkick pickup truck

Ratchet – Search and Rescue Hummer H2

Decepticons

Megatron – Stealth bomber~

Starscream – F-22 Raptor

Blackout – MH-53 Pave Low

Brawl – Modified M1 Abrams

Barricade – Saleen-modified Ford Mustang police car

Frenzy – CD player^

Bonecrusher – Buffalo H Mine-Protected Vehicle

Scorponok – Mechanical scorpion

* Changed from the cartoon's Volkswagen Beetle, due to rights issues

~ Changed from the cartoon's Walther P38 because turning into a giant gun would have looked really stupid

^ Changed from the original's cassette tape, because that's, like, so 80s, dude

THE MUSIC OF MARTY*

Song: 'Jumpin' Jack Flash' by The Rolling Stones
Film: Mean Streets (1973)
Where to find it: Johnny Boy (Robert De Niro) enters Tony's bar

Song: 'Mickey's Monkey' by Smokey Robinson And The Miracles
Film: Mean Streets (1973)
Where to find it: Johnny Boy dances before getting into a car

Song: 'Rubber Biscuit' by The Chips
Film: Mean Streets (1973)
Where to find it: Charlie (Harvey Keitel) gets drunk

Song: Intermezzo from *Cavaleria Rusticana* by Pietro Mascagni
Film: Raging Bull (1980)
Where to find it: Jake La Motta (De Niro) bounces round a ring

Song: 'Is That All That There Is?' by Peggy Lee
Film: After Hours (1985)
Where to find it: Paul Hackett (Griffin Dunne) dances with June (Verna Bllom)

Song: 'Werewolves Of London' by Warren Zevon
Film: The Color Of Money (1986)
Where to find it: Vincent (Tom Cruise) plays pool

Song: 'Sunshine Of Your Love' by Cream
Film: Goodfellas (1990)
Where to find it: Jimmy Conway (De Niro) decides to kill Morrie

Song: 'Rags To Riches' by Tony Bennett
Film: Goodfellas (1990)
Where to find it: Young Henry (Christopher Serrone) blows up a car

Song: 'The House Of The Rising Sun' by The Animals
Film: Casino (1995)
Where to find it: Mobsters get murdered

Song: 'I'm Shipping Up To Boston' by The Dropkick Murphys
Film: The Departed (2006)
Where to find it: The night-time drive

* Legendary director Martin Scorsese

EMMANUELLE

Based on Emmanuelle Arsan's scandalous 1957 novel, this franchise followed the erotic misadventures of Emmanuelle (Sylvia Kristel), the bored housewife of an embassy official based in Thailand. The influential films have spawned many rip-offs – Laura Gemser made enough imitations to be defined as another series – but here is the 'official' Emmanuelle filmography:

Film	Emmanuelle
Emmanuelle (1974)	Sylvia Kristel
Emmanuelle 2 (1975)	Sylvia Kristel
Goodbye, Emmanuelle (1977)	Sylvia Kristel
Emmanuelle 4 (1984)	Sylvia Kristel/Mia Nygren*
Emmanuelle V (1987)	Monique Gabrielle
Emmanuelle 6 (1988)	Natalie Uher
Emmanuelle Au 7ème Ciel (1993)	Sylvia Kristel

* Emmanuelle undergoes plastic surgery – Kristel emerges as Nygren

THE FIRST FILM TO BE PREMIERED UNDERWATER

The Incredible Mr Limpet (1964), shown on a submerged screen off Weeki Waka, Florida, to 250 viewers in a glass tank 20 feet below the surface.

CASTS OF THOUSANDS

Listed below are the films that have featured the largest number of real extras. With digital technology now creating crowd scenes, these records are unlikely to be broken.

Gandhi (1982)	294,560
Kolberg (1945)	187,000
Monster Wangmagwi (1967)	157,000
War And Peace (1968)	120,000
Ilya Muromets (1956)	106,000
Dun Huang (1998)	100,000
Razboiul Independentei (1912)	80,000
Around The World In 80 Days (1956)	68,894
Intolerance (1956)	60,000
Dny Zrady (1973)	60,000

YUPPIE NOSTALGIA

The college-friends-reuniting-in-their-thirties movie was a prevalent sub-genre in the 1980s and early 90s. Below are the friends (not partners) featured in three of the most famous examples:

The Return Of The Secaucus 7 (1980)

Mike Donnelly (Bruce MacDonald), Katie Sipriano (Maggie Renzi), Maura Tolliver (Karen Trott), JT (Adam LeFevre), Frances Carlson (Maggie Cousineau), Chip Hollister (Gordon Clapp), Irene Rosenblue (Jean Passanante)

The Big Chill (1983)

Sam (Tom Berenger), Sarah (Glenn Close), Harold (Kevin Kline), Michael (Jeff Goldblum), Nick (William Hurt), Meg (Mary Kay Place), Karen (JoBeth Williams)

Peter's Friends (1992)

Peter Morton (Stephen Fry), Roger Charleston (Hugh Laurie), Andrew Benson (Kenneth Branagh), Sarah Johnson (Alphonsia Emmanuel), Maggie Chester (Emma Thompson), Mary Charleston (Imelda Staunton)

RENOWNED PROSTHETIC* DESIGNERS

Designer	Effect to mention
Jack Pierce	Boris Karloff's Frankenstein make-up
William Tuttle	The seven faces Of Dr Lao in Seven Faces Of Dr Lao
John Chambers	The apes in Planet Of The Apes
Dick Smith	The spinning head in The Exorcist
Christopher Tucker	John Merrick's disfigurations in The Elephant Man
Rick Baker	The werewolf in An American Werewolf In London
Tom Savini	The undead in Dawn Of The Dead
Rob Bottin	The monster in The Thing
Chris Walas	The melting faces in Raiders Of The Lost Ark
Stuart Freeborn	Yoda in The Empire Strikes Back

* special effects make-up

CORRECT MOVIE PRONUNCIATION

Name	Pronounced
Kirsten Dunst	Keersten Dunst
Richard Dreyfuss	Richard Dry-fuss
Cinecitta	Chinny-Cheetah
Martin Scorsese	Martin Score-sez-ee (not Score-say-zee)
Steve Buscemi	Steve Buh-sem-ee
M Night Shyamalan	M Night Shah-ma-lawn
Ralph Fiennes	Rayf Fines
Annabella Sciorra	Annabella Shee-or-a
Pedro Almodóvar	Pay-dro Al-mo-doh-var
A lightsaber being turned on	Vvvmmm

TIME BANDITS

The time-travelling dwarfs from Terry Gilliam's 1981 fantasy flick.

Character	Actor	Characteristic
Randall	David Rappaport	The Leader
Fidgit	Kenny Baker	The Nice One

Strutter	Malcolm Dixon	The Strong One
Og	Mike Edmonds	The Stupid One
Wally	Jack Purvis	The Angry One
Vermin	Tiny Ross	The Gluttonous One

ELIZABETH TAYLOR'S MARRIAGES

Below is a list of the eight marriages of Elizabeth Taylor, followed by what she said at the time of each marriage.

Conrad 'Nicky' Hilton* (6 May 1950 – 1 February 1951)

'Your heart knows when you've met the right man. There is no doubt that Nicky is the one I want to spend the rest of my life with.'

Michael Wilding (21 February 1952 – 30 January 1957)

'I just want to be with Michael. This, for me, is the beginning of a happy end.'

Mike Todd (2 February 1957 – 22 March 1958)@

'This marriage will last forever. For me it will be third time lucky.'

Eddie Fisher (12 May 1959 – 6 March 1964)

'I have never been happier in my life. We will be on our honeymoon for thirty or forty years.'

Richard Burton (15 March 1964 – 26 June 1974)

'I'm so happy I can't believe it. I love him enough to stand by him no matter what he might do.'

Richard Burton (10 October 1975 – 1 August 1976)

'There will be no more marriages or divorces. We're stuck like chicken feathers to tar – for always.'

John W Warner (4 December 1976 – 7 November 1982)

'I don't think of John as Husband Number Seven. He's number one all the way – the best lover I've ever had. I want to spend the rest of my life with him and I want to be buried with him.'

Larry Fortensky (6 October 1991 – 31 October 1996)

'With God's blessing, this is it, forever.'

* Paris Hilton's grandfather

@ killed in a plane crash

$150

The weekly wage of Dooley Wilson, who played the pianist Sam in Casablanca (1942).

MEN-ON-A-MISSION WAR MOVIES

Film	Mission
Saving Private Ryan	To get James Ryan home after his brothers were killed
The Guns Of Navarone	To infiltrate Greek territory to destroy a massive gun-emplacement
Force 10 From Navarone	To destroy a dam in order to knock out a strategic bridge with torrents of water
Where Eagles Dare	To rescue an American general who has full knowledge of D-Day from SS HQ
Kelly's Heroes	To cross enemy lines and steal $16,000,000 in Nazi gold bullion
A Walk In The Sun	To head inland and take a fortified farmhouse
Castle Keep	To occupy an ancient castle and protect its artistic treasures
The Sea Wolves	To destroy Nazi radio ships in neutral waters while pretending to be on a fishing expedition
The Eagle Has Landed	To dress up as Polish soldiers and kidnap Winston Churchill during the PM's visit to a sleepy village
The Dirty Dozen	To parachute behind enemy lines and cause havoc for German generals on the eve of D-Day
The Wild Geese	To rescue an imprisoned politico, the enemy of an evil dictator, who is critically ill and due for execution

FAMOUS INTERNET-ONLY FILMS

Loose Change - 9/11 conspiracy documentary, now in its third revision to correct inaccuracies
http://www.question911.com/

405 The Movie - Short action movie about a hapless driver on a freeway where a DC-10 is trying to land
http://www.405themovie.com/

America: Freedom To Fascism - Web documentary about the erosion of civil liberties post 9/11
http://video.google.co.uk/videoplay?docid=-4312730277175242198
The Phantom Edit - A semi-mythical cut of The Phantom Menace, edited to remove all references to Jar Jar and still make sense
http://en.wikipedia.org/wiki/The_Phantom_Edit

NON-SINGERS IN SINGING ROLES

Audrey Hepburn - Breakfast At Tiffany's (1961)
Drew Barrymore, Ed Norton et al - Everyone Says I Love You (1996)
Marlon Brando - Guys And Dolls (1955)
Sissy Spacek - Coal Miner's Daughter (1980)
Tom Hanks - The Polar Express (2004)
Lee Marvin and Clint Eastwood - Paint Your Wagon (1969)
Meryl Streep - Postcards From The Edge (1991)
Ewan McGregor and Nicole Kidman - Moulin Rouge (2001)
Richard Attenborough - Doctor Dolittle (1967)
Sean Connery - Darby O'Gill And The Little People (1959)
Jack Nicholson - Something's Gotta Give (2003)
Natalie Wood - West Side Story (1961)
Rex Harrison - My Fair Lady (1964)
Gary Busey - The Buddy Holly Story (1978)
Michelle Pfeiffer - The Fabulous Baker Boys (1989)
Rod Steiger - Oklahoma (1955)
Jim Carrey - The Cable Guy (1996)

CHUCK NORRIS FACTS

Ginger action legend Chuck Norris has seen a post-millenium revival thanks to the website chucknorrisfacts.com, which spawned a series of outlandish 'facts' riffing on his mystique. Here are a few ...
Chuck Norris's tears cure cancer. Too bad he has never cried.
Chuck Norris counted to infinity - twice.
When the Boogeyman goes to sleep every night he checks his closet for Chuck Norris.

The chief export of Chuck Norris is pain.

Chuck Norris is currently suing NBC, claiming Law and Order are trademarked names for his left and right legs.

If you have five dollars and Chuck Norris has five dollars, Chuck Norris has more money than you.

When Chuck Norris had surgery, the anaesthesia was applied to the doctors.

Chuck Norris can touch MC Hammer.

Chuck Norris ordered a Big Mac at Burger King, and got one.

Chuck Norris does not sleep. He waits.

Superman owns a pair of Chuck Norris pyjamas.

The quickest way to a man's heart is with Chuck Norris's fist.

Chuck Noris puts the 'laughter' in 'manslaughter'.

Chuck Norris doesn't read books. He stares them down until he gets the information he wants.

Chuck Norris can divide by zero.

When Chuck Norris sends in his taxes, he sends blank forms and includes only a picture of himself, crouched and ready to attack. Chuck Norris has not had to pay taxes ever.

Water boils faster when Chuck Norris watches it.

Life is like a box of chocolates. You never know when Chuck Norris is going to kill you.

TOP TEN HIGHEST-GROSSING BOX-OFFICE STARS

Star	Total worldwide box office	Biggest hit
1. Tom Hanks	$3,104.9 million	Forrest Gump
2. Harrison Ford	$3,044.7 million	Star Wars
3. Eddie Murphy	$2,925.5 million	Shrek 2
4. Tom Cruise	$2,537.6 million	War Of The Worlds
5. Bruce Willis	$2,165.5 million	The Sixth Sense
6. Robert De Niro	$2,139.4 million	Meet The Fockers
7. Samuel L Jackson	$2,098.5 million	Revenge Of The Sith
8. Robin Williams	$2,094.4 million	Mrs Doubtfire
9. Julia Roberts	$2,093.9 million	Ocean's Eleven
10. Mel Gibson	$2,022.2 million	Signs

MOVIES THAT SOUND LIKE PORN BUT AREN'T

Ace In The Hole, The Black Hole, Blow, Bone Daddy, Bones, Carry On Dick, Chopper, Christie Malry's Own Double-Entry, Come And See, Deep Impact, Dick, Fanny And Alexander, Fanny By Gaslight, F.I.S.T., Fun With Dick And Jane, The Harder They Come, Harry Potter And The Chamber Of Secrets, Heat, Holes, The Insider, In & Out, I Went Down, The Jerk, Jugs & Speed, Kiss Kiss Bang Bang, Lethal Weapon, Manhunter, Nine Queens, Paradise Alley, Prize Puppies, The Rescuers Down Under, Riding In Cars With Boys, Shaft, Shag, A Shot In The Dark, Snatch, Stop! Or My Mom Will Shoot, Unlawful Entry, X-Men

SELECTED POP STAR MOVIES

S Club: Seeing Double – S Club
Spice World – The Spice Girls
A Hard Day's Night – The Beatles
Catch Us If You Can – Dave Clark Five
Head – The Monkees
Cool As Ice* – Vanilla Ice
ABBA: The Movie† – ABBA
Gonks Go Beat – Lulu
Cuckoo Patrol – Freddie & The Dreamers
Born To Boogie – Marc Bolan
Rude Boy – The Clash
From Justin To Kelly – Justin Guarini and Kelly Clarkson

* Shot by Oscar-winning cinematographer Janusz Kaminski (Schindler's List)

† Directed by Lasse Hallström (Chocolat)

SELECTED USES OF 'KLAATU BARADA NIKTO'*

Film	Use
Return Of The Jedi	The names of three creatures on Jabba's sail barge
Teenage Mutant Ninja Turtles (TV show)	The names of three visiting aliens
Toys Recited	To stop a runaway monster

Army Of Darkness	The words that will allow Ash to safely remove the Necronomicon, the Book Of The Dead†
Tron	Seen on a sign hanging in Alan's cubicle
Jimmy Neutron: Boy Genius	The words to a magic spell
Close Encounters Of The Third Kind	On a banner on the wall of an alien-research group

* Alien codewords from The Day The Earth Stood Still (1951)

† The div gets them wrong and unleashes a living-dead army

REJECTED NAMES FOR SNOW WHITE'S SEVEN DWARFS

Awful, Biggy, Blabby, Dirty, Gabby, Gaspy, Gloomy, Hoppy, Hotsy, Jaunty, Jumpy, Nifty, Shifty

FREAKY FAMILIES

Alexander: Colin Farrell is less than a year younger than screen mother Angelina Jolie.

Back To The Future: Michael J Fox is only ten days younger than screen mother Lea Thompson, and three years older than screen dad Crispin Glover.

Family Business: Sean Connery is just seven years older than screen son Dustin Hoffman.

Indiana Jones And The Last Crusade: Harrison Ford's screen dad, Sean Connery, is only twelve years his senior.

The Manchurian Candidate (1962): Angela Lansbury plays Laurence Harvey's mother, yet is only three years older than him.

Mean Girls: Rachel McAdams is only five years younger than Amy Poehler, who plays her mother.

North By Northwest: Cary Grant is only eight years younger than Jessie Royce Landis, who plays his mother.

WE WERE EXPECTING YOU ...

Bond's baddies plans/demands:

Dr No
Dr No (Joseph Wiseman) wants to wreck the US space programme by shooting down rockets

From Russia With Love
Red Grant (Robert Shaw) wants to kill James Bond

Goldfinger
Auric Goldfinger (Gert Frobe) wants to irradiate Fort Knox so Goldfinger's gold bullion supplies become more valuable

Casino Royale
Jimmy Bond (Woody Allen) wants to kill all men taller than him

Thunderball
Largo (Adolfo Celi) wants to steal nuclear warheads and blackmail the world

You Only Live Twice
Ernst Stavro Blofeld (Donald Pleasence) wants to wreck the US/USSR space programmes by kidnapping rocketships and start WWIII

On Her Majesty's Secret Service
Ernst Stavro Blofeld (Telly Savalas) wants to develop bacteriological weapons to kill off the world's population

Diamonds Are Forever
Ernst Stavro Blofeld (Charles Gray) wants to steal diamond lenses that will help him build a satellite laser weapon

Live And Let Die
Dr Kananga (Yaphet Kotto) wants to give away free heroin to create a market for his drugs business

The Man With The Golden Gun
Francisco Scaramanga (Christopher Lee) wants to steal a solar panel device

The Spy Who Loved Me
Stromberg (Curt Jurgens) wants to kidnap warships and start WWIII

Moonraker
Hugo Drax (Michel Lonsdale) wants to kill off the world's population so he can create a new race ... from space

Octopussy
Cenrel Orlöv (Steven Berkoff) wants to launch a strike against NATO and start WWIII

Never Say Never Again
Largo (Klaus Maria Brandauer) wants to steal nuclear warheads and blackmail the world (see Thunderball)

A View To A Kill
Max Zorin (Christopher Walken) wants to flood Silicon Valley and take over the computer industry

The Living Daylights
Brad Whittaker (Joe Don Baker) wants to sell arms to Afghanistan

Licence To Kill
Franz Sanchez (Robert Davi) wants to sell drugs to everyone in America

GoldenEye
Alec Trevelyan (Sean Bean) wants to detonate a satellite over London to hide the theft of money from the Bank Of England

Tomorrow Never Dies

Elliott Carver (Jonathan Pryce) wants to start a war between China and Britain to help market his new television news network

The World Is Not Enough

Renard (Robert Carlyle) and Elektra King (Sophie Marceau) want to contaminate the Bosporus Straits so the only outlet for petroleum is King's pipeline

Die Another Day

Gustav Graves (Toby Stephens) wants to use Icarus, a superweapon disguised as an orbital mirror system, to defend North Korea while it invades surrounding nations

Casino Royale

Le Chiffre (Mads Mikelsen) wants to get back the money he owes terrorist organisations by hosting a high-stakes poker game

WALLACE & GROMIT'S CRACKING CONTRAPTIONS

A series of short animations featuring the cheese lover and his dog that first appeared on the Internet and subsequently became an extra on the Curse Of The Were-Rabbit DVD. Each features a new invention.

Contraption	Use
Shopper 13	A remote-controlled, cheese-carrying shopping trolley
The Autochef	A mechanised fried-breakfast-maker
A Christmas Cardomatic	A Christmas card-maker
The Tellyscope	An overly elaborate remote control
The Snowmanotron	An overzealous snowman-maker
The Bully Proof Vest	A vest that fends off attackers
The 525 Crackervac	A vacuum cleaner specifically for cracker crumbs
The Turbo Diner	A machine that clears the table after a meal
The Snoozatron	A machine to aid sleep (not as effective as a dog dressed as a sheep)
The Soccamatic	A contraption to beat dogs at football

SELECTED LARRY KING CAMEOS

He's the American Michael Parkinson, and he's had more movie cameos than Parky's had bland dinners:

Ghostbusters, Lost In America*, Crazy People, The Exorcist III, Dave, We're Back! A Dinosaur's Story*, Spin, Open Season, The Long Kiss Goodnight, Contact, An Alan Smithee Film: Burn Hollywood Burn, Mad City, The Jackal, Primary Colors, Bulworth, Enemy Of The State, The Kid, The Contender, America's Sweethearts, John Q, The Stepford Wives, Shrek 2*†, Mr 3000

* Voice only

† As 'Ugly Stepsister'

CELEBRITY LA LAKERS FANS

Doris Day

Leonardo DiCaprio

Penny Marshall

Denzel Washington

Andy Garcia

Dyan Cannon

Michael Douglas

Rob Lowe

Rob Reiner

Ray Liotta

John Lithgow

Heather Locklear

Dennis Hopper

Eddie Murphy

Walter Matthau

Steven Spielberg

Dustin Hoffman

Joel Silver

Sherry Lansing

Jeffrey Katzenberg

Ice Cube

Tobey Maguire
Chris Rock
Peter Berg
Jessica Alba
Matthew Perry
Michael Clarke Duncan
Kevin James
Cuba Gooding Jr
David Arquette
Freddie Prinze, Jr
Charlize Theron
Adam Sandler
Edward Norton
Demi Moore
Chris Tucker
Cameron Diaz
Jim Carrey
Jack Black
Sylvester Stallone
Dean Martin
Ashton Kutcher
Jami Gertz
Salma Hayek
Larry David

CELEBRITY SHEFFIELD UNITED FANS

Sean Bean

ACTORS WHO WERE RECAST AFTER SHOOTING BEGAN

Michael J Fox replaced Eric Stoltz as Marty McFly in Back To The Future.
Viggo Mortensen replaced Stuart Townsend as Aragorn in The Fellowship Of The Ring.

Martin Sheen replaced Harvey Keitel as Captain Benjamin L Willard in Apocalypse Now.

Sandra Bullock replaced Lori Petty as Lt Lenina Huxley in Demolition Man.

Klaus Kinski replaced Jason Robards as Fitzcarraldo in Fitzcarraldo.

Yul Brynner replaced Tyrone Power as Solomon in Solomon And Sheba.

Elaine Stritch, Denholm Elliott and **Sam Shepard** replaced Maureen O'Sullivan, Charles Durning and Christopher Walken as Diane, Howard and Peter respectively in September (Shepard was then replaced by Sam Waterston).

Arthur Kennedy replaced Edmond O'Brien as Jackson Bentley in Lawrence Of Arabia.

Jack Haley replaced Buddy Ebsen as the Tin Man in The Wizard Of Oz*.

Betty Hutton replaced Judy Garland as Annie Oakley in Annie Get Your Gun.

William Devane replaced Roy Thinnes as Arthur Adamson in Family Plot.

* Ebsen was allergic to the metallic make-up. His voice can, however, still be heard during 'We're Off To See The Wizard'

ACTORS WHOSE PRIVATE SEX TAPES HAVE BEEN LEAKED TO THE PUBLIC

Colin Farrell, Pamela Anderson, Rob Lowe, Gena Lee Nolin, Steve Guttenberg, Tom Sizemore, Paris Hilton*

* She was in House Of Wax, so technically she has acted

GODZILLA VS. ... (AND WHO WON)

Many Godzilla movies have been produced over the years, but only a selection have been a straightforward rumble. Here follows the complete list of Godzilla title bouts:

Contest	Winner
King Kong Vs. Godzilla	King Kong
Mothra Vs. Godzilla	Mothra
Godzilla Vs. Hedorah	Godzilla
Godzilla Vs. Gigan	Godzilla

Godzilla Vs. Megalon	Godzilla
Godzilla Vs. Mechagodzilla	Godzilla
Godzilla Vs. Biollante	Biollante - although Godzilla later revives
Godzilla Vs. King Ghidorah	Godzilla
Godzilla Vs. Mothra	Mothra
Godzilla Vs. Mechagodzilla II	Godzilla
Godzilla Vs. Spacegodzilla	Godzilla
Godzilla Vs. Destoroyah	Godzilla - although Godzilla is still destroyed
Godzilla Vs. Megaguirus	Godzilla

THE COMPLETE 'MOTHER'
Actors who have played 'Mother' in the Psycho franchise:

Psycho - Virginia Gregg, Paul Jasmin, Jeanette Nolan (voice only)

Psycho II - Claudia Bryar*, Virginia Gregg (voice only)

Psycho III - Virginia Gregg (voice only)

Psycho IV: The Beginning - Olivia Hussey, Alice Hirson (living Norma Bates/
voice only)

* Mother impersonator

THE MARX BROTHERS – WHICH ONE'S WHICH?
The one with the glasses and moustache - Groucho (Julius Henry Marx)

The one with the hat and the Italian accent - Chico (Leonard Marx)

The mute one - Harpo (Adolph Marx)

The boring, good-looking one - Zeppo (Herbert Marx)

The one who wasn't in the films - Gummo (Milton Marx)

A DAY IN THE MOVIES
We Dive At Dawn, Breakfast At Tiffany's, A Walk In The Park, Naked Lunch, Love In
The Afternoon, Tea With Mussolini, Dinner At Eight, Dancing At The Blue Iguana,
Home Before Midnight

CARTOON CHARACTERS WHO CAMEO IN WHO FRAMED ROGER RABBIT

Disney

Mickey Mouse, Minnie Mouse, Donald Duck, Daisy Duck, Goofy, Pluto, Black Pete, Horace Horsecollar, Clarabelle Cow, Clara Cluck, Peter Pig, the hummingbirds from Song Of The South, Dumbo, the crows from Dumbo, the broomsticks from Fantasia, the dancing hippo from Fantasia, José Carioca, Snow White and the Seven Dwarfs, the Witch from Snow White And The Seven Dwarfs, Bambi, Bill the lizard with a ladder from Alice In Wonderland, the Big Bad Wolf and the Three Little Pigs, Maleficent's goons from Sleeping Beauty, Mr Toad, the penguins from Mary Poppins, Pinocchio, Jiminy Cricket, Tinkerbell

Warner Bros

Bugs Bunny, Daffy Duck, Porky Pig, Road Runner, Wile E Coyote, Yosemite Sam, Speedy Gonzales, Tweety Bird, Sylvester, Foghorn Leghorn, Marvin the Martian

Other

Droopy, Betty Boop, Koko The Clown, Woody Woodpecker

A SELECTION OF STARS WHO HAVE MADE THE SUCCESSFUL TRANSITION FROM CHILD ACTOR TO ADULT ACTOR

Kurt Russell, Drew Barrymore, Jodie Foster, Kirsten Dunst, Christian Bale, Anna Paquin, Diane Lane, Jackie Cooper, Sarah Polley, Elizabeth Taylor, Macaulay Culkin, Matt Dillon, Veronica Cartwright, Lindsay Lohan, Elijah Wood, Mickey Rooney

SELECTED RAPPERS TURNED ACTORS

Will Smith (I, Robot), Ice Cube (Three Kings), LL Cool J (Any Given Sunday), Queen Latifah (Chicago), Ice T* (Tank Girl), Tupac Shakur (Gridlock'd), Buster Rhymes (Shaft), DMX (Cradle 2 The Grave), Dr Dre (Training Day), Snoop Dogg (Starsky &

Hutch), Eminem (8 Mile), Vanilla Ice (Cool As Ice), 50 Cent (Get Rich Or Die Tryin'),
Eve (The Woodsman), Mos Def (The Hitchhiker's Guide To The Galaxy), Ja Rule
(Assault On Precinct 13), Coolio (Batman & Robin)

* Real name Tracy Marrow

THE WORST MOVIES EVER MADE*

1.	Anus Magillicutty (2003)
2.	In The Mix (2005)
3.	Going Overboard (1989)
4.	SuperBabies: Baby Geniuses 2 (2004)
5.	From Justin To Kelly (2003)
6.	Santa With Muscles (1996)
7.	Troll 2 (1990)
8.	3 Ninjas: High Noon At Mega Mountain (1998)
9.	Car 54, Where Are You? (1994)
10.	Glitter (2001)
11.	Son Of The Mask (2005)
12.	The Honeymooners (2005)
13.	Backyard Dogs (2000)
14.	You Got Served (2004)
15.	House Of The Dead (2003)
16.	Love In Paris (1997)
17.	Leonard Part 6 (1987)
18.	Kazaam (1996)
19.	The Shaggy Dog (2006)
20.	Chairman Of The Board (1998)

* According to the website IMDb.com, as voted for by the site's users

SONGS COVERED IN THE MOULIN ROUGE
SOUNDTRACK AND THE ARTISTS WHO ORIGINALLY
RECORDED THEM

Song	Artist
'The Sound Of Music'	Julie Andrews
'Lady Marmalade'	Patti LaBelle
'Nature Boy'	Nat King Cole
'Rhythm Of The Night'	DeBarge
'Material Girl'	Madonna
'Smells Like Teen Spirit'	Nirvana
'Diamonds Are A Girl's Best Friend'	Marilyn Monroe
'Diamond Dogs'	David Bowie
'Galop Infernal' (The Can-Can)	Jacques Offenbach (composer)
'One Day I'll Fly Away'	The Crusaders
'Children Of The Revolution'	T-Rex
'Gorecki'	Lamb
'Roxanne'	The Police
'The Show Must Go On'	Queen
'Like A Virgin'	Madonna
'Your Song'	Sir Elton John
'Love Is Like Oxygen'*	Sweet
'Love Is A Many Splendored Thing'*	Frank Sinatra
'Up Where We Belong'*	Joe Cocker and Jennifer Warnes
'All You Need Is Love'*	The Beatles
'Lover's Game'*	Chris Isaak
'I Was Made For Lovin' You'*	KISS
'Just One Night'*	Eric Clapton
'Pride (In The Name Of Love)'*	U2
'Don't Leave Me This Way'*	Harold Melvin & The Blue Notes
'Silly Love Songs'*	Paul McCartney And Wings
'Heroes'*	David Bowie
'I Will Always Love You'*	Dolly Parton

* Featured in the 'Elephant Love Medley'

OSCAR NOMINEES WHO DON'T EXIST

Robert Rich - The pseudonym for blacklisted writer Dalton Trumbo, who won the Best Screenplay Oscar for The Brave One (1957).

PH Vazak - The name of Robert Towne's sheepdog, under which he was nominated for a screenwriting Oscar for Greystoke: The Legend Of Tarzan, Lord Of The Apes (1984).

Donald Kaufman - Charlie's 'brother' was credited as co-writer of Adaptation (2002) and shared a Best Original Screenplay nomination with him - but doesn't actually exist. Donald is the only fictional nominee who isn't even a false name for a real person.

Roderick Jaynes - The Coen brothers' irascible English editor is credited on many of their films and was Oscar-nominated for Fargo (1997), but is actually a pseudonym for the brothers themselves.

BATMAN MOVIE VILLAINS
Batman: The Movie (1966)

The Joker (Cesar Romero), The Penguin (Burgess Meredith), The Riddler (Frank Gorshin), The Catwoman (Lee Meriwether)

Batman (1989)

The Joker a.k.a. Jack Napier (Jack Nicholson)

Batman Returns (1992)

The Penguin a.k.a. Oswald Cobblepot (Danny DeVito), Catwoman a.k.a. Selina Kyle (Michelle Pfeiffer), Max Shreck (Christopher Walken)

Batman Forever (1995)

The Riddler a.k.a. Edward Nygma (Jim Carrey), Two-Face a.k.a. Harvey Dent (Tommy Lee Jones), Sugar* (Drew Barrymore), Spice* (Debi Mazar)

Batman & Robin (1997)

Mr Freeze a.k.a. Dr Victor Fries (Arnold Schwarzenegger), Poison Ivy a.k.a. Dr Pamela Isley (Uma Thurman), Bane (Jeep Swenson)

Batman Begins (2005)

Ra's Al Ghul a.k.a. Henri Ducard (Liam Neeson), The Scarecrow a.k.a. Dr Jonathan Crane (Cillian Murphy), Carmine Falcone (Tom Wilkinson)

*Two-Face's sidekicks

BIG BOY CAPRICE'S HENCHMEN*

Mumbles (Dustin Hoffman), Pruneface (RG Armstrong), Flattop (William Forsythe), Influence (Henry Silva), Stooge (Jim Wilkey), 88 Keys (Mandy Patinkin), Shoulders (Stig Eldred), The Rodent (Neil Summers), The Brow (Chuck Hicks), Spud Spaldoni (James Caan), Little Face (Lawrence Steven Meyers), Itchy (Ed O'Ross), Numbers (James Tolkan)

* From Dick Tracy (1990) – Big Boy Caprice is played by Al Pacino

THE COMPLETE MOVIE WORKS OF HAYAO MIYAZAKI, A.K.A. THE JAPANESE WALT DISNEY

The Castle Of Cagliostro (1979), Mirai Shônen Conan Tokubetsu-Hen: Kyodaiki Giganto No Fukkatsu (1984), Nausicaä Of The Valley Of The Winds (1984), Laputa: Castle In The Sky (1986), My Neighbour Totoro (1988), Kiki's Delivery Service (1989), Porco Rosso (1992), Princess Mononoke (1997), Spirited Away (2001), Howl's Moving Castle (2004)

WHAT'S THE FILM IN WHICH JOHN WAYNE SAYS, 'GET OFF YOUR HORSE AND DRINK YOUR MILK'?

He never said it.

PHILIP K DICK STORIES THAT HAVE BEEN TURNED INTO FILMS

'Do Androids Dream Of Electric Sleep?' (Blade Runner, 1982), 'We Can Remember It For You Wholesale' (Total Recall, 1990), 'Confessions Of A Crap Artist' (Confessions D'Un Barjo, 1992), 'Second Variety' (Screamers, 1995), 'Impostor' (Impostor, 2000), 'Minority Report' (Minority Report, 2002), 'Paycheck' (Paycheck, 2003), 'A Scanner Darkly' (A Scanner Darkly, 2006)

GAMES OF DEATH*

Battleships, Clue (US version of Cluedo), NFL Super Bowl Electronic Football, Twister

* Games played by Bill and Ted against the Grim Reaper in Bill & Ted's Bogus Journey (1991)

HOLLYWOOD STARS THAT HAVE RELEASED PERFUMES

Jennifer Lopez (Glow, Still), Elizabeth Taylor (White Diamonds, Black Pearls, Passion, Forever, Gardenia), Antonio Banderas (Spirit), Mary-Kate and Ashley Olsen (Coast To Coast LA/NYC), Mariel Hemingway (Mariel), Sarah Jessica Parker (Lovely), Cher (Uninhibited), Kermit The Frog (Amphibia), Miss Piggy (Moi), Alan Cumming (Cumming)

AND ONE THAT ONLY EVER APPEARED IN A SIMPSONS EPISODE

Meryl Streep's Versatility

NUMBER OF TIMES ROSE AND JACK SAY EACH OTHER'S NAMES IN TITANIC (1997)

Jack says 'Rose' 50 times

Rose says 'Jack' 80 times

ROCKY HORROR AUDIENCE INTERACTION

Arguably the ultimate cult movie, The Rocky Horror Picture Show (1975) has developed a code of audience interaction at special screenings throughout the world. The following props are to be used at the instructed points in the film (fishnet stockings optional but encouraged).

Rice - To be thrown at the wedding of Ralph Hapschatt and Betty Munroe.

Water pistols - To be fired to simulate the storm Brad and Janet are caught in.

Newspapers - To shield one's head from the rain, à la Brad and Janet.

Rubber gloves - To be snapped along with Dr Frank-N-Furter during his creation speech.

Noisemakers - To be used to show approval of the creation speech.

Confetti - To be thrown as Rocky and Frank go to the bedroom following the Charles Atlas Song.

Toilet paper - To be thrown when Brad shouts, 'Great Scott!' (Scott is an American toilet paper brand.)

Toast (unbuttered) - To be thrown in the air when Frank proposes a toast.

Party hat - To be worn when Frank dons his own party hat.

Bell - When, during the 'Planet Schmanet' song, Frank asks, 'Did you hear a bell ring?', ring yours accordingly.

Cards - To be thrown in the air during the song 'I'm Going Home', when Frank sings, 'Cards for sorrow, cards for pain.'

RETIRED OSCAR CATEGORIES

Best Assistant Director	1934-38
Comedy Direction	1929 only*
Best Dance Direction	1936-38
Best Title Writing	1929 only†
Engineering Effects	1929 only~
Best Short Film (Colour)	1937-38
Best Short Film (Live Action - Two Reels)	1937-57
Short Film (Novelty)	1933-36
Best Story	1929-57
Unique and Artistic Production	1929 only°

* Won by Lewis Milestone for Two Arabian Nights

† Awarded for titles that appeared between scenes to convey story in silent films. Won by Joseph Farnham for Telling The World

~Won by Roy Pomeroy for Wings

°Won by William Fox for Sunrise

WHAT'S THE HITCHCOCK FILM WITH THE DALÍ DREAM SEQUENCE?

Spellbound (1945)

THE WORLD'S MOST FAMOUS STUDIO SPACES

Fox Studios Australia, Australia (The Star Wars prequels, the Matrix trilogy)
Barrandov Studios, Prague (Casino Royale (2006), The Bourne Identity)
Cinnecittà, Rome (Gangs Of New York, The Life Aquatic With Steve Zissou)
Estudios Churubusco, Mexico (Romeo + Juliet, The Matador)
Ealing Studios, UK (The Ladykillers (1955), Attack Of The Clones)
Elstree Studios, UK (Indiana Jones And The Temple Of Doom)
Leavesden Studios, UK (The Harry Potter series, Die Another Day)
Pinewood Studios, UK (The Bond series, Charlie And The Chocolate Factory (2005))
Shepperton Studios, UK (The Da Vinci Code, Batman Begins)
Film City, India (Many Bollywood productions)
Kamal Amrohi Studios, India (Many Bollywood productions)

HOLLYWOOD STREETS NAMED AFTER FILM STARS

Bob Hope Drive, [Rudolph] Valentino Place, Carmen Miranda Square, [Charles] Bronson Avenue, [Charlie] Chaplin Avenue, MarBro Avenue (named for the Marx Brothers), [Fred] Astaire Avenue, [Judy] Garland Drive, [Hedy] Lamarr Avenue, [Red] Skelton Circle, [Katharine] Hepburn Circle, [Douglas] Fairbanks Way, [Mary] Pickford Way, Gene Autry Way, [Clark] Gable Circle, [Humphrey] Bogart Circle, [Elvis] Presley Circle, George Burns Road

THE SOCIAL CLIQUES OF MEAN GIRLS

Plastics, Freshmen, ROTC Guys, Preps, J.V. (Junior Varsity) Jocks, Asian Nerds, Cool Asians, Varsity Jocks, Unfriendly Black Hotties, Girls Who Eat Their Feelings, Girls Who Don't Eat Anything, Desperate Wannabes, Burnouts, Sexually Active Band Geeks, Art Freaks

CRM 114

This phrase appears in several of Stanley Kubrick's movies and is also the name of an email filter.

2001: A Space Odyssey	The name on one of the space pods
A Clockwork Orange	Alex is injected with Serum (CRM – geddit?) 114

Dr Strangelove	The message decoder is called the CRM-114
Eyes Wide Shut	Tom Cruise visits Wing C, Room 114 of the morgue

NB It is also seen on the amplifier that Marty McFly plugs his guitar into in Back To The Future

A SHORT HISTORY OF POPCORN

The Western world's favourite movie snack originated as a foodstuff among Native Americans, who flavoured it with herbs and spices. The first commercial popping machine was invented by Charles Cretors of Chicago, Illinois, in 1885, and popcorn was first sold in cinemas in 1912. American cinema audiences now consume over 15 billion litres of popcorn per year.

ACTORS WHO WERE CUT OUT OF THE THIN RED LINE (1998)

Bill Pullman, Viggo Mortensen, Mickey Rourke, Lukas Haas, Gary Oldman, Billy Bob Thornton (narration)

SELECTED MOVIE STARS' HIGH SCHOOL AWARDS

Eddie Murphy	Most Popular
Sylvester Stallone	Most Likely To End Up In The Electric Chair
Gillian Anderson	Most Likely To Go Bald/Most Likely To Be Arrested
Sandra Bullock	Most Likely To Brighten Your Day
Meg Ryan	Cutest Girl In Class
Jack Nicholson	Class Clown
Trey Parker	Class Clown
Rosie O'Donnell	Class Clown
Cybill Shepherd	Most Attractive
Teri Hatcher	Most Likely To Become A Solid Gold Dancer
Halle Berry	Prom Queen
Natalie Portman	Most Likely To Be A Guest On Jeopardy
Chris Tucker	Most Humorous
Robin Williams	Most Humorous

Dennis Hopper — Most Likely To Succeed
Heather Graham — Most Talented
Joan Allen — Most Likely To Succeed
Jimmy Fallon — Most Likely To Replace David Letterman
Matthew McConaughey — Most Handsome

MOVIES THAT HAVE THEIR OWN LEGO RANGE

Harry Potter And The Philosopher's Stone, Harry Potter And The Chamber Of Secrets, Harry Potter And The Prisoner Of Azkaban, Harry Potter And The Goblet Of Fire, Spider-Man, Spider-Man 2, The Phantom Menace, Attack Of The Clones, Revenge Of The Sith, A New Hope, The Empire Strikes Back, Return Of The Jedi, Batman, SpongeBob SquarePants

SELECTED ACTOR SIBLINGS

Rosanna, Patricia, Alexis and David Arquette
William, Alec, Steven and Daniel Baldwin
Warren Beatty and Shirley MacLaine
John and Jim Belushi
David, Keith and Robert Carradine
Macaulay, Kieran and Rory Culkin
John, Ann, Bill, Susie and Joan Cusack
Zooey and Emily Deschanel
Catherine Deneuve and Françoise Dorléac
Joan Fontaine and Olivia de Havilland
Peter and Jane Fonda
Jake and Maggie Gyllenhaal
Ben and Casey Affleck
Matt and Kevin Dillon
Marlon, Keenan Ivory and Damon Wayans
Owen, Luke and Andrew Wilson
Angelica and Danny Huston
Edward and James Fox
Nicholas and Christopher Guest

Stacy and James Keach
The Marx Brothers
Ashley and Mary-Kate Olsen
River, Summer and Joaquin Phoenix
Randy and Dennis Quaid
Emilio Estevez and Charlie Sheen
Meg and Jennifer Tilly
Oliver and James Phelps (a.k.a. the Weasley twins)

THE COMPLETE OSCAR HOSTS

1929:	Douglas Fairbanks, William C de Mille
1930*:	William C de Mille
1930*:	Conrad Nagel
1931:	Lawrence Grant
1932:	Lionel Barrymore
1933:	Conrad Nagel
1934:	Will Rogers
1935:	Irwin S Cobb
1936:	Frank Capra
1937:	George Jessel
1938:	Bob Burns
1939:	None
1940-41:	Bob Hope
1942:	Frank Capra
1943:	Bob Hope
1944:	Jack Benny
1945:	Bob Hope, John Cromwell
1946:	Bob Hope, James Stewart
1947:	Jack Benny
1948:	None
1949:	Robert Montgomery
1950:	Paul Douglas
1951:	Fred Astaire

1952:	Danny Kaye
1953:	Bob Hope, Conrad Nagel
1954:	Donald O'Connor, Fredric March
1955:	Bob Hope, Thelma Ritter
1956:	Jerry Lewis, Claudette Colbert, Joseph L Mankiewicz
1957:	Jerry Lewis, Celeste Holm
1958:	Bob Hope, David Niven, James Stewart, Jack Lemmon, Rosalind Russell
1959:	Bob Hope, David Niven, Tony Randall, Mort Sahl, Laurence Olivier, Jerry Lewis
1960-62:	Bob Hope
1963:	Frank Sinatra
1964:	Jack Lemmon
1965-68:	Bob Hope
1969:	'The Friends Of Oscar' - multiple stars
1970:	'The Friends Of Oscar' - multiple stars
1971:	Multiple stars
1972:	Helen Hayes, Alan King, Sammy Davis Jr, Jack Lemmon
1973:	Carol Burnett, Michael Caine, Charlton Heston, Rock Hudson
1974:	John Huston, Burt Reynolds, David Niven, Diana Ross
1975:	Sammy Davis Jr, Bob Hope, Shirley MacLaine, Frank Sinatra
1976:	Goldie Hawn, Gene Kelly, Walter Matthau, Robert Shaw
1977:	Warren Beatty, Ellen Burstyn, Jane Fonda, Richard Pryor
1978:	Bob Hope
1979-82:	Johnny Carson
1983:	Liza Minnelli, Dudley Moore, Richard Pryor, Walter Matthau
1984:	Johnny Carson
1985:	Jack Lemmon
1986:	Alan Alda, Jane Fonda, Robin Williams
1987:	Chevy Chase, Goldie Hawn, Paul Hogan
1988:	Chevy Chase
1989:	No official host
1990-93:	Billy Crystal
1994:	Whoopi Goldberg

1995:	David Letterman
1996:	Whoopi Goldberg
1997:	Billy Crystal
1998:	Billy Crystal
1999:	Whoopi Goldberg
2000:	Billy Crystal
2001:	Steve Martin
2002:	Whoopi Goldberg
2003:	Steve Martin
2004:	Billy Crystal
2005:	Chris Rock
2006:	Jon Stewart
2007:	Ellen DeGeneres

* Yes, there were two ceremonies in 1930, one covering 1928-29, the other 1929-30

FICTIONAL MOVIE PRIME MINISTERS

Unless indicated, characters are credited only as 'Prime Minister'

Michael Gambon – Ali G Indahouse

Hugh Grant – Love Actually

Peter Porteous – Lifeforce

Faith Brook – North Sea Hijack

George Arliss – The Tunnel

Robbie Coltrane – Stormbreaker

Harry H Corbett – Percy's Progress

Robert Dorning – Carry On Emmanuelle

Edward Fielding – Random Harvest

Colin Gordon – Heavens Above!

Maureen Lipman – Water: The Movie

Tony Doyle – Damage

Peter Cook (Sir Mortimer Chris) – Whoops Apocalypse

Ronald Adam (Arthur Lytton) – Seven Days To Noon

WHAT'S THE FILM IN WHICH THE DRAG QUEEN EATS POO?

Pink Flamingos (1972)

MOVIES THAT SOUND LIKE THEY'RE ABOUT ANIMALS
BUT THEY AREN'T

Film	Theme
Cat Ballou	About a Wild West farm girl
Dog Day Afternoon	About a bank robber
Bird On A Wire	It's a rubbish romcom
They Shoot Horses, Don't They?	About a dance marathon
Bull Durham	About baseball
What's Up, Doc?	Nothing to do with Bugs Bunny
Elephant	About gun violence in schools
Animal House	About drunken fraternities
The Taming Of The Shrew (multiple productions)	It's a Shakespeare play
The Mouse That Roared	A comedy war movie
Bunny Lake Is Missing	About a young girl's kidnapping
The Silence Of The Lambs	About a serial killer
A Cock And Bull Story	About filming an unfilmable book
The Squid And The Whale	About divorce in 1970s New York
Cat On A Hot Tin Roof	About familial dramas
The Duchess And The Dirtwater Fox	There is no fox, wet, dirty or otherwise
Three Blind Mice	About three sisters searching for husbands
The Wisdom Of Crocodiles	About vampires

MOST FOUL-MOUTHED FILMS

Films with the most prolific use of the F-word

Film	Times used
Casino	422
Born On The Fourth Of July	289

The Big Lebowski	281
Pulp Fiction	271
Dead Presidents	247
Boondock Saints	246
GoodFellas	246
Jay And Silent Bob Strike Back	228
Scarface (1983)	218
American History X	205

NB South Park: Bigger, Longer And Uncut features 399 instances of swearing.
However, only 146 of those were 'fuck'.

A ROUND TABLE OF KNIGHTED ACTORS AND ACTRESSES*

Sirs

Richard Attenborough

Michael Caine

Sean Connery

Tom Courtenay

Michael Gambon

Ian Holm

Anthony Hopkins

Bob Hoskins

Derek Jacobi

Ben Kingsley†

Ian McKellen

Roger Moore

Ridley Scott

Anthony Sher

Dames

Julie Andrews

Eileen Atkins

Judi Dench

Helen Mirren

Joan Plowright

Diana Rigg

Maggie Smith

Elizabeth Taylor

* Living ones only

† Is said to insist on being addressed as 'Sir'

SELECTED ACTORS WHO PLAYED BOTH IDENTICAL TWINS

Olivia de Havilland - The Dark Mirror

Hayley Mills - The Parent Trap (1961)

Elvis Presley - Kissin' Cousins

Bette Davis - Stolen Life and Dead Ringer

Gene Wilder and Donald Sutherland - Start The Revolution Without Me

Jim Dale - Hot Lead And Cold Feet

Jeremy Irons - Dead Ringers

Lily Tomlin and Bette Midler - Big Business

Jean-Claude Van Damme - Double Impact

Matthew Modine - Equinox

Lindsay Lohan - The Parent Trap (1998)

Eddie Murphy - Bowfinger

Leonardo DiCaprio - The Man In The Iron Mask

Chris Rock - Bad Company

Nicolas Cage - Adaptation

THE FRONT PAGE

This play, written by Ben Hecht and Charles MacArthur, concerns a reporter, Hildy Johnson, bored of the newspaper game and ready to quit and get married, and his scheming editor, Walter Burns, who wants him to stick around. When a guilty but insane murderer is sentenced to death, Hildy is persuaded to stay and break the story. The play has been adapted into several film adaptations:

The Front Page (1931), His Girl Friday* (1940), The Front Page (1974), Switching Channels* (1988)

* Changed the lead character to a woman and made the story a romantic comedy

THE MANY HUSBANDS OF ZSA ZSA GABOR

Burhan Belge, 1937-41

Conrad Hilton*, 1942-47

George Sanders, 1949-54

Herbert Hutner, 1962-66

Joshua S Cosden Jr, 1966-67

Jack Ryan#, 1975-76

Michael O'Hara, 1976-82

Felipe de Alba†, 1982 (for one day!)

Frédéric, Prinz von Anhalt, 1986-present

* Founder of the Hilton Hotel chain

Designer of the Barbie doll

† Marriage was annulled as Gabor was still married to Michael O'Hara

BETTE DAVIS VS. JOAN CRAWFORD

Two of the biggest stars of the 1930s and 40s, Joan Crawford and Bette Davis became equally well known for their rivalry. Davis was irked by what she saw as Crawford's falseness and dependence on her looks, and the pair would continually belittle each other in the press. The very public feud was seen on screen in What Ever Happened To Baby Jane? (1962), in which the pair played aging stars bitterly enduring each other's company.

Davis on Crawford

'I can only assume that she wasn't a much better wife than a mother' – when asked why she thought Crawford's marriages hadn't lasted.

'I wouldn't piss on her if she was on fire.'

'She has slept with every male star at MGM except Lassie.'

'You hang around that woman long enough and you'll pick up all kinds of useless shit.'

'You should never say bad things about the dead, you should only say good … Joan Crawford is dead – good.'

'There may be a heaven, but if Joan Crawford is there, I'm not going.'

Crawford on Davis

'So I had no great beginnings in legitimate theatre, but what the hell had she become if not a movie star? With all her little gestures with the cigarette, the clipped speech, the big eyes, the deadpan? I was just as much an actress as she was, even though I wasn't trained for the stage.'

'I am aware of how Miss Davis felt about my make-up in Baby Jane, but my reasons for appearing somewhat glamorous were just as valid as hers, with all those layers of rice powder she wore and that ghastly lipstick. But Miss Davis was always partial to covering up her face in motion pictures. She called it "art". Others might call it camouflage – a cover-up for the absence of any real beauty.'

'Bette likes to rant and rave. I just sit and knit. She yelled and I knitted a scarf from Hollywood to Malibu.'

DAFTLY NAMED JERRY BRUCKHEIMER MOVIE HEROES

Axel Foley (Beverly Hills Cop), Cole Trickle (Days Of Thunder), Stanley Goodspeed (The Rock), Cameron Poe (Con Air), Randall 'Memphis' Raines (Gone In 60 Seconds), Rafe McCawley (Pearl Harbor)

ACTORS WHOSE NATIONALITIES WE GET WRONG

Name	Sounds	Actually
Mel Gibson	Australian	American
Sienna Miller	English	American

Kim Cattrall	American	British
Russell Crowe	Australian	New Zealand
Jean Reno	French	Moroccan/Spanish
Audrey Hepburn	American	Belgian
Bob Hope	American	British
Charlize Theron	American	South African

FILM FOLK WHO HAVE APPEARED IN REALITY TV SHOWS*

Jackie Chan (*The Disciple*)

Gary Busey (*I'm With Busey*)

Matt Damon and Ben Affleck (*Project Greenlight*)

Steven Spielberg (*On The Lot*)

Vincent Pastore (*Dancing With The Stars*)

Joel Silver (*Next Action Star*)

Faye Dunaway (*The Starlet*)

Jeff Conaway (*Celebrity Fit Club*)

Ken Russell (*Celebrity Big Brother*)

Shilpa Shetty (*Celebrity Big Brother*)

Brigitte Nielsen (*Celebrity Big Brother*)

Cheech Marin (*Celebrity Duets*)

Cameron Diaz (*Trippin'*)

Jamie Kennedy (*Blowin' Up*)

Ryan O'Neal (*Chasing Farrah*)

Daniel Baldwin (*Celebrity Fit Club*)

Kelly LeBrock (*Celebrity Fit Club*)

Sylvester Stallone (*The Contender*)

Kevin Spacey (*Going Hollywood*)

Forest Whitaker (*American Idol*)

Keira Knightley (*American Idol*)

Hugh Grant (*American Idol*)

Daniel Radcliffe (*American Idol*)

Helena Bonham Carter (*American Idol*)

*Not counting *Punk'd*

TRADITIONAL CINEMA SNACKS FROM AROUND THE WORLD*

Toasted leaf cutter ants - Colombia

Dried reindeer meat - Norway

Poppadoms - Pakistan

Pickled gherkins - Poland

Tortilla chips - Mexico

Beef jerky - Argentina

Falafel - Egypt

Boerewors bites (spicy sausage snacks) - South Africa

Rice cakes - South Korea

Chilli crackers - The Philippines

* Until globalisation meant everyone started eating popcorn and nachos

MOVIES IN WHICH TOM HANKS AND MEG RYAN HAVE STARRED TOGETHER

Joe Versus The Volcano (1990)*

Sleepless In Seattle (1993)

You've Got Mail (1998)

* She played DeDe, Angelica Graynamore and Patricia Graynamore

THE AMICUS ANTHOLOGY HORROR FILMS*

Founded by American producer and screenwriter Milton Subotsky and Max J Rosenberg, Amicus Productions was a company based at Shepperton Studios that became famous for its horror anthologies, which each featured a number of horror shorts linked by a narrator. Individual chapters are listed:

Dr Terror's House Of Horrors (1965)

Based on original stories by writer-producer Milton Subotsky†

'Werewolf', 'Creeping Vine', 'Voodoo', 'Disembodied Hand', 'Vampire'

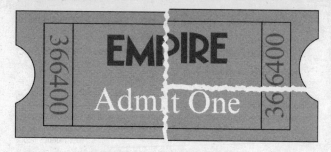

Torture Garden (1967)
Based on stories by Robert Bloch
'Enoch', 'Terror Over Hollywood', 'Mr Steinway', 'The Man Who Collected Poe'

The House That Dripped Blood (1970)
Based on stories by Robert Bloch
'Method For Murder', 'Waxworks', 'Sweets To The Sweet', 'The Cloak'

Asylum (1972)
Based on stories by Robert Bloch
'Frozen Fear', 'The Weird Tailor', 'Lucy Comes To Stay', 'Mannikins Of Horror'

Tales From The Crypt (1972)
Based on EC horror comics
'And All Through The House', 'Reflection Of Death', 'Poetic Justice', 'Wish You Were Here', 'Blind Alleys'

The Vault Of Horror (1973)
Based on EC horror comics
'Midnight Mess', 'A Neat Job', 'This Trick'll Kill You', 'Bargain In Death', 'Drawn And Quartered'

From Beyond The Grave (1974)

Based on stories by R Chetwynd-Hayes

'The Gatecrasher', 'An Act Of Kindness', 'The Elemental', 'The Door'

† At least one of these 'originals' is a straight lift from someone else's work – 'Voodoo' is based without credit on Cornell Woolrich's short story 'Papa Benjamin'. Naughty naughty …

* This one's for Gary Watson

KNOW YOUR COMPOSERS

Composer	Most Famous Score
John Williams	Star Wars
Bernard Herrmann	Psycho
Jerry Goldsmith	The Omen
James Horner	Titanic
Alan Silvestri	Back To The Future
Howard Shore	The Lord Of The Rings
Maurice Jarre	Lawrence Of Arabia
John Barry	Goldfinger
Max Steiner	Gone With The Wind
Miklos Rosza	Ben-Hur
Danny Elfman	Batman
Ennio Morricone	The Good, The Bad and The Ugly
Alex North	A Streetcar Named Desire
Nino Rota	The Godfather
Michael Nyman	The Piano
Elmer Bernstein	The Great Escape
Henry Mancini	Breakfast At Tiffany's
Alfred Newman	Wuthering Heights
Thomas Newman	American Beauty
Randy Newman	Toy Story

SHAKESPEAREAN ROLES PLAYED BY LAURENCE OLIVIER ON SCREEN

Orlando - As You Like It (1936)

Henry V - Henry V (1944)

Hamlet* - Hamlet (1948)

Richard III - Richard III (1955)

Othello - Othello (1965)

Narrator - Romeo & Juliet (1968)

Shylock - The Merchant Of Venice† (1973)

King Lear - King Lear† (1983)

* Won him an Oscar

† On TV

PIRATES OF THE CARIBEEAN BY NUMBERS

1,065,659,812 - the worldwide gross in dollars of Dead Man's Chest

350,000 - the cost in dollars of damage caused by a fire on the soundstage

1,800 - The weight in pounds of the gigantic wheel that Sparrow, Turner and Norrington fight on top of in Dead Man's Chest

225 - The budget in millions of dollars of At World's End

140 - The budget in millions of dollars of The Curse Of The Black Pearl

82 - number of characters who die in Dead Man's Chest

60 - Size in feet of the Black Pearl replica used for the desert scenes in At World's End

26 - The chart position of Curse Of The Black Pearl in the highest grossing films list of all time

5 - Oscar nominations received by the original film

3 - the number of the lead characters named after birds: Jack Sparrow, Elizabeth Swann and Will Turner (a famous ornithologist)

2 - The number of capuchin monkeys who play the monkey 'Jack' (also the number of days Dead Man's Chest took to reach $100 miliion at the US box office)

SAM RAIMI'S CAR

Sam Raimi's 1973 Oldsmobile Delta 88 has made an appearance in every one of his films except for The Quick And The Dead (not many cars in the Old West), although Bruce Campbell has said it was disguised as a covered wagon.

Film	Car's role
Evil Dead	Ash's car
Crimewave	The getaway car
Evil Dead II	Still Ash's car
Darkman	In collision with Liam Neeson, while being driven by Joel and Ethan Coen
Army Of Darkness	Yup, still Ash's car
A Simple Plan	Parked outside the feed store
For Love Of The Game	Its appearance was shot but cut in editing
The Gift	Cate Blanchett's car
Spider-Man	Uncle Ben's car
Spider-Man 2	Parked in Aunt May's driveway

STAGE TO SCREEN

The fickle world of film has little time for stage stars. Despite making roles famous on Broadway, the following were dumped when the move to screen was made:

Character (show)	Stage Star	Film Star
Eliza Doolittle (My Fair Lady)	Julie Andrews	Audrey Hepburn
The Phantom (The Phantom Of The Opera)	Michael Crawford	Gerard Butler
Tevye (Fiddler On The Roof)	Zero Mostel	Topol
Maria (The Sound Of Music)	Mary Martin	Julie Andrews
Rose Hovick (Gypsy)	Ethel Merman	Rosalind Russell
Dolly (Hello, Dolly!)	Carole Channing	Barbra Streisand
Mimi (Rent)	Daphne Rubin-Vega	Rosario Dawson
Valmont (Dangerous Liaisons)	Alan Rickman	John Malkovich
Regina Giddens (The Little Foxes)	Tallulah Bankhead	Bette Davis

Judith Traherne (Dark Victory)	Tallulah Bankhead	Bette Davis
Frankie (Frankie & Johnny)	Kathy Bates	Michelle Pfeiffer
Sally Bowles (Cabaret)	Jill Haworth	Liza Minnelli
Willy Loman (Death Of A Salesman)	Lee J Cobb	Fredric March

SELECTED MOVIE CHARACTERS AND THEIR TIPPLES

The Dude (The Big Lebowski) – White Russian

James Bond – Martini; shaken, not stirred

Fast Eddie (The Hustler) – JTS Brown; no ice, no glass

Count Dracula (Dracula, 1931) – Not wine*

Marty McFly (Back To The Future) – Pepsi Free

Frank Booth (Blue Velvet) – Pabst Blue Ribbon

Forrest Gump – Dr Pepper

Nick and Nora Charles (The Thin Man) – Martinis

Aunt Beru (Star Wars) – Blue milk

Jack Torrence (The Shining) – Bottle of bourbon, a little glass and some ice

Det. Samuel 'George' Francisco (Alien Nation) – Sour milk

Captain Jack Sparrow (Pirates Of The Caribbean) – Rum

Ron Burgundy (Anchorman) – Three fingers of Glenlivet with a little bit of pepper …
and some cheese

* 'I never drink … wine.'

A SELECTION OF MOVIE STARS WHO'VE PLAYED MOVIE STARS

Cate Blanchett played Katharine Hepburn in The Aviator

Kate Beckinsale played Ava Gardner in The Aviator

Jude Law played Errol Flynn in The Aviator

Vincent D'Onofrio played Orson Welles in Ed Wood

Martin Landau played Bela Lugosi in Ed Wood

Liev Schreiber played Orson Welles in RKO 281

Angus Macfadyen played Orson Welles in Cradle Will Rock

Jennifer Love Hewitt played Audrey Hepburn in The Audrey Hepburn Story*

James Cagney played Lon Chaney in Man Of A Thousand Faces

Brian Aherne played David Garrick in The Great Garrick

James Brolin played Clark Gable in Gable And Lombard

Jill Clayburgh played Carole Lombard in Gable And Lombard

Robert Downey Jr played Charlie Chaplin in Chaplin

Eddie Izzard played Charlie Chaplin in The Cat's Meow

John Gavin played Cary Grant in Sophia Loren: Her Own Story*

Rudolf Nureyev played Rudolph Valentino in Valentino

Ray Liotta played Frank Sinatra in The Rat Pack*

Joe Mantegna played Dean Martin in The Rat Pack*

Don Cheadle played Sammy Davis Jr in The Rat Pack*

Judy Davis played Judy Garland in Life With Judy Garland: Me And My Shadows*

* TV movie

GIMMICK RELEASE DATES

Omen 666	06.06.06
Independence Day	Independence Day weekend, 1996*
Freddy Vs. Jason	Friday the 13th, August 2003 (US premiere)
V For Vendetta	5 November 2005†
Terminator 2 Special Edition VHS	29 August 2000º

* Actually the day before Independence Day, but allowed for a longer box-office weekend.

† Scheduled date, which was then bumped to 17 March 2006. The film concerns an imitator of Guy Fawkes, who famously tried to blow up parliament on 5 November.

º The day the world ended in the film, albeit in 1997, not 2000.

NB None of the Star Wars movies was ever released on May the 4th, despite the obvious gimmick potential

THE MOST EXPENSIVE MOVIES EVER MADE

(adjusted for inflation)

1. Cleopatra (1963)	$286,400,000
2. Titanic (1997)	$247,000,000
3. Waterworld (1995)	$229,000,000
4. Terminator 3 (2003)	$216,400,000

5. Spider-Man 2 (2004)	$210,000,000
6. King Kong (2005)	$207,000,000
7. Wild Wild West (1999)	$203,400,000
8. Speed 2: Cruise Control (1997)	$198,800,000
9. The 13th Warrior (1999)	$190,700,000
10. Troy (2004)	$184,300,000

THE MYSTERY MEN AND THEIR POWERS

The characters are taken from the *Flaming Carrot* comic series by Bob Burden. The film, however, omits the titular vegetable and The Strangler (whose talent is strangling people).

Character	Ability
The Shoveller (William H Macy)	Can shovel really well (has own spade)
Mr Furious (Ben Stiller)	Can become very angry and achieve superhuman strength (once)
The Blue Raja (Hank Azaria)	Hurls silverware (no knives, only forks and spoons) and wears no blue whatsoever
The Bowler (Janeane Garofalo)	Wields a flying bowling ball containing the skull (and soul) of her murdered father
The Invisible Boy* (Kel Mitchell)	Can become invisible, but only when no one's watching
The Spleen (Paul Reubens	Can unleash noxious farts at will thanks to a gypsy curse
The Sphinx* (Wes Studi)	Can cut things in half with his mind and displays a flare for cryptic aphorisms
Dr Heller (Tom Waits)	Eccentric scientist with a talent for inventing non-lethal weaponry

* Created for the film

OSCAR-WINNING DEBUTS*

Julie Andrews - Best Actress (Mary Poppins)
Michael Arndt - Best Original Screenplay (Little Miss Sunshine)

Alan Ball - Best Original Screenplay (American Beauty)
Shirley Booth - Best Actress (Come Back, Little Sheba)
James L Brooks - Best Director (Terms Of Endearment)
Mel Brooks - Best Original Screenplay (The Producers)
Kevin Costner - Best Director (Dances With Wolves)
Matt Damon and Ben Affleck - Best Original Screenplay (Good Will Hunting)
Julian Fellowes - Best Original Screenplay (Gosford Park)
Goldie Hawn - Best Supporting Actress (Cactus Flower)
Jennifer Hudson - Best Supporting Actress (Dreamgirls)
Callie Khouri - Best Original Screenplay (Thelma & Louise)
Ben Kingsley - Best Actor (Gandhi)
Marlee Matlin - Best Actress (Children Of A Lesser God)
Mercedes McCambridge - Best Supporting Actress (All The King's Men)
Sam Mendes - Best Director (American Beauty)
Haing S Ngor - Best Supporting Actor (The Killing Fields)
Tatum O'Neal - Best Supporting Actress (Paper Moon)
Anna Paquin - Best Supporting Actress (The Piano)
Katina Paxinou - Best Supporting Actress (For Whom The Bell Tolls)
The Pink Panther - Best Animated Short (The Pink Phink)
Robert Redford - Best Director (Ordinary People)
Harold Russell - Best Supporting Actor (The Best Years Of Our Lives)
Eva Marie Saint - Best Supporting Actress (On The Waterfront)
Gale Sondergaard - Best Supporting Actress (Anthony Adverse)
Barbra Streisand - Best Actress (Funny Girl)
Steve Tesich - Best Original Screenplay (Breaking Away)
Emma Thompson - Best Adapted Screenplay (Sense And Sensibility)
Miyoshi Umeki - Best Supporting Actress (Sayonara)
Jo Van Fleet - Best Supporting Actress (East Of Eden)

* Major categories only

THE SONGS OF 9 SONGS

What they're listening to when not having dull sex in Michael Winterbottom's 2004 film:

'Whatever Happened To My Rock 'N' Roll' – Black Rebel Motorcycle Club
'Love Burns' – Black Rebel Motorcycle Club
'C'mon, C'mon' – The Von Bondies
'Jacqueline' – Franz Ferdinand
'Movin' On Up' – Primal Scream
'The Last High' – The Dandy Warhols
'Slow Life' – Super Furry Animals
'Nadia' – Michael Nyman
'Fallen Angel' – Elbow

ASTEROIDS NAMED AFTER MOVIE FOLK

Astronomers give asteroids numbers and names. Many have been named after cinema's finest, including:

4,238	Audrey (Audrey Hepburn)
4,659	Roddenberry (Gene Roddenberry)
6,377	Cagney (James Cagney)
6,546	Kaye (Danny Kaye)
7,032	Hitchcock (Alfred Hitchcock)
7,037	Davidlean
8,299	Téaleoni
8,353	Megryan
9,341	Gracekelly
9,342	Carygrant
9,617	Grahamchapman
9,618	Johncleese
9,619	Terrygilliam
9,620	Ericidle
9,621	Michaelpalin
9,622	Terryjones
10,221	Kubrick (Stanley Kubrick)
10,378	Ingmarbergman
11,333	Forman (Milos Forman)
11,548	Jerrylewis

13,070	Seanconnery
17,744	Jodiefoster
19,291	Karelzeman
19,578	Kirkdouglas

SELECTED HIGHEST-GROSSING FILMS, BY COUNTRY

Country	Film	Gross
Australia	Titanic	$58 million
Canada	Titanic	$68 million
China	Titanic	$38.6 million
Egypt	Booha	$2.6 million
France	Titanic	$138.9 million
Germany	Titanic	$118 million
India	Sholay	$48 million
Japan	Spirited Away	$250 million
Russia	Turetskii Gambit	$20 million
Singapore	Titanic	$6.46 million
Spain	Titanic	$35.5 million
Thailand	Suriyothai	$12 million
UK	Titanic	$119.2 million
USA	Titanic	$600.8 million

SERVING HEAVEN AND HELL

Actors who have worked for both sides in the eternal struggle:

Max von Sydow

Jesus in The Greatest Story Ever Told, the devil in Needful Things

Christopher Walken

An angel in The Prophecy, a vampire in The Addiction

Gabriel Byrne

A priest in Stigmata, the devil in End Of Days

Robert De Niro
A priest in True Confessions, the devil in Angel Heart

Claude Rains
An angel in Here Comes Mr Jordan, the devil in Angel On My Shoulder

Thomas Kretschmann
The Pope in Have No Fear: The Life Of John Paul II, a vampire in Blade II

Sam Neill
The Pope in From A Far Country, the Antichrist in The Final Conflict

Christian Bale
Jesus in Mary, Mother Of Nazareth, serial killer in American Psycho

Willem Dafoe
Jesus in The Last Temptation Of Christ, a vampire in Shadow Of The Vampire

John Hurt
Jesus in History Of The World: Part 1, the Horned King in The Black Cauldron

Jennifer Jones
A saint in The Song Of Bernadette, a sinner in Duel In The Sun

Chris Sarandon
Jesus in The Day Christ Died, a vampire in Fright Night

Olivia Hussey
The Virgin Mary in Jesus Of Nazareth, Mrs Bates in Psycho IV: The Beginning

George Burns
God in Oh, God!, the devil in Oh, God! You Devil

ACTRESSES WHO WERE BEAUTY QUEENS

Michelle Yeoh - Miss Malaysia 1983

Cybill Shepherd - Miss Teenage Memphis 1966

Zsa Zsa Gabor - Miss Hungary 1936

Michelle Pfeiffer - Miss Orange County 1978

Sophia Loren - Queen Of The Sea, 1948

Sharon Stone - Saegertown High School's Spring Festival Queen, Miss Crawford County 1975

Halle Berry - Miss Teen All American 1985, Miss Ohio 1986

Cloris Leachman - Miss Chicago 1946

Raquel Welch - Miss Fairest Of The Fair 1957, Miss Photogenic, Miss Contour and Miss Maid Of California (all in her teens)

Eva Longoria - Miss Corpus Christi 1998

Aishwarya Rai - Miss World 1994

INAUSPICIOUS MOVIE DEBUTS

Star	Role	Film
Sharon Stone	Pretty girl on train	Stardust Memories
Harrison Ford	Bellhop	Dead Heat On A Merry-Go-Round
Brad Pitt	Waiter	No Man's Land
Jack Lemmon	Plasterer	The Lady Takes A Sailor
Joan Crawford	Twin Double for Norma Shearer	Lady Of The Night
Robert De Niro	Client at the diner	Three Rooms In Manhattan
Dennis Quaid	Bellhop	Crazy Mama
Kevin Spacey	Subway thief	Heartburn
Matthew McConaughey	Guy #2	My Boyfriend's Back
Michael Douglas	Jeep driver	Cast A Giant Shadow
Bruce Willis	Man entering diner	The First Deadly Sin
Pierce Brosnan	Last victim	The Carpathian Eagle
Maggie Smith	Party guest	Child In The House
Jude Law	Young man #1	The Crane

A SELECTION OF ACTORS WHO HAVE LOST/GAINED SIGNIFICANT WEIGHT FOR A ROLE

Actor	Film	Weight change
Vincent D'Onofrio	Full Metal Jacket	+70lb
Robert De Niro	Raging Bull	+60lb
Sylvester Stallone	Cop Land	+40lb
Toni Collette	Muriel's Wedding	+40lb
George Clooney	Syriana	+35lb
Will Smith	Ali	+35lb
Shelley Winters	The Poseidon Adventure	+35lb
Minnie Driver	Circle Of Friends	+30lb
Christopher Reeve	Superman	+30lb
Charlize Theron	Monster	+30lb
Renée Zellweger	Bridget Jones's Diary	+25lb
Johnny Depp	Edward Scissorhands	-25lb
Ewan McGregor	Trainspotting	-30lb
Matt Damon	Courage Under Fire	-40lb
Jerry Lewis	The Day The Clown Cried	-40lb
Russell Crowe	Cinderella Man	-50lb
Tom Hanks	Cast Away	-50lb
Christian Bale	The Machinist	-63lb

A CLUTCH OF MOVIE DRAGONS

Name	Film
Vermithrax Pejorative*	Dragonslayer (1981)
None given	Reign of Fire (2002)
'Dragon'	Shrek (2001)
Draco*	Dragonheart (1996)
Hungarian Horntail*	Harry Potter and the Goblet Of Fire (2005)
Red dragons/gold dragons	Dungeons and Dragons (2000)
Saphira*	Eragon (2006)
Elliot	Pete's Dragon (1977)
Mushu	Mulan (1998)

Maleficent   Sleeping Beauty (1959)
None given   The 7th Voyage of Sinbad (1958)

* Indicates special effects by ILM (Industrial Light and Magic)

A SELECTION OF MOVIE ISLANDS

Isla Nublar – Jurassic Park

Cutthroat Island – Cutthroat Island

Crab Key Island – Dr No

Summerisle – The Wicker Man

Hirta – The Edge Of The World

The Island Of Dr Moreau – The Island Of Dr Moreau

Snape* – Tower Of Evil

Balfe – Doomwatch

Fara – Night Of The Big Heat

Indian Island – And Then There Were None

St Sebastian – I Walked With A Zombie

Skull Island – King Kong

Monster Island – Son Of Godzilla

Dryland – Waterworld

The Island Of Lost Dreams – Spy Kids 2

Todday – Whisky Galore

Fantasy Island – Fantasy Island

Almanzora – Would You Kill A Child?

Blood Island – Mad Doctor Of Blood Island

Terminal Island – Terminal Island

Lilliput and Brobdignag – The 3 Worlds Of Gulliver

Isla Sorna – Jurassic Park: The Lost World

The Island – The Island

Molukk – Zombie Holocaust

Treasure Island – Treasure Island

Matul Island – Zombie

* Not to be confused with the teacher from Harry Potter, because no man is an island

SCARY MOVIE TAGLINES

Scary Movie – No mercy. No shame. No sequel.

Scary Movie 2 – No more mercy. No more shame. No more sequels – honest! – we lied.

Scary Movie 3 – Great trilogies come in threes.

Scary Movie 4 – The fourth and final chapter of the trilogy.

THE SEVEN CHAPTERS OF EVERYTHING YOU ALWAYS WANTED TO KNOW ABOUT SEX*

Do Aphrodisiacs Work?

Court jester battles with queen's chastity belt

What Is Sodomy?

Doctor falls in love with sheep

Do Some Women Have Trouble Reaching Orgasm?

Michelangelo Antonioni homage

Are Transvestites Homosexuals?

Middle-aged man cross-dresses

What Are Sex Perverts?

Sex game-show

Are The Findings Of Doctors And Clinics Who Do Sexual Research Accurate?

A giant breast attacks

What Happens During Ejaculation?

Woody plays a sperm in a space-travel parody

* But Were Afraid To Ask

MOVIES IN WHICH PERENNIAL GOOD GUYS/GIRLS PLAY VILLAINS

James Stewart – After The Thin Man

Tom Hanks – The Ladykillers

Tom Cruise – Collateral, Interview With The Vampire

Harrison Ford – The Conversation, What Lies Beneath

Gregory Peck – The Boys From Brazil

Charlie Chaplin – Monsieur Verdoux

Alan Alda – Whispers In The Dark

Robin Williams – Insomnia, One Hour Photo

Henry Fonda – Once Upon A Time In The West

Denzel Washington – Training Day

Jenny Agutter – Dominique

Christopher Reeve – Deathtrap

Olivia de Havilland – Hush … Hush, Sweet Charlotte

Jamie Lee Curtis – Mother's Boys

Jim Carrey – The Cable Guy

Clint Eastwood – The Beguiled

Michael Keaton – Pacific Heights, Desperate Measures

Richard Dreyfuss – Dillinger

Ben Johnson – The Getaway

Bing Crosby – Dr Cook's Garden

Macaulay Culkin – The Good Son

Mark Lester – Night Hair Child

Timothy Dalton – The Rocketeer

Sean Connery – The Avengers

Pierce Brosnan – The Fourth Protocol

Hugh Grant – An Awfully Big Adventure, Bridget Jones's Diary

THE GANGS IN WEST SIDE STORY
The Jets

Riff (Russ Tamblyn)

Tony (Richard Beymer)

Ice (Tucker Smith)
Action (Tony Mordente)
Baby John (Eliot Feld)
A-Rab (David Winters)
Snowboy (Bert Michaels)
Joyboy (Robert Banas)
Big Deal (Scooter Teague)
Gee-Tar (Tommy Abbott)
Mouthpiece (Harvey Evans)
Tiger (David Bean)

The Sharks

Bernardo (George Chakiris)
Chino (Jose De Vega)
Pepe (Jay Norman)
Indio (Gus Trikonis)
Luis (Robert Thompson)
Juano (Eddie Verso)
Chile (Andre Tayir)
Toro (Nick Covvacevich)

THE COMPLETE ELVIS PRESLEY MOVIES

Hail to the King, baby ...

Film	Character
Love Me Tender (1956)	Clint Reno
Loving You (1957)	Jimmy Tompkins
Jailhouse Rock (1957)	Vince Everett
King Creole (1958)	Danny Fisher
G. I. Blues (1960)	Tulsa McLean
Flaming Star (1960)	Pacer Burton
Wild In The Country (1961)	Glenn Tyler
Blue Hawaii (1961)	Chad Gates
Follow That Dream (1962)	Toby Kwimper

Kid Galahad (1962)	Walter Gulick a.k.a. Kid Galahad
Girls! Girls! Girls! (1962)	Ross Carpenter
It Happened At The World's Fair (1963)	Mike Edwards
Fun In Acapulco (1963)	Mike Windgren
Kissin' Cousins (1964)	Josh Morgan/Jodie Tatum
Viva Las Vegas (1964)	Lucky Jackson
Roustabout (1964)	Charlie Rogers
Girl Happy (1965)	Rusty Wells
Tickle Me (1965)	Lonnie Beale/Panhandle Kid
Harum Scarum (1965)	Johnny Tyronne
Frankie And Johnny (1966)	Johnny
Paradise, Hawaiian Style (1966)	Rick Richards
Spinout (1966)	Mike McCoy
Easy Come, Easy Go (1967)	Lt Ted Jackson
Double Trouble (1967)	Guy Lambert
Clambake (1967)	Scott Heyward/'Tom Wilson'
Stay Away, Joe (1968)	Joe Lightcloud
Speedway (1968)	Steve Grayson
Live A Little, Love A Little (1968)	Greg Nolan
Charro! (1969)	Jess Wade
The Trouble With Girls (1969)	Walter Hale
Change Of Habit (1969)	Dr John Carpenter

FEARFUL FILM TITLES

Movie titles based on phobias:

Acrophobia a.k.a. Don't Look Down	Fear of heights
Arachnophobia	Fear of spiders
Chromophobia	Fear of colour
Claustrophobia	Fear of enclosed spaces
Freewayphobia #1*	Fear of freeways†

* Disney Goofy short

† Not scientifically recognised

SIDEWAYS WINE LIST

Actual wines name-checked in Alexander Payne's 2005 movie.

1992 Byron sparkling Pinot Noir*

Bien Nacido local wine*

Foxen Winery estate Chardonnay*

Foxen Winery Cabernet Franc (fifth year of varietal)

Foxen Winery estate Syrah

Fiddlehead Cellars Sauvignon Blanc*

Whitcraft Winery 2001 Pinot Noir

Sea Smoke Botella

Kistler Sonoma County Chardonnay

Pommard 1st Cru

Andrew Murray M. Syrah*

Hitching Post Highliner (blend of various Pinot Noirs)

Frass Canyon local wine

1961 Saint-Emilion Chateau Cheval Blanc +

* Heartily recommended

+ Serve with a burger and onion rings

SELECTED ACTORS WHO PLAY/SING IN BANDS

Russell Crowe (Singer), 30 Odd Foot Of Grunts*†

Jason Schwartzman (Drummer), Phantom Planet*†

Kevin Bacon (Singer), The Bacon Brothers†

Jack Black (Singer/guitarist), Tenacious D†

Keanu Reeves (Bass guitarist), Dogstar†

Juliette Lewis (Singer), Juliette And The Licks†

Johnny Depp (Guitarist), Tonto's Giant Nuts

Dennis Quaid (Singer), The Sharks

Anthony Michael Hall (Singer/drummer), Hall Of Mirrors†

Mark Wahlberg (Rapper), Marky Mark And The Funky Bunch*†

Jada Pinkett Smith (Singer), Wicked Wisdom†

Jeff Goldblum (Jazz piano), The Mildred Snitzer Orchestra°

Bruce Willis (Singer), Bruce Willis & The Accelerators†

Shane West (Guitarist), Johnny Was
Miguel Ferrer (Drums), Jenerator
David Arquette (Singer), EAR2000
Taryn Manning (Singer), Boomkat
Gary Busey (Drummer), Carp*
Jared Leto (Singer), 30 Seconds To Mars
Woody Harrelson (Singer), Manly Moondog And The Three Kool Hats

* Has since left

† Have released material commercially

º With Peter Weller (RoboCop) on horns!

POLITICAL GROUPS IN THE LIFE OF BRIAN

The Judean People's Front
The People's Front Of Judea*
The Judean Popular People's Front#
Campaign For Free Galilee

* The group Brian joins

\# Only has one member

THE SEQUENCES OF FANTASIA

Music	Scene
Toccata And Fugue In D Minor (Bach)	Excitable squiggles
Nutcracker Suite (Tchaikovsky)	Fairies, fish and Chinese mushrooms
The Sorcerer's Apprentice (Dukas)	Mickey and the brooms
The Rite Of Spring (Stravinsky)	Dino-death
Symphony No. 6 (Beethoven)	Randy centaurs
Dance Of The Hours (Ponchielli)	Ballerina hippos
Night On Bald Mountain (Mussorgsky)	Scary winged demon
Ave Maria (Schubert)	Morning after scary winged demon
Symphony No. 5 (Beethoven)	Butterflies*
Pines Of Rome (Respighi)	Flying whales*
Rhapsody In Blue (Gershwin)	Al Hirschfeld New York*
Piano Concerto No. 2: Allegro (Shostakovich)	The Steadfast Tin Soldier*

The Carnival Of The Animals (Saint-Saens)   Yo-yoing flamingo*
Pomp And Circumstance Marches (Elgar)   Donald Duck's Ark*
The Firebird (Stravinsky)   The Firebird*

* From Fantasia 2000

M-I-C-K-E-Y M-O-U-S-E

Stars who got their big break on the 1990s American TV show The Mickey Mouse Club.

Britney Spears (Crossroads), Keri Russell (Mission: Impossible 3), Justin Timberlake (Alpha Dog), Ryan Gosling (The Notebook)

SELECTED HOLLYWOOD ACTRESSES' VITAL STATISTICS

Angelina Jolie	36C-27-36
Cameron Diaz	34B-23-36
Sandra Bullock	33B-24-34
Marilyn Monroe	37C-24-35
Jane Russell	38D-25-36
Jessica Alba	34-24-34
Rita Hayworth	36.5C-24-36
Julia Roberts	34B-23-34
Jane Fonda	34C-25-34
Jennifer Connelly	34D-22-34
Halle Berry	36C-22-37
Pamela Anderson	34C-24-34
Carmen Electra	36C-23-35
Monica Bellucci	35C-24-35
Jennifer Aniston	34C-23-35
Nicole Kidman	34B-23-36
Salma Hayek	36C-25-37

AGES OF WOODY ALLEN COMPARED TO LOVE INTEREST

Film	Allen	Co-Star	Difference
Everything You Always Wanted To Know About Sex (But Were Afraid to Ask)	36	29 (Lynn Redgrave)	-7
Sleeper	37	27 (Diane Keaton*)	-10
Manhattan	43	18 (Mariel Hemingway)	-25
Stardust Memories	44	35 (Charlotte Rampling)	-9
A Midsummer Night's Sex Comedy	46	37 (Mia Farrow†)	-9
Hannah And Her Sisters	50	32 (Barbara Hershey)	-18
Husbands And Wives	56	19 (Juliette Lewis)	-37
Mighty Aphrodite	59	29 (Helena Bonham Carter)	-30
Everyone Says I Love You	60	31 (Julia Roberts)	-29
Deconstructing Harry	61	36 (Kirstie Alley)	-25
Small Time Crooks	64	41 (Tracey Ullman)	-23
The Curse Of The Jade Scorpion	65	38 (Helen Hunt)	-27
Hollywood Ending	66	36 (Téa Leoni)	-30

* Also love interest in Love And Death, Annie Hall and Manhattan Murder Mystery

† Also love interest in Broadway Danny Rose, New York Stories, Crimes And Misdemeanours, Shadows And Fog and Husbands And Wives

ACTORS WHO HAVE WON AN OSCAR AND A RAZZIE*

Actor	Oscar	Razzie
Halle Berry	Monster's Ball	Catwoman
Faye Dunaway	Network	Mommie Dearest, The Temp
Liza Minnelli	Cabaret	Arthur 2: On The Rocks
Roberto Benigni	Life Is Beautiful	Pinocchio
Laurence Olivier	Hamlet (1948)	Inchon, The Jazz Singer (1980)
Marlon Brando	The Godfather, On The Waterfront	The Island Of Dr Moreau
Charlton Heston	Ben-Hur	Cats & Dogs

* For acting performances only

FILM-SET LINGO

ADR (Automatic Dialogue Replacement): The process of re-recording lines after shooting to replace poor-quality sound or change delivery. Also occasionally used to re-dub one actor's voice with another. Otherwise known as 'looping'.

Blocking: The process of running through a scene to decide where the actors will move and where lighting and cameras will be placed.

Boom: The large fuzzy microphone on the end of a pole that looks a bit like an old dog.

Call sheet: A list, usually created by the first assistant director, of actors who will be required on set for each day's shooting.

Clean speech: A take in which there were no errors with dialogue recording.

Craft service: Catering. Often serve apple crumble and chips with everything.

Dailies: The prints of footage shot the previous day, often viewed by the director and lead actors at the end of each day to monitor progress. Also known as 'rushes'.

Dope sheet: A list of scenes that have already been filmed.

Honeywagons: Portaloos to you and me.

Magic hour: The short time just before sunset when light levels change dramatically and very quickly and enable shots that will look 'very Terrence Malick'.

Overcranking: The act of speeding up the frame rate on a camera, so that more frames are captured. Enables the footage to be played in slow motion. Undercranking has the opposite effect.

Pick-up: Footage shot after shooting wraps, usually minor.

Squib: A small explosive device used to simulate a bullet hit or very small explosion.

Unit publicist: The poor soul who sets up press visits to a film set and handles all press matters relating to the film during shooting.

Rhubarb: Background conversation made by extras. So-called as extras were often asked to mutter the word to produce the desired effect. Also known as 'walla'.

Winnebago: The giant trailers that stars occupy when not required on set.

Wrap: End of shooting.

POORLY TRANSLATED MOVIE TITLES

Sliding Doors	Two-Faced Lovers (China)
Thunderball	007 Against Atomic Blackmail (Brazil)
G. I. Jane	Satan Female Soldier (China)
Free Willy	A Very Powerful Whale Runs To Heaven (China)
Austin Powers: The Spy Who Shagged Me	The Spy Who Treated Me Nicely (Singapore)
Risky Business	Just Send Him To University Unqualified (China)
Babe	I'm Not Stupid, I Have Something To Say (China)
Never Say Never Again	Don't Say No Twice (Finland)
Them!	Spiders!*(Sweden)
Annie Hall	The Urban Neurotic (Germany)
Boogie Nights	His Powerful Device Makes Him Famous (China)
The Horse Whisperer	The Man Who Murmured Into The Ears Of Horses (France)
Gone With The Wind	The Confused World Of A Beautiful Woman (China)
On Her Majesty's Secret Service	007 Seized The Snow Mountain Castle (China)
Groundhog Day	Monday The Whole Week (Sweden)
Vertigo	From Out Of The Kingdom of the Dead (Germany)
Airplane	The Unbelievable Trip In A Wacky Plane (Germany)
Airplane II	The Unbelievable Trip In A Wacky Spaceship (Germany)
Good Will Hunting	Bright Sun, Just Like Me (China)

* It's about giant ants

NORMAN WISDOM FILMS IN WHICH HE PLAYS A CHARACTER CALLED NORMAN

Trouble In Store (1953), One Good Turn (1954), Man Of The Moment (1955), Up In The World (1956), Just My Luck (1957), The Square Peg (1958), Follow A Star (1959), The Bulldog Breed (1960), On The Beat (1962), A Stitch In Time (1963), The Early Bird (1965), Press For Time (1966)

STEVEN SPIELBERG FEATURES NOT SCORED BY JOHN WILLIAMS

Duel (1971) - Billy Goldenberg
Twilight Zone: The Movie (1983) - Jerry Goldsmith
The Color Purple (1985) - Quincy Jones

ACTORS' PRODUCTION COMPANIES

Accomplice Films (Hilary Swank and Chad Lowe)
Big Town Productions (Bill Pullman)
Black And White Productions (Jack Black and Mike White)
Blaspheme Films (Christina Ricci)
Blueprint Films (Nicole Kidman)
Cheyenne Enterprises (Bruce Willis, Danny Glover, Whoopi Goldberg)
Coquette Productions (Courtney Cox Arquette and David Arquette)
Cosmic Entertainment (Kate Hudson)
Denver & Delilah Films* (Charlize Theron)
Dualstar Entertainment Group (Mary-Kate and Ashley Olsen)
Egg Pictures (Jodie Foster)
El Dorado Pictures (Alec Baldwin)
First Cold Press Productions (Stanley Tucci)
Fleece Productions (Jason Patric)
Flower Films (Drew Barrymore)
Fort Hill Productions (Matt LeBlanc)
Fortis Films (Sandra Bullock)
Furthur Films (Michael Douglas)
=Happy Madison Productions (Adam Sandler)
Huntaway Films (Sam Neill)
Icon Productions (Mel Gibson)
Infinitum Nihil (Johnny Depp)
Jersey Films (Danny DeVito)
J. K. Livin Productions (Matthew McConaughey)
Maguire Entertainment (Tobey Maguire)

Malpaso Productions (Clint Eastwood)

Moving Pictures (Demi Moore)

New Crime Productions (John Cusack)

Nine Stories (Jake Gyllenhaal)

Pit Bull Productions (Jim Carrey)

Plan B (Brad Pitt, and formerly Jennifer Aniston)

Playtone (Tom Hanks)

Prufrock Productions (Meg Ryan)

Red Hour Films (Ben Stiller)

Red Om Films (Julia Roberts)

Saturn Films (Nicolas Cage)

Section Eight (George Clooney, with Steven Soderbergh)

Seed Productions (Hugh Jackman)

Simian Films (Hugh Grant and Elizabeth Hurley)

Tig Productions (Kevin Costner)

Tribeca Films (Robert De Niro)

Two Drivers (Minnie Driver, with her sister, Kate)

Type A (Reese Witherspoon)

Vandalia Films (Jennifer Garner)

Ventanarosa Productions (Salma Hayek)

* Named after her cocker spaniels

THE GOONIES CHARACTERS' NICKNAMES AND REAL NAMES

Chunk	Lawrence Cohen
Mouth	Clark Devereaux
Data	Richard Wang†
Sloth	Lotney Fratelli

† If you were Dick Wang you'd change your name too

STEVE OEDEKERK'S THUMB

Steve Oedekerk, writer of Bruce Almighty among others, has produced a number of spoof films featuring decorated thumbs in place of actors. The titles in the thumb series are:

Thumb Wars: The Phantom Cuticle* (1999)

The Godthumb (2001)

Bat Thumb (2001)

Frankenthumb (2002)

The Blair Thumb (2002)

Thumbtanic (2002)

* Featuring Oobedoob Benubi

THE NERDS OF REVENGE OF THE NERDS (1984)

Nerds	Actor
Louis Skolnick	Robert Carradine
Gilbert Lowell	Anthony Edwards
Arnold Poindexter	Timothy Busfield
Harold Wormser	Andrew Cass
Dudley 'Booger' Dawson	Curtis Armstrong
Lamar Latrell	Larry B Scott
Toshiro Takashi	Brian Tochi

THE COMPLETE ED WOOD

Widely considered the worst director of all time and subject of a 1994 biopic directed by Tim Burton.

Necromania: A Tale Of Weird Love* (1971)

Excited (1970)

Take It Out In Trade (1970)

The Sinister Urge (1961)

Plan 9 From Outer Space (1959)

Night Of The Ghouls (1959)

Final Curtain (1957)

The Night The Banshee Cried (1957)

Bride Of The Monster (1955)

Jail Bait (1954)

Boots (1953)

Crossroad Avenger: The Adventures Of The Tucson Kid† (1953)

Glen Or Glenda˜ (1953)

Trick Shooting With Kenne Duncan (1953)

The Sun Was Setting† (1951)

* As Don Miller

† TV short

˜ Features Wood cross-dressing

GRANGE HILL GRADUATES

People who started their careers on the perennial children's soap opera.

Graduate (role)	Biggest success
Anthony Minghella (script supervisor)	The English Patient (director)
Desmond Askew (Richard)	Go (as Simon Baines)
Ashley Walters (Andy Phillips)	Bullet Boy (as Ricky)
Todd Carty ('Tucker' Jenkins)	Krull (as Oswyn)
Amma Asante (Cheryl Webb)	A Way Of Life (director)
Kevin Bishop (Sam Spalding)	Muppet Treasure Island (as Jim Hawkins)
Danny Cunningham (Liam Brady)	24 Hour Party People (as Shaun Ryder)
Alex Kingston (Jill Harcourt)	Croupier (as Jani de Villiers)
Michael Sheard (Mr Bronson)	The Empire Strikes Back (as Admiral Ozzel)

CAST MEMBERS OF HOLLYOAKS WHO WENT ON TO BECOME FILM CRITICS

Shebah Ronay (Natasha Anderson) who became co-critic, with Paul Ross, at the *News Of The World*.

SHOT MISCELLANY

Aerial shot - An exterior shot filmed from a bird's-eye view.

Arc shot - A shot in which the subject is circled by the camera.

Boom shot - A shot using a boom (long counterbalanced pole upon which the camera is mounted) that can film from many different angles or levels in one continuous shot. Most of Alfred Hitchcock's Rope was shot this way.

Bridging shot - A shot used to denote change of time or place between scenes, e.g. the move across the map in Raiders Of The Lost Ark.

Close-up shot - Only the subject's face is in frame.

Cowboy shot - A shot framed from mid-thigh up. The name comes from its common usage in Westerns.

Crane shot - Like a boom shot, but using an extendable mechanical arm to reach greater heights.

Crowd shot - Lots and lots of people bustle.

Cutaway shot - A brief shot that interrupts continuous action, often showing a character's reaction. See also 'reaction shot'.

Deep-focus shot - Foreground, middle-ground and background all in sharp focus.

Discovery shot - A moving shot in which a moving camera 'discovers' a previously unnoticed object or person.

Establishing shot - Often the opening shot of a scene, which shows the location at its fullest to give the viewer a sense of where and when the action is taking place.

Handheld shot - The camera is held by the cameraman in motion to create the kind of jerky action much loved by Steven Soderbergh.

Head-on shot - The action moves directly towards the camera.

High-angle shot - The camera is positioned above the scene, pointing down at the action. Often used by Orson Welles.

Insert shot - A brief shot inserted into a larger scene that offers a closer view of a key detail, such as a hand hovering above a gun in a shoot-out.

Library shot - Previously shot footage of a location, wild animal etc. taken from a film library, in order to save time/money. Also known as a 'stock shot'.

Locked-down shot - The camera is fixed in one position while something dramatic happens off-screen, often a murder.

Long shot - An object or character filmed from a distance.

Low-angle shot - The subject is filmed from below to appear larger.

Master shot - A continuous take of an entire scene providing a basic view of the action, which is then intercut with more interesting shots.

Matte shot - A shot that incorporates foreground action with a painted background. In older films, the camera would shoot through a sheet of glass upon which painted scenery was carefully positioned to appear to be an extension of the set. Nowadays it mostly involves actors being shot on blue/greenscreen, which is then replaced with CGI.

Medium shot - Standard framing of a subject that shows less than their whole body but more than just their face.

Over-the-shoulder shot - The camera is positioned behind one subject's shoulder, showing them interacting with another.

Panning shot - The camera moves continuously right or left. Abbreviation of 'panorama'.

POV shot - Filmed from the subject's point-of-view, so we see what they see.

Reaction shot - A quick shot that shows the effect an action has had on a character or characters.

Reverse-angle shot - The subject is filmed from the opposite angle to that in which they're facing to give a different perspective.

Static shot - The camera does not move.

Steadicam shot - Motion is filmed using a hydraulically balanced camera apparatus that allows for smooth action, rather than the wobbly images of handheld.

Tracking shot - The camera moves alongside the subject. Also known as a 'following shot'.

Two-shot - A medium shot that contains two people.

Wide-angle shot - A larger lens is used to give a wider field of view and give the image greater depth.

THE REAL NAMES OF X-MEN CHARACTERS
The X-Men

Professor X	Professor Charles Xavier
Wolverine	Logan a.k.a. James Howlett

Storm	Ororo Monroe
Rogue	Marie D'Ancanto
Angel~	Warren Worthington III
Pyro†	John Allerdyce
Cyclops	Scott Summers
Beast~	Dr Hank McCoy
Shadowcat~	Kitty Pryde
Colossus†	Peter Rasputin
Jubilee	Jubilation Lee
Nightcrawler†	Kurt Wagner
Iceman†	Bobby Drake
Multiple Man	Jamie Madrox
Siryn	Theresa Rourke

The Villains

Magneto	Eric Lensherr
Phoenix~	Dr Jean Grey
Mystique	Raven Darkholme
Juggernaut~	Cain Marko
Lady Deathstrike†	Yuriko Oyama
Sabretooth	Victor Creed
Toad	Mortimer Toynbee
Psylocke	Elizabeth 'Betsy' Braddock

† First appeared in X-Men 2

~ First appeared in X-Men 3

ACTRESSES WHO UNSUCCESSFULLY AUDITIONED TO PLAY SCARLETT O'HARA IN GONE WITH THE WIND

Jean Arthur, Lucille Ball, Tallulah Bankhead, Bette Davis, Claudette Colbert, Joan Crawford, Paulette Goddard, Susan Hayward, Katharine Hepburn, Olivia de Havilland, Carole Lombard, Norma Shearer, Barbara Stanwyck, Margaret Sullavan

THE BUG'S LIFE POSSE

From Pixar's insect-centric take on The Magnificent Seven.

Flik (Dave Foley)	Ant
Slim (David Hyde Pierce)	Stick insect
Heimlich (Joe Ranft*)	Caterpillar/butterfly
Gypsy (Madeline Kahn)	Butterfly
Dim (Brad Garrett)	Elephant beetle
Rosie (Bonnie Hunt)	Spider
Manny (Jonathan Harris)	Praying mantis
Tuck/Roll (Mike McShane)	Pill bugs
Francis (Denis Leary)	Ladybird

* Co-wrote the film

THE LONGEST FILMS EVER SHOWN

1. The Cure For Insomnia (1987), USA	87 hrs
2. The Longest Most Meaningless Movie In The World (1970), UK	48 hrs
3. The Burning Of The Red Lotus Temple (1931), China	27 hrs
4. Heimat 2 (1992), Germany	25 hrs 32 mins
5. ****† (1967), USA	25 hrs
6. Heimat (1984), Germany	15 hrs 40 mins
7. Berlin Alexanderplatz (1980), Germany/Italy	15 hrs 21 mins
8. The Journey (1987), Sweden	14 hrs 33 mins
9. How Yukong Moved The Mountains (1976), France	12 hrs 43 mins
10. Out 1: Noli Me Tangere (1971), France	12 hrs 9 mins

† This is not an official Empire star mark

MOVIE STARS' FIRST JOBS

Jim Carrey	Janitor
Sean Connery	Coffin polisher
Kate Winslet	Deli assistant
Steven Spielberg	Fruit-tree whitewasher
Bette Midler	Worker at a pineapple processing plant
Danne DeVito	Hairdresser

Harrison Ford	Carpenter
Jerry O'Connell	Landscaper
Jennifer Jason Leigh	Gift wrapper in a department store
Rob Schneider	Dishwasher at an ice-cream parlour
Lucy Liu	Aerobics instructor
Keanu Reeves	Skate sharpener at the local ice rink
Kevin Spacey	Stand-up comedian
Whoopi Goldberg	Make-up artist at a funeral parlour
Sylvester Stallone	Lion-cage cleaner
Warren Beatty	Rat-catcher
Michael Douglas	Gas-pump attendant
Mickey Rourke	Cinema usher*

* Fired for brawling with his workmates

THE TERMINATORS

T-800 (Arnold Schwarzenegger) - Terminator
T-1000 (Robert Patrick) - Terminator 2: Judgment Day
T-X (Kristanna Loken) - Terminator 3: Rise Of The Machines

A CLOWDER† OF MOVIE CATS

Mr Bigglesworth	The Austin Powers trilogy
Cat	Breakfast At Tiffany's
The Cat In The Hat	The Cat In The Hat
Garfield	Garfield
O'Malley*, Duchess, Toulouse, Berlioz and Marie	The Aristocats
Cheshire Cat	Alice In Wonderland
Crookshanks and Mrs Norris	The Harry Potter series
Fritz	Fritz The Cat
Gideon	Pinocchio
Shere Khan and Bagheera	The Jungle Book
Jones	Alien
Snowbell	Stuart Little
Mr Tinkles	Cats And Dogs

Rajah	Aladdin
Patrina	A Tiger Walks
Baby	Bringing Up Baby
King Leonidas	Bedknobs And Broomsticks
Elsa	Born Free

† Yes, that's the name for a group of cats

* Full name Abraham de Lacy Giuseppe Casey Thomas O'Malley

THE ALIASES OF THE GREAT ESCAPEES

Hilts (Steve McQueen)	The Cooler King
Lt Hendley (James Garner)	The Scrounger
Lt Velinski (Charles Bronson)	The Tunnel King
Captain Ramsay (James Donald)	The SBO
Roger Bartlett (Richard Attenborough)	Big X
Flying Officer Louis Sedgwick (James Coburn)	The Manufacturer
Lt Cmdr Eric Ashley-Pitt (David McCallum)	Dispersal
Flight Lt William Dickes (John Leyton)	The Tunneler
Flying Officer Archibald Ives (Angus Lennie)	The Mole
Flight Lt Denys Cavendish (Nigel Stock)	The Surveyor
Flight Lt Sandy MacDonald (Gordon Jackson)	Intelligence

GUY RITCHIE'S MOCKNEY RHYMING SLANG*

Slang	Translation
Aristotle	Bottle
Battle cruiser	Boozer
Bird's nest	Chest
Chevy Chase	Face
Bubble and squeak	Greek
Custard (custard and jelly)	Telly
Jam roll	Arsehole
Iron (rusted)	Busted
Nuclear sub	Pub
Ping pong	Strong

Tiddly(wink)	Drink
Roger Mellie	Smelly

* From Lock, Stock And Two Smoking Barrels

THE RED CURTAIN TRILOGY

A trilogy of films directed by Baz Luhrmann that all ascribe to a deliberately artificial, grandly theatrical mood and aesthetic inspired by highly technical Hollywood movies of the 1930s and 40s (e.g. Singin' In The Rain, Citizen Kane). Though unrelated by character or plot, each film tells a classical story, using a thematic device to highlight the emotional elements. The trilogy, their stories and their thematic devices are:

Film	Story	Device
Strictly Ballroom	David and Goliath/ The ugly duckling	Dancing
Romeo + Juliet	Young love vs. society	Shakespearean dialogue in the modern world
Moulin Rouge	Orpheus in the underworld	Musical

ACTORS TURNED POLITICIANS

Clint Eastwood	Mayor of Carmel, California (1986)
Ronald Reagan	US President (1981-89)
Arnold Schwarzenegger	Governor of California (2003-present)
Jesse Ventura	Governor of Minnesota (1999-2003)
Glenda Jackson	Labour MP for Hampstead & Highgate (1992-present)
Amitabh Bachchan	Member of Congress for Ahallabad (1984-87)

FAMOUS LAST WORDS

'Die? I should say not, dear fellow. No Barrymore would allow such a conventional thing to happen to him.'
- **John Barrymore**, died 29 May 1942
'I should never have switched from Scotch to Martinis.'

- Humphrey Bogart, died 14 January 1957

'Damn it, don't you dare ask God to help me!'

- Joan Crawford (to her praying housekeeper), died 10 May 1977

'I've never felt better.'

- Douglas Fairbanks, died 12 December 1939

'I've had a hell of a lot of fun and I've enjoyed every minute.'

- Errol Flynn, died 14 October 1959

'Nothing matters. Nothing matters.'

- Louis B Mayer, died 29 October 1957

'Don't worry, chief, it will be all right.'

- Rudolph Valentino, died 23 August 1926

'I am leaving you with your worries. Good luck.'

- George Sanders, died 25 April 1972

'Channel Five's all shit, isn't it?'

- Adam Faith, died 8 March 2003

'That was a great game of golf, fellas.'

- Bing Crosby, died 14 October 1977

'Goodnight, my darlings. I'll see you tomorrow.'

- Noel Coward, died 26 March 1973

'Die, my dear? Why, that's the last thing I'll do.'

- Groucho Marx, died 19 August 1977

'My fun days are over.'

- James Dean, died 30 September 1955

'I hope I haven't bored you.'

- Elvis Presley, died 16 August 1977

THE FATES OF THE CHILDREN IN WILLY WONKA'S CHOCOLATE FACTORY*

Augustus Gloop	Sucked into the chocolate river
Violet Beauregard	Turns into a human blueberry
Veruca Salt	Rejected as a bad egg after trying to steal a golden goose*/
	Pushed down a rubbish chute by squirrels†

| Mike Teavee | Shrunk after being transported via TV waves |
| Charlie Bucket | Wins the factory |

* In Mel Stuart's Willy Wonka & The Chocolate Factory (1971)

† In Tim Burton's Charlie And The Chocolate Factory (2005)

WRITERS WHO WON OSCARS FOR ADAPTING THEIR OWN BOOKS

James Goldman (The Lion In Winter, 1968), Mario Puzo (The Godfather and The Godfather Part II, 1972 and 1974), William Peter Blatty (The Exorcist, 1974), Ernest Thompson (On Golden Pond, 1982), Peter Shaffer (Amadeus, 1984), Alfred Uhry (Driving Miss Daisy, 1990), Michael Blake (Dances With Wolves, 1991), Billy Bob Thornton (Sling Blade, 1996), John Irving (The Cider House Rules, 1999)

THE WORDS THAT STUMPED THE SPELLING BEE CONTESTANTS IN SPELLBOUND

Ted	Distractible
Ashley	Ecclesiastical
Harry	Banns
Neil	Hellebore
Angela	Heleoplankton
Emily	Clavecin
April	Terrene
Nupur	Won with logorrhea*

* US spelling

SELECTED MOVIE ACTORS WHO STARTED ON SOAP OPERAS

Actor (character)	Soap
Rose Byrne (Belinda O'Connor)	Echo Point
Diego Luna (Luis)	El Abuelo Y Yo
Jude Law (Nathan Thompson)	Families
Hayden Christensen (Skip McDeere)	Family Passions
Melissa George (Angel Brooks/Parish)	Home And Way

Simon Baker (James Healey)	Home And Away
Isla Fisher (Shannon Reed)	Home And Away
Julian McMahon (Ben Lucini)	Home And Away
Naomi Watts (Julie Gibson)	Home And Away
Russell Crowe (Kenny Larkin)	Neighbours
Guy Pearce ('Motorbike' Mike Young)	Neighbours
Radha Mitchell (Catherine O'Brien)	Neighbours
Jesse Spencer (Billy Kennedy)	Neighbours
Holly Valance (Felicity 'Flick' Scully)	Neighbours
Brandon Routh (Seth Anderson)	One Life To Live
Heath Ledger (Snowy Bowles)	Sweat
Salma Hayek (Teresa)	Teresa
Gael García Bernal (Peluche)	Teresa

TERMITE TERRACE

Termite Terrace was the name given to the Hollywood studio where the Looney Tunes animated shorts were created between 1935 and 1937. The Looney Tunes cartoons were originally produced by an independent company, Leon Schlesinger Productions. Schlesinger's company employed such animation gods as Tex Avery, Friz Freleng, Bob Clampett and Chuck Jones. The company was bought by Warner Bros in 1944 and renamed Warner Bros Cartoons, Inc. Though Termite Terrace was eventually abandoned and torn down, the name stuck as a nickname for the Warner Bros animation facility as a whole.

NUMBER OF SPEAKING ROLES IN THE ENTIRE LORD OF THE RINGS TRILOGY

114

CARRY ON ... ALTERNATIVE TITLES
Carry On Up The Jungle
or The African Queen
or Stop Beating Around The Bush
or Show Me Your Waterhole And I'll Show You Mine

Carry On Abroad
or What A Package
or It's All In
or Swiss Hols In The Snow

Carry On Again Doctor
or Where There's A Pill There's A Way
or The Bowels Are Ringing
or If You Say It's Your Thermometer I'll Have To Believe You, But It's A Funny Place
To Put It

Carry On Doctor
or Nurse Carries On Again
or Death Of A Daffodil
or Life Is A Four Lettered Word

Carry On At Your Convenience
or Down The Spout
or Ladies Please Be Seated
or Up The Workers
or Labour Relations Are The People Who Come To See You When You're Having A Baby

Carry On Camping
or Let Sleeping Bags Lie

Carry On Henry
or Mind My Chopper

Carry On Matron
or From Here To Maternity
or Familiarity Breed
or Womb At The Top
or The Pregger's Opera

Carry On Up The Khyber
or The British Position In India

THE TRAVELLING GNOME

In Jean-Pierre Jeunet's Amélie, the title character sends her father's garden gnome off on a trip around the world with an air stewardess, from which he sends Polaroids of his exploits. The places he visits are: Moscow, New York (Statue Of Liberty and the Empire State Building), Rome, Angkor Wat, Monument Valley and Istanbul.

THE SEXIEST MEN ALIVE

Every year since 1985, *People* magazine has crowned one of Hollywood's possessors of the XY chromosome its Sexiest Man Alive. The complete list of sexy men and their ages at time of being deemed especially shaggable can be seen below.

1985	Mel Gibson (29)
1986	Mark Harmon (34)
1987	Harry Hamlin (35)
1988	John F Kennedy Jr* #(27)
1989	Sean Connery (59)
1990	Tom Cruise (28)
1991	Patrick Swayze (39)
1992	Nick Nolte (51)
1993	Richard Gere (44) and Cindy Crawford† (27)
1994	No award given – men just weren't sexy that year
1995	Brad Pitt (31)
1996	Denzel Washington (41)
1997	George Clooney (36)
1998	Harrison Ford (56)
1999	Richard Gere (50)
2000	Brad Pitt (36)
2001	Pierce Brosnan (48)
2002	Ben Affleck (30)

2003	Johnny Depp (40)
2004	Jude Law (32)
2005	Matthew McConaughey (36)
2006	George Clooney (45)

* The only non-actor to ever win

No longer alive

† Eagle-eyed readers will notice that Cindy Crawford is not a man - 1993 was the only year that the magazine gave a Sexiest Couple award

THE COMPLETE INDIANA JONES

Actors who have portrayed the world's favourite archaeologist:

Corey Carrier* (aged 9-11)

River Phoenix (aged 13)

Sean Patrick Flanery* (aged 16-20)

Harrison Ford (aged 36-39 and aged 50†)

George Hall* (aged 93)

* Appeared in the TV series *The Young Indiana Jones Chronicles* (1992-93) only

† In a cameo in *The Young Indiana Jones Chronicles*

ROMAN À CLEF MOVIES

From the French for 'novel with a key', *roman à clef* movies purport to be about a fictional person, but are actually thinly veiled biographies of historical characters.

Film	Says it's about	Is actually about
The Great Dictator	Adenoid Hinkel	Adolf Hitler
Scarface (1932/1983)	Tony Camonte/Tony Montana	Al Capone
Citizen Kane	Charles Foster Kane	William Randolph Hearst (newspaper magnate)
All The King's Men	Willie Stark	Governor Huey Long (Louisiana Governor)
Primary Colors	Governor Jack Stanton	Bill Clinton
The Barefoot Contessa	Maria Vargas	Rita Hayworth*

The Last Tycoon.	Monroe Stahr	Irving G Thalberg (Hollywood tycoon)
After The Fall	Maggie and Quentin	Arthur Miller and Marilyn Monroe
North Dallas Forty	North Dallas Bulls	The Dallas Cowboys c. 1970s
Blessed Event	Alvin Roberts	Walter Winchell (New York journalist)
Sweet Smell Of Success	JJ Hunsecker	Walter Winchell again
The Greek Tycoon	Liz Cassidy	Jackie Kennedy Onassis
The Harder They Fall	Eddie Willis	Harold Conrad (boxing promoter)
White Hunter Black Heart	John Wilson	John Huston and the making of The African Queen
Young Man With A Horn	Rick Martin	Bix Beiderbecke (trumpeter)
The Manchurian Candidate	Bennett Marco	Joe McCarthy (or at least his hearings)
Winter Kills	The Kegans	The Kennedys

* Also features a producer based on Howard Hughes

A YEAR IN THE MOVIES

The January Man

15 Février 1839

March Of The Penguins

Pieces Of April

Seven Days In May

Henry & June

Born On The Fourth Of July

The Whales Of August

One Day In September

The Hunt For Red October

Sweet November

December Bride

MASSIVE GAPS BETWEEN MOVIE AND SEQUEL*

The Wizard Of Oz (1939) to Return To Oz (1985)	46 years
The Hustler (1961) to The Color Of Money (1986)	25 years
Carrie (1976) to The Rage: Carrie 2 (1999)	23 years
Superman II (1980) to Superman Returns† (2006)	26 years
Psycho (1960) to Psycho 2 (1983)	23 years
The Last Picture Show (1971) to Texasville (1990)	19 years
Chinatown (1974) to The Two Jakes (1990)	16 years
A Man And A Woman (1966) to A Man And A Woman: 20 Years Later (1986)	20 years
The Decline Of The American Empire (1986) to The Barbarian Invasions (2003)	17 years
Star Wars Episode III (2005) and Star Wars Episode IV (1977)	-28 years

* Not counting straight-to-DVD sequels

† This ignores III and IV, as should you

BILL MURRAY'S MEANS OF DEATH

In the movie Groundhog Day (1993), which sees Murray live the same day over and over again:

Electrocution (toaster + bath = death)

Jumping off a tall building

Driving a pick-up truck off a cliff

Being hit by a truck

NB He is also stabbed, shot, poisoned, frozen, hanged and burned, though these are reported rather than witnessed first-hand

THE HITCHCOCK BLONDES

Alfred Hitchcock expressed a preference for sophisticated blondes in his films – 'the real ladies, who become whores once they're in the bedroom'. They were:

Grace Kelly	Dial M For Murder, Rear Window, To Catch A Thief
Ingrid Bergman*	Notorious, Spellbound, Under Capricorn
Tippi Hedren	The Birds, Marnie
Kim Novak	Vertigo

Anny Ondra	Blackmail, The Manxman
Eva Marie Saint	North By Northwest
Madeleine Carroll	The 39 Steps, Secret Agent
Anne Baxter	I Confess
Barbara Harris	Family Plot
Janet Leigh	Psycho
Doris Day	The Man Who Knew Too Much
Barbara Leigh-Hunt	Frenzy
Karen Black	Family Plot

* Actually more 'mousey' than blonde

THE ST TRINIAN'S SERIES

The girls' school created by Ronald Searle.

The Belles Of St Trinian's (1954), Blue Murder At St Trinian's (1957), The Pure Hell Of St Trinian's (1960), The Great St Trinian's Train Robbery (1966), The Wildcats Of St Trinian's (1980), St Trinian's (2007)

A ROALD DAHL FILMOGRAPHY

Charlie and The Chocolate Factory (1971*, 2005)	Mel Stuart, Tim Burton
Danny The Champion of the World (1989)	Gavin Millar
The BFG (1989)~	Brian Cosgrove
The Silent Hunt (1990)	Kiumars Poorahmad
The Witches (1990)	Nicolas Roeg
James and the Giant Peach (1996)~	Henry Selick
Matilda (1996)	Danny DeVito
Fantastic Mr Fox (2008)	Wes Anderson

* Released as Willy Wonka and the Chocolate Factory

~ Animated

SELECT FILMIC FOLK WHO HAVE HAD ANIMALS NAMED AFTER THEM

Charlie Chaplin	Campsicnemius charliechaplini (dolichopodid fly)
Laurel and Hardy	Baeturia laureli and B. hardyi (cicadas)

Abbott and Costello	Sula abbotti costelloi (a subspecies of Abbott's booby, a kind of gannet)
John Cleese	Avahi cleesei (woolly lemur)
Harrison Ford	Calponia harrisonfordi (caponiid spider)/ Pheidole harrisonfordi (ant)
Orson Welles	Orsonwelles othello, O. macbeth, O. falstaffius, O. ambersonorum (giant Hawaiian linyphiid spiders)
Greta Garbo	Rostropria garbo (diapriid wasp)
Steven Spielberg	Utahraptor spielbergi (theropod dinosaur)

REASONS WHY DAPHNE CAN'T MARRY OSGOOD*

'I can't get married in your mother's wedding dress. We're not built the same way.'

'I'm not a natural blonde.'

'I smoke. I smoke all the time.'

'I have a terrible past. For three years now I've been living with a saxophone player.'

'I'm a MAN.'

* As said by Jack Lemmon in Some Like It Hot (1959). But, of course, nobody's perfect

ZAZ* END CREDITS TOMFOOLERY
Airplane!

Foreez ... A Jolly Good Fellow

In case of tornado ... Southwest corner of basement

Worst Boy	Adolf Hitler
Focus Loader	Jack Williams
Focus Puller	Tony Strachan
Clapper Loader	John Fletcher
Clapper Puller	Tom Brown
Puller Clapper	Joe Taylor
Clapper Clapper	Edward Davis
Flipper Flapper	Jane Thomas
Author of A Tale Of Two Cities	Charles Dickens
Generally in charge of a lot of things	Mike Finnell

Top Secret!
Hey Diddle Diddle The Cat And The Fiddle
This Space For Rent

The Third Man   *Guido Reidy*

IF YOU HAD LEFT THIS THEATER WHEN THESE CREDITS BEGAN, YOU'D BE HOME NOW

Hot Shots†
THINGS TO DO AFTER THE MOVIE
Start a story hour at the local library
Help someone learn to read
Teach someone to use a computer
Help someone learn to speak a new language
Organize a physical fitness program
Visit a dairy and see how milk is handled and prepared for delivery

Hot Shots Part Deux†
The secret of Crying Game: She's a guy
Answer to tonight's scrambled movie title: 'T-2'
Fun Fact: Actor Richard Crena invented tartar sauce

Naked Gun

General Foreman	John Hoskins
General Schwarzkopf	Welcome Home
Foremen	Guy A. MacLaury, Joseph Santre, Michael Bunch
George Foreman	6'4", 250lbs. Age: 42 Won: 60 Lost: 3 KO's: 65
Production Painters	Nick Bridwell, Donnie R. Puga
Impressionist Painters	Vincent Van Gogh, Edgar 'Skip' Degas
Stock Librarian	Suzy Lafer
Stock Answer	'I'll have it ready in the morning.'

* Zucker Abrahams Zucker

† Abrahams only

THE END CREDITS COPYRIGHT NOTICE

The events, characters and firms depicted in this photoplay are fictitious. Any similarity to any persons living or dead or to actual events or firms is purely coincidental. Ownership of this motion picture is protected by copyright and any other applicable laws and any unauthorised duplication, distribution or exhibition of this motion picture could result in criminal prosecution as well as civil liability.

INDEX OF FILM TITLES

STAY IN YOUR SEAT

Selected films that have 'treats' in their end credits:

The Adventures Of Buckaroo Banzai Across The Eighth Dimension

Amazon Women On The Moon

Analyze That

Bruce Almighty

The Cannonball Run

Demon Knight

Dogma

Dude, Where's My Car?

Ferris Bueller's Day Off

Finding Nemo (plus most Pixar films)

Four Weddings And A Funeral

Gremlins 2: The New Batch

Harry Potter And The Chamber Of Secrets

The Hot Chick

The Howling

Inspector Gadget

Jackass: The Movie

Johnny English

A Knight's Tale

L.A. Story

Lethal Weapon 4

Lolita

Matinée

The Matrix Reloaded

The Mission

Natural Born Killers

Old School

Pirates Of The Carribean: Dead Man's Chest

Planes, Trains And Automobiles

Private Parts

Rush Hour (plus most Jackie Chan films)